STATE LAWS

RELATIVE TO THE

Making and Perfecting Assessments,

APPLICABLE TO THE

CITY OF NEW YORK:

CONTAINING SUCH PORTIONS OF THE GENERAL PROVISIONS OF THE REVISED STATUTES, AND THE AMENDMENTS THERETO, AS ARE APPLICABLE TO THE CITY AND COUNTY OF NEW YORK.

COMPILED BY THOMAS STEPHENS.

TO WHICH IS APPENDED A COMPILATION OF THE

LAWS

OF THE

STATE OF NEW YORK,

RELATIVE TO THE

ASSESSMENT AND COLLECTION OF TAXES IN THE CITY AND COUNTY OF NEW YORK:

CONTAINING SUCH PORTIONS OF THE GENERAL PROVISIONS OF THE REVISED STATUTES, AND THE AMENDMENTS THERETO, AS ARE APPLICABLE TO THE CITY AND COUNTY OF NEW YORK; THE LAWS RELATING EXCLUSIVELY TO THE CITY AND COUNTY OF NEW YORK; AND NOTES OF CASES RELATING TO THE SUBJECT OF TAXATION.

COMPILED BY A. R. LAWRENCE, JR., COUNSELLOR AT LAW.

PRINTED BY ORDER OF THE

BOARD OF COUNCILMEN, CITY OF NEW YORK.

Document No. 22.

NEW YORK:
EDMUND JONES & CO., PRINTERS TO BOARD OF COUNCILMEN,
No. 26 JOHN STREET.
1859.

DOCUMENT No. 22.

Board of Councilmen,
November 14th, 1859.

The following resolution was adopted:

Resolved, That 5,000 copies of the State Laws relative to the making and perfecting assessments applicable to the city of New York, and furnished by the Clerk of this Board, be printed for the use of the city—manuscript copy herewith accompanying—the printing and proof to be under the direction and supervision of the Clerk of this Board.

C. T. McCLENACHAN,
Clerk.

STATE LAWS

APPLICABLE TO THE LEVYING AND COLLECTION OF

TAXES AND ASSESSMENTS

IN THE

CITY AND COUNTY OF NEW YORK.

Sec. 175 of Act April 9th, 1813.

⁂

PAVING AND REGULATING STREETS, ETC.

Corporation to cause sewers to be made, streets paved and cleansed, and vacant lots filled in, etc.

CLXXV. *And be it further enacted,* That it shall be lawful for the said Mayor, Aldermen, and Commonalty, to cause common sewers, drains, and vaults to be made in any part of the said city, and to order and direct the pitching and paving the streets thereof, and the cutting into any drain or sewer, and the altering, amending, cleansing, and scouring of any street, vault, sink, or common sewer, within the said city; and the raising, reducing, leveling, or fencing in any vacant or adjoining lots in the said city; and to cause estimates of the expenses of conforming to such regulations to be made, and a just and equitable assessment thereof among the owners or occupants of all the houses and lots intended to be benefited thereby, in proportion, as nearly as may be, to the advantage which each shall be deemed to acquire; and the said Mayor, Aldermen, and Commonalty shall appoint such skillful and competent disinterested persons as they shall or may think proper, to make every such estimate and assessment, who, before they enter upon the execution of their trust, shall severally take

Expenses thereof, how estimated and assessed.

an oath before the Mayor or Recorder of the said city, to make the said estimate and assessment fairly and impartially, according to the best of their skill and judgment; and the said persons, after having made such estimate and assessment, shall certify the same in writing to the said Mayor, Aldermen, and Commonalty, in Common Council convened, and being ratified by the said Council, shall be binding and conclusive upon the owners and occupants of such lots so to be assessed, respectively, and shall be a lien or charge on such lots as aforesaid; and such owners or occupants shall, also, respectively, be liable, upon demand, to pay the sum at which such houses or lots, respectively, shall be so assessed, to such person as the said Common Council shall appoint to receive the same; and in default of such payment, or any part thereof, it shall be lawful for the Mayor, Recorder, and Aldermen of the said city, or any five of them, of whom the Mayor or Recorder shall be one, by warrant, under their hands and seals, to levy the same by distress and sale of the goods and chattels of such owner or occupant refusing or neglecting to pay the same, rendering the overplus (if any), after deducting the charges of such distress and sale, to such owner or occupant, and the money, when paid or recovered, shall be applied toward making, altering, amending, pitching, paving, cleansing, and scouring such streets, and making and repairing such vaults, drains, and sewers, as aforesaid, and raising, reducing, levelling, or fencing in such lots as aforesaid:

Assessments to be ratified by Common Council.

And in default of payment, to be levied by distress and sale.

Provided, however, That nothing herein contained shall affect any agreement between any landlord and tenant, respecting the payment of any such charges, but they shall be answerable to each other in the same manner as if this act had never been made; and if any money, so to be assessed, be paid by any person, when, by agreement or by

Agreement between landlord and tenant not affected.

law, the same ought to have been borne and paid by some other person, it shall then be lawful for the person paying, to sue for and recover the money so paid, with interest and costs, as so much money paid for the use of the person who ought to have paid the same; and the assessment aforesaid, with proof of payment, shall be conclusive evidence in such suit.

Persons paying for others to recover back.

CLXXVI. *And be it further enacted*, That if, upon completing any such regulation, it shall appear to the said Mayor, Aldermen, and Commonalty, that a greater sum of money had been *bona fide* expended in making such regulation than the sum estimated and collected as aforesaid, it shall then be lawful for the said Mayor, Aldermen, and Commonalty, to cause a further assessment, equal to such excess, to be made and collected in manner aforesaid; and in case the sum actually expended shall be less than the sum expressed in such estimate, and collected as aforesaid, the surplus shall forthwith be returned to the persons from whom the same was collected, or their legal representatives.

Further assessments, how made.

OPENING AND LAYING OUT STREETS, ETC.

CLXXVII. *And be it further enacted*, That whenever and as often as the Mayor, Aldermen, and Commonalty of the City of New York shall be desirous to open any street, avenue, square, or public place, or any particular part or section of any street or avenue laid out by the Commissioner of Streets and Roads in the City of New York, under and by virtue of the act, entitled, "An act relative to improvements touching the laying out of streets and roads in the city of New York, and for other purposes," passed April 3d, 1807; and also, whenever and as often as so many proprietors of lands

Streets, avenues, and squares, how to be opened.

fronting on any such street, avenue, square, or public place, or any particular part or section of any such street, avenue, square, or public place, as shall together own *three fourth parts of all the lands fronting* on such street, avenue, square, or public place, or on such part or section of any such street, avenue, square, or public place, shall by petition desire the said Mayor, Aldermen, and Commonalty to open any such street, avenue, square, or public place, or any such particular part or section of any such street, avenue, square, or public place, and the said Mayor, Aldermen, and Commonalty shall deem the opening thereof to be necessary or useful; it shall be lawful for the said Mayor, Aldermen, and Commonalty to cause the same to be opened, and the lands, tenements, and hereditaments that may be required for the purpose of opening the same, may be taken for that purpose, and compensation and recompense made to the parties and persons, if any such there shall be, to whom the loss and damage thereby shall be deemed to exceed the benefit and advantage thereof, for the excess of the damage over and above the value of the said benefit in the manner hereinafter for that purpose directed and prescribed; and whenever and as often, also, as it shall, in the opinion of the said Mayor, Aldermen, and Commonalty, in Common Council convened, be necessary or desirable for the public convenience or health, to lay out, form, and open any street or streets, or public place or places in any part of the said city, not laid out into streets, avenues, squares, and public places, by the Commissioners of Streets and Roads in the City of New York, under and by virtue of the act aforesaid, or to extend, enlarge, straighten, alter, or otherwise improve any street or streets, or part of a street, or public place or places, already laid out, or hereafter to be laid out, and formed or open in any part of the said city not laid out into streets, avenues, squares, and public places, by the Commissioners aforesaid, it shall be lawful for the said Mayor, Aldermen, and Commonalty of the City of New York, to order and direct the same to be done, and to cause the same to be done accordingly, in such manner as they shall think most advisable, notwithstanding it may become necessary for that purpose to remove any building or buildings, or to take any lands, tenements, hereditaments, or premises whatsoever; and if the said Mayor, Aldermen, and Commonalty shall require any lands, tenements, hereditaments, or premises of any person or persons, or body politic or corporate, for any such purpose, the same may be taken and appropriated to such use, and compensation and recompense made to the parties and persons respectively, if any such there shall be, to whom the loss and damage thereby shall be deemed to exceed the benefit and advantage thereof, for the excess of the said damage above the said benefit, in the manner for that purpose hereinafter mentioned and provided.

On application of Corporation, Supreme Court to appoint three commissioners to ascertain damage, etc.

CLXXVIII. *And be it further enacted*, That whenever and as often as any lands, tenements, hereditaments, or premises whatsoever, shall be required for the said purpose of opening any such public square, place, street, or avenue, or part or section of a street or avenue, in the said city of New York, laid out by the Commissioners aforesaid, under and by virtue of the act aforesaid, so to be opened, or for the said purpose of laying out and forming, or extending, enlarging, straightening, altering, or otherwise improving, in any part of the said city not laid out into streets, avenues, squares, and public places, by the Commissioners aforesaid, under the act aforesaid, or for any or either of the said purposes, it shall be lawful for the said Mayor, Aldermen, and Commonalty, to make application, or to cause application to be made, to the Supreme Court of Judicature, of this State, for the appointment of Commissioners.

And it shall be lawful for the said court to whom such application shall be made, on any such application, to nominate and appoint three discreet and disinterested persons, being citizens of the United States, Commissioners of estimate and assessment, for the purpose of performing the duties hereinafter, in that behalf, prescribed; which said Commissioners, before they enter upon the performance of the duties of their appointment, shall severally take and subscribe an oath or affirmation, before some person authorized by law to administer oaths, "faithfully to perform the trusts and duties required of them by this act;" which oaths or affirmations shall be filed in the Clerk's Office of the city of New York. And it shall be the duty of the said Commissioners, after having viewed the lands, tenements, hereditaments, and premises so required for the purpose of opening the said public square or place, street, avenue, or part or section of a street or avenue so to be opened, or for the purpose of laying out and forming the street or streets, or public place so to be laid out and formed, or for the purpose of extending, enlarging, straightening, altering, or otherwise improving the street or public place so to be extended, enlarged, straightened, altered, or otherwise improved, as the case may be, and the lands, tenements, hereditaments, and premises on each side of the same, half way to the next street or avenue thereto (if they shall deem such view to be necessary or useful); and after causing all such surveys, maps, profiles, plans, and other things as they may judge necessary to be made, done, and prepared for their use, to proceed to, and make a just and equitable estimate and assessment of the loss and damage, if any, over and above the benefit and advantage, or of the benefit and advantage, if any, over and above the loss and damage, as the case may be, *to the respective owners, lessees, parties, and*

Commissioners to be sworn.

Duty of commissioners.

To make estimate of damage and benefit to parties interested in land required for streets, etc.

persons, respectively, entitled unto or interested in the lands, tenements, hereditaments, and premises so required, for the purpose, by and in consequence of opening such public square or place, street, avenue, or part or section of a street or avenue so to be opened, or by and in consequence of laying out or forming such public street or place so to be laid out and formed, or by and in consequence of extending, enlarging, or otherwise improving the street or public place so to be extended, enlarged, or otherwise improved, as the case may be, and a just and equitable estimate and assessment also of the value of the benefit and advantage of such public square or place, street, avenue, or part or section of a street or avenue so to be opened, or such street or public place so to be laid out and formed, or of such extension, enlargement, or other improvement of the street or public place so to be extended, enlarged, or otherwise improved, as the case may be, *to the respective owners, lessees, parties, and persons respectively entitled unto or interested in the said respective lands, tenements, hereditaments, and premises not required* for the purpose of opening, laying out, and forming or extending, enlarging, or otherwise improving the same, but fronting or to front thereon, or being at and within half the distance of the next street or avenue thereto from the same on each side thereof, and which the said Commissioners may deem to be benefited by such public square or place, street, avenue, or part or section of a street or avenue to be opened, or such street or public place so to be laid out and formed, or so to be extended, enlarged, or otherwise improved, in respect to the respective estates and interest of such said owners, lessees, parties, and persons respectively, so entitled unto or interested in such said lands, tenements, hereditaments, and premises, so benefited thereby; and to report to the said Supreme And report to Supreme Court.

When the damage exceeds the benefit, commissioners to report only the excess of damage.

Court of Judicature without unnecessary delay; and, in making such estimate and assessment and report in the premises, it shall be the duty of the said Commissioners in all cases where the loss and damage to the owners, lessees, parties, and persons entitled unto or interested in any such lands, tenements, hereditaments, or premises, so required for the purpose of any such said operation or improvement, that is to say, the operation and improvement of opening such said public square or place, street or avenue, or part or section of a street or avenue so to be opened, or the operation and improvement of laying out and forming any such street or public place so to be laid out and formed, or the operation and improvement of extending, enlarging, or otherwise improving such said street or public place to be extended, enlarged, or otherwise improved as the case may be, by and in consequence of such said operation and improvement, shall, in the opinon of the said Commissioner, exceed the value to him, her, or them, of the benefit and advantage of such said public square or place, street or avenue, or part or section of a street or avenue so to be opened, or of such street or public place so to be laid out and formed, or of such extension, enlargement, or other improvement of the said street or public place so to be extended, enlarged, or otherwise improved, as the case may be, to estimate and report the excess and surplus only, of the said loss and damage over and above the value of the said benefit and advantage, as and for the compensation and recompense, and the same shall be the compensation and recompense to be made to such ower or owners, lessee or lessees, parties and persons, respectively, for his, her, or their loss and damage by and in consequence of the said operation and improvement of opening, laying out, and forming or extending, enlarging, or otherwise improving such said public square, place, avenue, street, or part or section of a street or avenue to be opened, laid out and formed, or extended, enlarged, or otherwise improved, as the case may be, and relinquishing the said lands, tenements, hereditaments, and premises so required of him, her, or them, for that purpose; and in all cases where the benefit and advantage of such said public square, place, street, or avenue, or part or section of a street or avenue so to be opened, or of such said street or public place so to be laid out and formed, or of such extension, enlargement, or other improvement of the street or public place so to be laid out and formed, or of such extension, enlargement, or other improvement of the street or public place so to be extended, enlarged, or otherwise improved, as the case may be, to any owner or owners, lessee or lessees, party or person or persons so entitled unto or interested in any such lands, tenements, hereditaments, or premises so required for the purpose of the said operation of opening, laying out, and forming, or extending, enlarging, or otherwise improving the same, will, in the opinion of the said Commissioners, be equal and equivalent to the loss and damage of such owner or owners, lessee or lessees, party or parties, person or persons, respectively, by and in consequence of the said operation of opening, laying out and forming, or extending, enlarging, or otherwise improving the same, and the relinquishment of the lands, tenements, hereditaments, and premises required for that purpose, to report that such owners, lessees, parties, and persons, respectively, will suffer no damage by or in consequence of making such said operation and improvement, and relinquishing the lands, tenements, hereditaments, and premises so required of him, her, or them, respectively, for that purpose, the benefit and advantage thereof to him, her, or them, being equal and equivalent to the loss and damage that will be sustained by him, her, or

When damage and benefit, it will be equal, commissioners to report accordingly.

them, thereby; but in all cases where the benefit and advantage of such said operation and improvement to any such owner or owners, lessee or lessees, party, or person or persons so entitled unto or interested in any lands, tenements, hereditaments, and premises required for the purpose of making the same, will, in the opinion of the said Commissioners, exceed the loss and damage which he, she, or they will respectively sustain by and in consequence of the making of the same and the relinquishment by him, her, or them, of the said lands, tenements, hereditaments, and premises so required of him, her, or them respectively for that purpose, to estimate, assess, and report the excess and surplus only of the value of the said benefit and advantage over and above the said loss and damage, as and for the sum or allowance to be allowed and paid, and the same shall be the sum on allowance to be allowed and paid by him, her, or them respectively, for the benefit and advantage of the said public square, place, street, or avenue, or part or section of a street or avenue so to be opened, or of the said street or public place so to be laid out and formed, or of the said extension, enlargement, or other improvement of the street or public place so to be extended, enlarged, or otherwise improved, as the case may be, to him, her, or them, respectively.

When the benefit exceeds the damage, commissioners to report only the excess of benefit.

And in all cases, also, where any owner or owners, lessee or lessees, party, or person or persons who may be interested in or entitled unto any lands, tenements, hereditaments or premises, not included within the limits of such public square or place, street, avenue, or part or section of a street or avenue so to be opened, or such street or public place so to be laid out and formed or extended, enlarged, or otherwise improved, but fronting or to front upon or being within half the distance of the next street or avenue thereto from the same or either side thereof, will, in the opinion of

Commissioners to include in their assessments adjacent to the street.

the said Commissioners, be benefited by opening, laying out, and forming, or extending, enlarging, or otherwise improving the same, as the case may be, to estimate, assess, and report the value of such benefit to such owner or owners, lessee or lessees, parties and persons respectively in respect to the said lands, tenements, and hereditaments and premises wherein he, she, or they may respectively be so interested; *and in which said report the Commissioners who shall make the same shall set forth the names of the respective owners, lessees, parties, and persons entitled unto or interested in the said lands, tenements, hereditaments, and premises mentioned in the said report, and each and every part and parcel thereof, as far forth as the same shall be ascertained by them*, and an apt and sufficient designation or description of the respective lots or parcels of lands and other tenements, hereditaments, and premises that may be required for the purpose of opening such public square, place, street, or avenue, or part or section of a street or avenue so to be opened, or laying out and forming, or extending, enlarging, or otherwise improving such street or public place, or to be laid out and formed, or so to be extended, enlarged, or otherwise improved, as the case may be, and also of the said respective lots or parcels of land, and other tenements, hereditaments, and premises not included within, but deemed to be benefited by the same, and so assessed by the said Commissioners, for the said benefit, as aforesaid, and also the several and respective sums estimated and assessed as and for the compensation and recompense, or the allowance to be made for the loss and damage, or for the benefit, as the case may be, of the respective owners of the fee or inheritance of such said lands, tenements, hereditaments, and premises, respectively, and for the loss and damage, or for the benefit, as the case may be, of the respective owners of the leasehold, estate, or other

Names of parties interested in, and description of lands required for streets, to be set forth in report.

The like as to adjacent land included in assessment.

interests therein, separately ; but in all and each and every case and cases, where the owners and parties interested, or their respective estates and interests, are unknown or not fully known, to the said Commissioners, it shall be sufficient for them to *estimate and assess*, and *to set forth* and state in their said report, in general terms, the respective *sums to be allowed* and *paid* to or by the owners and proprietors generally of *such said lands, tenements, hereditaments, and premises*, and parties interested therein, for the loss and damage, or for the benefit and advantage, as the case may be, to such owners, proprietors, and parties interested, in respect of the whole estate and interest of whomsoever may be entitled unto or interested in the said lands, tenements, hereditaments, and premises, respectively, by and in consequence of the said operation and improvement of opening the said public square, or place, street, avenue, or part or section of a street or avenue so to be opened, or so to be laid out and formed or extended, enlarged, or otherwise improved, as the case may be, *without specifying the names*, or the *estates or interests*, of such owners, proprietors, and parties interested, or of any or either of them; and upon the coming in of the said report, signed by the said Commissioners, or any two of them, the said court shall by rule or order, *after hearing any matter which may be alleged against the same*, either confirm the said report, or refer the same to the same Commissioners for revisal and correction, or to new Commissioners, to be appointed by the said court to reconsider the subject-matter thereof, and the said Commissioners, to whom the said report shall be so referred, shall return the same report corrected and revised, or a new report to be made by them in the premises, to the said court, without unnecessary delay; and the same, on being so returned, shall be confirmed or again referred by the said court, in manner aforesaid,

Report, how to be made, when parties interested, or other estates, are not known.

Report to be confirmed by Supreme Court, or referred to the commissioners for revisal, or to new commissioners.

as right and justice shall require, and so from time to time until a report shall be made or returned in the premises, *which the said court shall confirm;* and such report, when so confirmed by the said court, shall be *final and conclusive*, as well upon the said Mayor, Aldermen, and Commonalty of the City of New York, as upon the owners, lessees, persons, and parties interested in, and entitled unto the lands, tenements, hereditaments, and premises mentioned in the said report, *and also upon all other persons whomsoever;* and on such final confirmation of such report by the said court, the said Mayor, Aldermen, and Commonalty of the City of New York shall become and be seized in fee of all the said lands, tenements, hereditaments, and premises in the said report mentioned, that shall or may be so required for the purpose of opening the said public square or place, street or avenue, or part or section of a street or avenue, so to be opened, or for the purpose of laying out and forming the said street or public place so to be laid out and formed, or for the purpose of extending, enlarging, or otherwise improving the street or public place so to be extended, enlarged, or othewise improved, as the case may be, the same to be appropriated, converted, and used to and for such said purpose accordingly ; and thereupon the said Mayor, Aldermen, and Commonalty, or any person or persons acting under their authority, may immediately, or at any time or times thereafter, take possession of the same, or any part or parts thereof, without any suit or proceeding at law for that purpose : *In trust nevertheless*, that the same may be appropriated and kept open for, or as part of a public street, avenue, square, or place forever, in like manner as the other public streets, avenues, squares, and places in the said city are, and of right ought to be ; *Provided*, that the said Mayor, Aldermen, and Commonalty may permit any building which shall be either

Report, when confirmed, to be final and conclusive.

Corporation thereupon to take possession of the premises required for streets, etc.

May permit certain buildings to remain unremoved.

partly or wholly included within the limits of any such street, avenue, public square or place laid out in the said city by the Commissioners of Streets and Roads in the City of New York, under and by virtue of the before-mentioned act, entitled "An act relative to improvements touching the laying out of streets and roads in the city of New York, and for other purposes" (1), and so to be opened as aforesaid, to remain unremoved for such time or times as they shall think proper; *Provided also:* That it shall not be lawful for the said Commissioners of Estimate and Assessment, to be appointed under and by virtue of this act, to allow any sum or compensation whatsoever for any building or buildings which, at any time subsequent to the filing of the maps mentioned in the fifth section of the said last-mentioned act, may have been built, placed, or erected, or which at any time hereafter may be built, placed, or erected, in part or in whole, on any such street, avenue, public square or place laid out by the said Commissioners of Streets and Roads in the City of New York, under and by virtue of the said last-mentioned act.

No compensation allowed for certain buildings.

But provided further, that compensation and recompense shall be made to the owners thereof, and parties interested therein, for all buildings and improvements erected, placed, or made wholly or in part upon any part of any such street, avenue, square, or public place, so to be opened, at any time before the time of the filing of the maps aforesaid:

Commissioners to assess a part of the value of buildings on Corporation.

And further, that it shall be lawful for the said Commissioners of estimate and assessment, if they shall deem it just and equitable under the circumstances to do so, but not otherwise, to assess any part, not exceeding one-third part of the estimated value of any such building or buildings,

(1) Act of April 3, 1807, p. 431.

but not of any other improvement, upon the said Mayor, Aldermen, and Commonalty of the City of New York :

When lands belonging to Corporation are required for aforesaid purposes, commissioners are to assess damages or benefit, in the usual manner.

And provided also, that if it should become necessary for the purpose of laying out, and forming or extending, enlarging, or otherwise improving any street or public place in any part of the said city of New York, not laid out into streets, avenues, squares, and public places, by the said Commissioners of Streets and Roads in the City of New York, under and by virtue of the said last-mentioned act, to remove any building or buildings, it shall and may be lawful to and for the said Commissioners of estimate and assessment, at their discretion, if they shall deem it equitable and just to do so, but not otherwise, to assess any part not exceeding one-third part of the estimated value of such building or buildings, upon the said Mayor, Aldermen, and Commonalty of the City of New York :

And provided, also, that if any lands, tenements, hereditaments, or premises, belonging to the said Mayor, Aldermen, and Commonalty of the City of New York, or wherein they may be interested, shall be required for any of the purposes aforesaid, or shall be benefited by any such operation and improvement as hereinbefore mentioned, the said Mayor, Aldermen, and Commonalty shall be entitled to compensation and recompense for the loss and damage they may sustain, and shall be bound to allow and pay for the benefit and advantage they may be deemed to acquire thereby, in like manner as other owners and proprietors of lands and premises required for the purpose of making the said operation and improvement, or deemed to be benefited thereby ; and it shall be lawful for the said Commissioners of estimate and assessment, and they are hereby directed in such each and every case, to estimate and assess upon the principles and in

2

the manner herein aforesaid; and to report the sum or sums which, in their opinion, ought to be allowed and paid to or by the said Mayor, Aldermen, and Commonalty for the said loss and damage, or for the said benefit and advantage, as the case may be, to the said Mayor, Aldermen, and Commonalty, by and in consequence of such said operation and improvement of opening the said public square, place, street, avenue, or part or section of a street or avenue so to be opened, or laying out and forming, or extending, enlarging, or otherwise improving the said street or public place so to be laid out and formed, or extended, enlarged, or otherwise improved, as the case may be.

Corporation may agree with parties interested, for cession of the lands required for tr eets, etc.

And provided also, that it shall be lawful for the said Mayor, Aldermen, and Commonalty, at any time or times, either before or after the appointment of Commissioners in the premises, for any of the purposes aforesaid, to agree with the owners, lessees, parties, and persons, entitled unto or interested in, the lands, tenements, hereditaments, and premises, that either will be benefited by, or may be required for, the purpose of making the operation and improvement intended to be made, or with any or with either of such owners or other parties interested therein, for and about the cession of the lands, tenements, hereditaments, and premises required of him, her, or them, respectively, for the purpose of making such said intended operation and improvement, and for and about the compensation and recompense to be made to him, her, or them, for the same, or for and about the allowance or sum or sums to be allowed and paid by such owners and parties, respectively, or by any or either of them, for the benefit and advantage of the public square, place, street, avenue, or part or section of a street or avenue so to be opened, or the street or public place, so to be laid out and formed, or the extension, enlargement, or other improvement of the street or public place so to be extended, enlarged, or otherwise improved, to him, her, or them, over and above the value of the lands, tenements, hereditaments, and premises, that may be required, if any lands, tenements, hereditaments, or premises shall be required of him, her, or them, for the purpose of opening, laying out, and forming or extending, enlarging, or otherwise improving the same; and in case of any such agreement or agreements with part only of the said owners and parties entitled unto and interested in the said lands, tenements, hereditaments, and premises so required for the purpose of making any such operation and improvement as aforesaid, or to be benefited thereby, the same shall be valid and binding upon the parties thereto; and the said Commissioners shall, nevertheless, enter upon and make, or proceed with their said estimate and assessment, and make report to the said court as to the residue of the said lands, tenements, hereditaments, and premises, required for the said purpose of making such operation and improvement, or to be benefited thereby, concerning which the owners thereof and parties interested therein shall not agree; and the said report, when confirmed, shall be of like force and effect in regard to the matter comprised therein, as if no such agreement, as to part of the premises, had been made.

[Sections 179 and 180, repealed by sec. 11, chap. 209, laws of 1839.]

CLXXXI. *And be it further enacted*, that in all cases where the whole of any lot or parcel of lands or other premises under lease or other contract, shall be taken for any of the purposes aforesaid, by virtue of this act, all the covenants, contracts, and engagements between landlord and

Contracts between landlord and tenant, to cease in certain cases.

tenant, or any other contracting parties, touching the same or any other part thereof, shall, upon the confirmation of such report in the premises as shall be confirmed by the court aforesaid, respectively, cease and determine, and be absolutely discharged; and in all cases where part only of any lot or parcel of land, or other premises so under lease or other contract, shall be so taken for any of the purposes aforesaid, all contracts and engagements respecting the same shall, upon the confirmation of such report in the premises, as shall be so confirmed, as aforesaid, cease, determine, and be absolutely discharged, as to the part thereof so taken, but shall remain valid and obligatory as to the residue thereof; and the rents, considerations, and payments, reserved or payable, and to be paid for or in respect to the same, shall be so apportioned as that the part thereof justly and equitably payable, or that ought to be paid for such said residue thereof, and no more, shall be demanded, or paid, or recoverable, for or in respect of the same.

CLXXXII. *And be it further enacted*, that the said Commissioners of estimate and assessment, to be appointed under and by virtue of this act, for any of the purposes aforesaid, after completing their said estimate and assessment, and at least fourteen days before they make their report to the said court, shall deposit a true copy or transcript of such estimate and assessment in the Clerk's Office of the city of New York, for the inspection of whomsoever it may concern, and shall give notice by advertisement, to be published in at least two of the public newspapers printed in the city of New York, of the said deposit thereof in the said office, and of the day on which their report will be presented to the said court; and any person or persons whose rights may be affected thereby, and who shall object to the same or any part thereof, may, within ten days after the first publication of the said notice, *state his, her, or their objections to the same in writing*, to the said *Commissioners;* and the said Commissioners, or such of them as shall make such estimate or assessment, in case any objections shall be made to the same, and stated in writing as aforesaid, shall reconsider their said estimate and assessment, or the part or parts thereof so objected to, and in case the same shall appear to them to require correction, but not otherwise, they shall and may correct the same accordingly.

Commissioners may correct assessment.

CLXXXIII. *And be it further enacted*, that the said Mayor, Aldermen, and Commonalty shall, within four calendar months after the confirmation of the report of the Commissioners in the premises by the court, pay to the respective persons and bodies, politic or corporate, mentioned or referred to in the said report, in whose favor any sum or sums of money shall be estimated and reported by the said Commissioners, the respective sum or sums so estimated and reported in their favor respectively; and in case of neglect or default in the payment of the same within the time aforesaid, the respective person or persons, or party or parties in whose favor the same shall be so reported, his, her, or their executors, administrators, or successors, at any time or times, after application first made by him, her, or them, to the said Mayor, Aldermen, and Commonalty, in Common Council convened, for payment thereof, may sue for and recover the same, with lawful interest, from and after the said application therefor, and the costs of suit, in any proper form of action against the said Mayor, Aldermen, and Commonalty, in any court having cognizance thereof, and in which it shall be sufficient to declare generally for so much money due to the plaintiff or plaintiffs therein by virtue of this act, for premises taken for the purpose herein mentioned, and it shall be lawful for the plaintiff or plaintiffs to give any

Damages awarded, when to be paid by Corporation.

In case of [illegible] payment, parties entitled may sue for the same.

special matter in evidence under such general declaration, and this act, and the report of the said Commissioners, with proof of the right and title of the plaintiff or plaintiffs to the sum or sums demanded, shall be conclusive evidence in such suit or action: *Provided*,

If parties entitled are infants, *non compos mentis*, feme covert, absent, or unknown, money may be paid into court.

CLXXXIV. *And be it further enacted*, That whenever the owners and proprietors of any such lands, tenements, hereditaments, and premises, so to be taken for any of the purposes aforesaid, or the party or parties, person or persons, interested therein, or any or either of them, the said owners, proprietors, parties, or persons in whose favor any such sum or sums, or compensation shall be so reported, shall be under the age of twenty-one years, *non compos mentis*, feme covert, or absent from the city of New York; and also in all cases where the name or names of the owner or owners, parties or persons entitled unto or interested in any lands, tenements, hereditaments, or premises, that may be so taken for any of the purposes aforesaid, shall not be set forth or mentioned in the said report, or where the said owners, parties, or persons, respectively, being named therein, cannot upon diligent inquiry be found, it shall be lawful for the said Mayor, Aldermen, and Commonalty to pay the sum or sums mentioned in the said report, payable, or that would be coming to such owners, proprietors, parties, and persons, respectively, into the said Supreme Court of Judicature, to be secured, disposed of, and improved, as the said court shall direct, and such payment shall be as valid and effectual, in all respects, as if made to the said owners, proprietors, parties and persons, respectively, themselves, according to their just rights, if they had been known, and had all been present, of full age, discreet, and *compos mentis*.

And provided also, That in all, and each, and every case and cases, where any such sum or sums, or compensation, so to be reported by the said Commissioners in favor of any person or persons, or party or parties whatsoever, whether named or not named in the said report, shall be paid to any person or persons, or party or parties whomsoever, when the same shall of right belong, and ought to have been paid, to some other person or persons, or party or parties, it shall be lawful for the person or persons, party or parties, to whom the same ought to have been paid, to sue for and recover the same, with lawful interest and costs of suit, as so much money had and received to his, her, or their use, by the person or persons, party or parties, respectively, to whom the same shall have been so paid.

Compensat'n due to one person, but received by another, may be recovered by the former from the latter.

CLXXXV. *And be it further enacted*, that all the moneys which the said Mayor, Aldermen, and Commonalty shall pay, disburse, and expend, or become liable or bound to pay, disburse, or expend, for cessions by agreement, and in discharge or on account of the sums or estimates of compensation or recompense that may be reported by the Commissioners in favor of the respective persons and parties deemed to be entitled thereto, and the charges and expenses of the estimate and assessment, and report that may be made in the premises, and all such other expenses, disbursements, and charges, also, as may arise or take place by and in consequence of the provisions of this act, for and about the opening of any such public square or place, street, avenue, or part or section of a street or avenue so to be opened, and laying out and forming or extending, enlarging, or otherwise improving, as the case may be, and the acquisition of the lands, tenements, hereditaments, and premises required for that purpose (except such sum or sums as may be assessed upon the said Mayor, Aldermen, and Commonalty, according to the provisions of this act in that behalf), shall be borne, and reimbursed,

All moneys expended by Corporation for said purposes, to be assessed upon persons benefited.

and paid to the said Mayor, Aldermen, and Commonalty by the parties and persons interested and entitled, as owners or otherwise, unto and in the lands, tenements, hereditaments, and premises deemed to be benefited thereby, and the same or the excess and balance thereof, if any such excess and balance thereof there shall be, over and above the amount of the sums or assessments that may be assessed upon the parties and persons, lands and tenements, assessed by the Commissioners in the premises for the benefit of such public square or place, street or avenue, or part or section of a street or streets so to be opened, or of such street or public place so to be laid out and formed, or of the extension, enlargement, or other improvement of the street or public place so to be extended, enlarged, or otherwise improved, as the case may be, together with the charges of the after-mentioned assessment and collection thereof, shall and may be estimated and assessed upon and among all the owners, occupants, and parties seized or possessed of, or interested in all the lands, tenements, hereditaments, and premises not assessed by the said Commissioners of estimate and assessment, nor included in their said report, that may be benefited by the said public square or place so to be laid out and formed, or the extension, enlargement, or other improvement of the public street or place, so to be extended, enlarged, or otherwise improved, as the case may be, in proportion, as nearly as may be, to the advantage which each shall be deemed to acquire thereby. And the said Mayor, Aldermen, and Commonalty shall appoint three disinterested freeholders to make such estimate and assessment, who, before they enter upon the duties of their appointment, shall severally take an oath before the Mayor, Recorder, or one of the Aldermen of the said city, to make the said estimate and assessment fairly and impartially, according to the best of

Three freeholders to be appointed assessors for the purpose. To be sworn.

their skill and judgment; and the said freeholders, or any two of them, after having made such estimate and assessment, shall certify the same, and make return thereof in writing, to the said Mayor, Aldermen, and Commonalty, in Common Council convened, and the same, when ratified and confirmed by the said Common Council, shall be binding and conclusive upon the parties and persons so to be assessed respectively, and upon all other persons whomsoever.

Assessments, when ratified by Common Council, to be conclusive.

Provided, however, that no part of such said moneys so to be estimated and assessed by the said assessors, shall be assessed upon any party or person whomsoever, for or on account of any lands, tenements, hereditaments, or premises, included in the aforesaid report of the Commissioners of estimate and assessment, and by them made the subject of their said estimate and assessment; but if any such party or persons shall be entitled unto or interested in any other lands, tenements, hereditaments, or premises, not included in the said report, that may be deemed to be benefited as aforesaid, such party or person shall be assessed therefor in proportion to the advantage deemed to be acquired in respect to the same.

Premises included in commissioners' report, not to be assessed by the assessors.

CLXXXVI. *And be it further enacted*, that as well the respective sums so to be assessed by the said assessors upon the owners, occupants, or parties seized or possessed of or interested in the lands, tenements, hereditaments, and premises mentioned in the said certificate and return of them, the said assessors; as also the respective sums or assessments so to be assessed and reported by the said Commissioners of estimate and assessment as, and for the allowance to be made by the parties and persons respectively in the said report mentioned or referred to, and intended as owners and proprietors of, or parties interested in, lands and premises deemed to be benefited for the

Sums assessed by commissioners and assessors, to be a lien on the premises assessed.

benefit and advantage of the public square, or place, street, avenue, or part or section of a street or avenue, or of the extension, enlargement, or other improvement of the street or public place mentioned in the said report, *shall be a lien or charge on the lands, tenements, hereditaments, and premises, in the said certificate and return of the said assessors, or in the said report of the said Commissioners mentioned*, or upon the estate and interest of the respective owners, lessees, and parties interested in such said lands, tenements, hereditaments, and premises, for, or on account of which, the said respective sums shall be so assessed by the said Commissioners or assessors, as the case may be, upon the said respective owners and proprietors thereof, or parties interested therein ; and as well the said owners and proprietors thereof, and parties interested therein, and also all the occupants, and each and every of them, shall moreover be respectively liable to pay on demand the respective sum or sums, or assessments mentioned in the said certificate and return of the assessors, or in the said report of the Commissioners, as the case may be, at which the respective lands, tenements, hereditaments, and premises so owned, or occupied by him, her, or them, or wherein he, she, or they are so interested, or at which the owners and proprietors thereof shall be so assessed, to such person or persons as the said Mayor, Aldermen, and Commonalty shall appoint to receive the same ; and in default of payment of the same or of any part thereof, it shall be lawful for the said Mayor, Aldermen, and Commonalty, or any five of them, of whom the Mayor or Recorder shall be one, by warrant under their hands and seals, to levy the same, with lawful interest thereon, from and after the expiration of thirty days from the time of the confirmation of the said report of the Commissioners by the court, or of the

Liable to pay.

In default of payment, may be levied by distress and sale.

said return of the assessors by the Common Council, as the case may be, and together also with all the charges and expenses of the proceedings to be had for the collection thereof, by distress and sale of the goods and chattels of such owner or owners, occupant or occupants, or party or parties interested, so refusing or neglecting to pay the same; rendering the overplus (if any overplus there shall be) after deducting all just charges, to such owner or owners, occupant or occupants, or party or parties interested, or the said respective sums or assessments, with such lawful interest as aforesaid, may be recovered, with all costs and charges, by the said Mayor, Aldermen, and Commonalty, *from* and against the parties assessed, or the owner or owners of the respective lands, tenements, hereditaments, and premises whereon or in respect of which the same may be assessed, or set forth in the said report of the Commissioners, or return of the assessment, as the case may be, or from or against any or either of the said parties or owners, without joining any other or others of them, the said parties or owners therein, by action of debt or assumpsit, in which it shall be sufficient to declare generally,, for so much money due by virtue of this act to the said Mayor, Aldermen, and Commonalty; and any matter may be given in evidence under such general declarations.

Or recovered by action of debt or assumpsit.

Provided, That nothing herein contained shall affect any agreement between landlord and tenant, or any other contracting parties, respecting the payment of any such assessment or charges, but they shall be answerable to each other in the same manner as if the provisions in this act contained concerning the same had never been made; and if any money so to be assessed be paid by or collected or recovered from any person or persons, when by agreement or by law the same ought to have been borne and paid by

Agreement between landlord and tenant not affected.

Persons paying assessment for others, who ought to pay, may recover same back.

some other person or persons, it shall be lawful for the person or persons paying the same, or from whom the same shall be recovered by distress, suit, or otherwise, to sue for and recover the money so paid by or recovered from him or them, with interests and costs, as so much money paid for the use of the person or persons who ought to have paid the same, and the said report of the Commissioners, with proof of payment, shall be conclusive evidence in such suit.

Vacancy in office of Commissioner, how to be filled.

CLXXXVII. *And be it further enacted*, that in case of the death, resignation, or refusal to act of any such Commissioner of estimate and assessment, to be appointed under and by virtue of this act for any such aforesaid purpose, it shall and may be lawful for the court aforesaid, or any one of the justices thereof, on the application of the Mayor, Aldermen, and Commonalty of the City of New York, as often as such event shall happen, to appoint a discreet and disinterested person, being a citizen of the United States, in the place and stead of such Commissioner so dying, resigning, or refusing to act, and that the surviving or acting Commissioners, as the case may be, shall have full power to proceed in the execution of the duties of their appointment, until a successor of the Commissioner so dying, resigning, or refusing to act, shall be appointed.

Any two Commissioners may act.

CLXXXVIII. *And be it further enacted*, That in all and every case of the appointment of Commissioners by the Court aforesaid, for any of the purposes aforesaid, it shall be competent and lawful for any two of such said Commissioners, so to be appointed, to proceed to, and execute and perform the trusts and duties of their said appointment, and their acts shall be as valid and effectual as the acts of all the Commissioners so to be appointed for such said purpose, if they had acted therein, would have been. *And further*, that in all cases, the acts, decisions, and proceedings of the major part of such of the Commissioners, to be appointed for any of the purposes aforesaid, as shall be acting in the premises, shall always be as binding, valid, and effectual as if the said Commissioners named and appointed for such purpose, had all concurred and joined therein.

CLXXXIX. *And be it further enacted*, That the Commissioners to be appointed under and by virtue of this act, for any of the purposes aforesaid, who shall enter upon the duties of their appointment, shall be entitled to receive the sum of not more than four dollars, besides all reasonable expenses, for maps, surveys, and plans, clerk hire, and other necessary expenses and disbursements for each day they shall respectively be actually employed in the duties of their appointment; the same to be paid by the Mayor, Aldermon, and Commonalty of the City of New York, and included in the before-mentioned assessment upon the persons and parties deemed to be benefited by the operation and improvement which shall have occasioned the appointment of the said Commissioners.

Compensation to be paid to Commissioners.

CXC. *And be it further enacted*, That all debts and expenses incurred by the said Mayor, Aldermen, and Commonalty, for or on account of the opening of any street, avenue, square, or public place, or any particular part or section of any street or avenue laid out by the said Commissioners of Streets and Roads in the City of New York, under and by virtue of the act, entitled "An act relative to improvements touching the laying out of streets and roads in the city of New York, and for other purposes," passed April 3d, 1807, may be funded at such interest, in like manner, and under the same limitations and restrictions, as is authorized by the act, entitled "An act to regulate the finances of the city of New York," passed June 8th,

Debts incurred by Common Council, for opening streets, may be funded.

1812. *And whereas*, the Commissioners constituted by the act, entitled "An act relative to improvements touching the laying out of streets and roads in the city of New York, and for other purposes," have completed the business assigned to them by the said act,

Corporation authorized to run out streets, over lands of private persons, and fix monuments, etc.

CXCI. *Be it further enacted*, That it shall and may be lawful for such persons as shall be appointed for that purpose by the Mayor, Aldermen, and Commonalty of the City of New York, in Common Council convened, to enter upon the lands of private persons, and to run out streets and to fix the the boundaries thereof, and to erect monuments, designating such streets and boundaries according to the maps and plan of the said Commissioners, and generally the said persons shall be invested with power to do all such matters as may be necessary to carry the said plan into execution.

Provided, that the provisions contained in the 17th section of the act, entitled "An act respecting streets in the city of New York," shall be, and hereby are extended and applied to the proceedings authorized by this section.

Rights of the State to streets and highways in New York, granted to Corporation.

CXCII. *And be it further enacted*, That all the estate, right, title, interest, claim, and demand whatsoever of the people of this State, of, in, and to all lands at any time heretofore left for streets or highways in the city of New York, by any person or persons whomsoever, shall be and hereby is vested in the Mayor, Aldermen, and Commonalty of the City of New York, and their successors, for the use of streets and highways.

WELLS AND PUMPS.

CC. *And be it further enacted*, That whenever, in the opinion of the Mayor, Aldermen, and Commonalty of the said city, in Common Council convened, it shall be expedient to make a public well and pump in any street or road of the said city, it shall be lawful for the said Common Council to order the same to be done accordingly, in such manner and at such place as they shall think most advisable, and the expense thereof shall be estimated and assessed among all the owners or occupants of the houses and lots of ground intended to be benefited thereby, in the manner directed in and by the one hundred and seventy-fifth section of this act, and shall be binding and conclusive in the manner therein prescribed, and shall be collected in the manner therein directed, or in the manner directed in the two hundred and fifty-ninth section of this act.

Expense, how estimated, assessed, and collected.

CCLXVII. *And be it further enacted*, That the Mayor, Aldermen, and Commonalty of the said city, in Common Council convened, shall have full power and authority to make and pass such by-laws and ordinances as they shall, from time to time, deem necessary and proper for the filling up, draining, and regulating of any grounds, yards, or cellars, within the said city, that may be sunken, damp, or unwholesome, or which they may deem proper to fill up, drain, raise, lower, or regulate; and, also, for causing all such lots of ground in the said city adjoining to Hudson's river, or to the East river or sound, as they may, from time to time, think proper to be filled up with wholesome earth or other solid materials, so far into the said rivers, respectively, as they shall, from time to time, deem expedient for promoting the health of the said city, and for compelling the proprietors of such lots to make suitable

To pass laws for filling up and regulating grounds, yards, and cellars.

For filling up lots adjoining the rivers.

For compelling bulkheads to be made.

bulkheads on, adjoining, or opposite to such lots, and to raise and fill up the same with such materials, and in such manner, and within such times as the Mayor, Aldermen, and Commonalty shall, from time to time, direct; and, also, for filling up, altering, and amending, of all public slips in the said city, at such times and in such manner as they may deem proper; and for filling up, altering, and amending all sinks and privies within the said city, and for directing the mode of constructing them in future, and for causing subterraneous drains to be made from the same, where they may think it necessary; and for regulating, or, if they find it necessary, preventing, the interment of the dead within the said city.

For filling up slips.

For cleansing privies and sinks.

Regulating interment of the dead.

Expense of certain works, how estimated and assessed.

Common Council to pay one-third part of the expense of filling up slips.

CCLXIX. *And be it further enacted*, That, in all cases where the said by-laws or ordinances shall require any thing to be done by or with respect to the property of several persons, or in relation to the filling up, altering or amending any of the public slips in the said city, the said Mayor, Aldermen, and Commonalty, in Common Council convened, shall cause the expense of such works to be estimated and assessed in the same manner as is directed in and by this act, with respect to the paving or regulating the public streets in the said city; and where the same shall relate to the filling up, altering, or amending the public slips as aforesaid, one-third of the expense attending the same shall be borne by the said Mayor, Aldermen, and Commonalty, and the residue by the persons in the vicinity who may be benefited thereby, and in other cases such expenses shall be borne by the persons, respectively, upon whom the same may be assessed as aforesaid.

CCLXX. *And be it further enacted*, That it shall and may be lawful for the said Mayor, Aldermen, and Commonalty, in all cases where they may deem it necessary for the more speedy execution of the said by-laws and ordinances, or any of them, to cause all such works as may be necessary for any of the purposes aforesaid, or any part thereof, to be executed and done at their own expense, on account of the persons, respectively, upon whom the same may be assessed, and shall have full power, and are hereby authorized to levy the same, with lawful interest, and all reasonable costs and expenses attending such proceedings, by distress and sale of the goods and chattels of the proprietors or occupants of the property, upon or by reason of which any such sum shall have been assessed, or to recover the amount of every such expense by action of debt, in any court of record, from the persons, respectively, on whose account the same shall have been incurred, their respective heirs, executors, or administrators, in all which actions they shall also recover lawful interest upon the said amount, with full costs of suit.

Common Council may cause work to be done, and recover expense from parties interested.

By distress and sale.

Or by action of debt.

CCLXXI. *And be it further enacted,* That the amount of every such expense which the said Mayor, Aldermen, and Commonalty shall pay as aforesaid, on account of others, shall be a real incumbrance upon the houses and lots in respect to which such assessment, as aforesaid, shall have been made, and shall bear lawful interest until paid, and that the same may be recovered, or the payment thereof, with costs, enforced in like manner as if the said houses and lots were mortgaged to the said Mayor, Aldermen, and Commonalty, for the payment thereof.

Such expenses a lien on property assessed.

1815.—CHAPTER CLII.

AN ACT *relative to Public Squares and Places in the City of New York.* Passed April 11, 1815.

Whereas, the Mayor, Aldermen, and Commonalty of the

Preamble.

City of New York have, by their memorial to the Legislature, prayed, for the reasons therein contained, that the act to reduce several laws relating particularly to the city of New York into one act, passed April 9th, 1813, may be amended in the manner hereinafter specified; *And whereas*, such prayer appears proper to be granted, Therefore

Powers of the Commissioners of estimate and assessment extended.

I. *Be it enacted by the People of the State of New York, represented in Senate and Assembly*, that whenever, and as often as Commissioners may hereafter be appointed by the Supreme Court of Judicature of this State, or by any one of the justices thereof, under and by virtue of the one hundred and seventy-eighth section, or one hundred and eighty-seventh section, of the act hereby amended, for the purpose of opening any or either of the public squares or places (other than except the streets and avenues) laid out by the Commissioners of Streets and Roads in the City of New York, under and by virtue of the act entitled, "An act relative to improvements touching the laying out of streets and roads in the city of New York, and for other purposes," passed April 3d, 1807, or any or either of the said public squares or places, as altered by the Legislature, the said Commissioners of Estimate and Assessment shall not, in making their estimate and assessment of the value of the benefit and advantage of such public square or place, be confined to the lands, tenements, hereditaments, and premises fronting thereon, and lying within half the distance of the next street or avenue thereto from the same on each side thereof, but on the contrary thereof, after having made their estimate and assessment of the loss and damage over and above the benefit and advantage, and of the benefit and advantage over and above the loss and damage, and of the equality of the benefit and advantage to the loss and damage, as the case may be, to the respective owners, lessees, parties, and persons, respectively, entitled unto or interested in the lands, tenements, hereditaments, and premises so required for the purpose by and in consequence of opening such public square or place, the said Commissioners shall proceed to make a just and equitable estimate and assessment of the value of the benefit and advantage of such public square or place so to be opened by the respective owners, lessees, parties, and persons respectively entitled unto or interested in the lands, tenements, hereditaments, and premises lying out of the limits of such public square or place, and which the said Commissioners may deem to be benefited by such public square or place, in respect to the respective estates and interest of such owners, lessees, parties, and persons, respectively, so entitled to or interested in such said lands, tenements, hereditaments, and premises so deemed benefited thereby. And the said Commissioners shall and may extend their said assessments to any such lands, tenements, hereditaments, and premises as they may deem to be benefited by the opening of the said public square or place, notwithstanding such said lands, tenements, hereditaments, and premises may be situated without and beyond half the distance of the next street or avenue thereto from such said public square or place or any side thereof.

Certain expenses to be paid by the Corporation

II. *And be it further enacted*, That no such assessment as is directed in and by the one hundred and eighty-fifth section of the act hereby amended, shall be made after the confirmation of the report of the Commissioners, in cases of the opening of such public squares or places as aforesaid, but all the excess and balance of the sums or estimates of compensation and recompense that may be reported by the said Commissioners, in favor of the respective persons and parties entitled thereto, and of the expenses and charges of the estimate and assessment and report that may be made in the premises, and all other expenses, disbursements, and charges in the premises over and above the amount of the sums or assessments which may be assessed by the said Commissioners upon the persons and parties, lands and tenements, for the benefit of such public square or place, shall be borne and paid by the Mayor, Aldermen, and Commonalty of the City of New York, without any such assessment and collection as is directed in and by the said one hundred and eighty-fifth section of the said act.

Commissioners, how to proceed.

III. *And be it further enacted*, That the said Commissioners shall in all things, except as above mentioned, proceed in the execution of the duties of their appointment in manner directed in and by the act hereby amended; and the report to be made by them shall, except as aforesaid, be made in the manner specified by the said act, and the like proceedings shall be had as to the deposit of the said report in the Clerk's Office of the city of New York, and notice thereof, and the confirmation of such report by the Court, or the reference back to the said Commissioners, or to new Commissioners, as are prescribed in and by the said act.

Sections of a former act applicable to opening public squares, etc. Treasury.

IV. *And be it further enacted*, that all and singular the provisions of the act hereby amended, as to the conclusive effect of the report, the right accruing to, and liabilities imposed upon, the corporation of New York thereupon, and all and every the other provisions contained in the one hundred and seventy-seventh, one hundred and seventy-eighth, one hundred and seventy-ninth, one hundred and eightieth, one hundred and eighty-first, one hundred and eighty-second, one hundred and eighty-third, one hundred and eighty-fourth, one hundred and eighty-sixth, one hundred and eighty-seventh, one hundred and eighty-eighth, one hundred and eighty ninth, and one hundred and ninetieth sections of the said act shall be, and they are hereby declared to be applicable to the opening of any public square or place in the city of New York, excepting only that the Commissioners appointed for that purpose, shall not be confined in their estimate and assessment of benefits to any limit or limits whatsoever, and excepting also that the damages awarded by the said Commissioners, and the expenses, disbursements, and charges in the premises, shall be borne and paid by the Mayor, Aldermen, and Commonalty of the City of New York, out of the amount or sums that may be assessed by the said Commissioners upon the parties and persons, lands and tenements, deemed by them benefited by the opening of such public square or place, so far as such amounts or sums assessed may extend, and the surplus of such damage, expenses, disbursements, and charges, shall be defrayed out of the city treasury. Treasury

---

1816.—CHAPTER CXV.

AN ACT *for the more effectual Collection of Taxes and Assessments in the City of New York.* Passed April 12, 1816.

I. *Be it enacted by the People of the State of New York, represented in Senate and Assembly:* that whenever any tax, of any description, on lands or tenements in the said city, shall remain unpaid on the day upon which the collectors are limited by law to account for the collection of the same, and the collector of the ward in which the same shall be charged, shall make such affidavit in relation to the said tax as is specified in the eleventh section of the act, entitled, "An act for the assessment and collection of taxes," Taxes, how to be levied.

passed April 5th, 1813; it shall be lawful for the Mayor, Recorder, and Aldermen of the said city, or any five of them, of whom the Mayor or Recorder shall be one, to issue a warrant, under their hands and seals, directed to and requiring some proper person to levy the said tax, by distress and sale of the goods and chattels of the owner or owners of such lands or tenements respectively, wheresoever the said goods and chattels may be found in the said city, together with the costs and charges of such distress and sale, rendering the overplus, if any, to the person or persons whose goods and chattels shall be so distrained and sold.

Proceedings in cases where taxes remain unpaid.

II. *And be it further enacted*, that whenever any such tax shall remain unpaid as aforesaid, and the collector shall make such affidavit as is above; and also wherever and whenever any assessment upon any lands or tenements in the said city, hath heretofore been, or hereafter shall be made and confirmed according to law, and the amount of such assessment hath not been or shall not be collected, and the collector shall make affidavit of his demanding the money two several times of such owner or owners of the said lands or tenements as may reside in the said city, and that they have neglected or refused to pay the same, or shall make affidavit that the owner or owners of any such lands or tenements cannot upon diligent inquiry, be found in the said city, then and in any such case it shall and may be lawful for the Mayor, Aldermen, and Commonalty of the City of New York, to take order for advertising the said lands and tenements, or any of them, for sale, in two or more of the public newspapers printed in the said city, for three months, once in each week; and by such advertisements the owner or owners of such lands and tenements, respectively, shall be required to pay the amount of such tax or assessment so remaining

Notice to be published.

unpaid, together with interest thereon, at the rate of seven per cent. per annum (the interest on said tax to be calculated from the time of making the above-mentioned affidavit, and the interest on such assessment to be calculated from the time of the confirmation of the said assessment) to the time of payment, with the charges of such notice and advertisement to the Treasurer or Chamberlain of the said city, and notice shall be given by such advertisements, that if default shall be made in such payment, such lands and tenements will be sold at public auction, at a day and place therein to be specified, for the lowest term of years at which any person or persons shall offer to take the same in consideration of advancing the said tax or assessment, and the interest thereon as aforesaid, to the time of sale, and together with the charges of the above-mentioned notice and advertisement, and the hereinafter-mentioned certificate, lease, and advertisement, and all other costs and charges accrued thereon. And if notwithstanding such notice, the owner or owners shall refuse or neglect to pay such tax or assessment, with interest as aforesaid, and the charges attending such notice and advertisement, then it shall and may be lawful to and for the said Mayor, Aldermen, and Commonalty, to cause such lands and tenements to be sold at public auction, for a term of years, for the purpose and in the manner expressed in the said advertisements; and such sales shall be made on the day for that purpose mentioned in the said advertisements, and shall be continued from day to day, if necessary, until all the lands and tenements so advertised shall be sold. And the said Mayor, Aldermen, and Commonalty shall give to the purchaser or purchasers of any such lands and tenements, a certificate in writing, describing the lands and tenements so purchased, the term of years for which the same shall have been sold, the sum paid therefor, and the

Lands may be sold for a term of years.

time when the purchaser will be entitled to a lease for the the said lands and tenements.

And the Mayor, Aldermen, and Commonalty of the City of New York shall, at least six months before the expiration of two years after any such sale, cause an advertisement to be published, at least once in each week, for four weeks successively, in the newspaper printed by the printer to this State, and in one of the public newspapers printed in the city of New York, in such form as they shall deem best calculated to give notice of such sale, and that unless the lands sold be redeemed by a certain day, they would be conveyed to the purchaser.

And if the person claiming title to the said lands and tenements, or some one on his or her behalf, shall not, within two years from the date of the above-mentioned certificate, pay to the Street Commissioner of the City of New York, for the use of the purchaser, his executors, administrators, or assigns, the sum mentioned in such certificate, together with the interest thereof, at the rate of twenty per cent. per annum, from the date of such certificate, the Mayor, Aldermen, and Commonalty of the said city shall, at the expiration of the said two years, execute to the purchaser, his executors, administrators, or assigns, a lease, under the common seal of the said city, of the lands and tenements so sold for such term of years as the same shall have been sold, and such lease shall be conclusive evidence that the sale was regular, according to the provisions of this act. And such purchaser or purchasers, his, her, or their executors, administrators, or assigns, shall by virtue thereof and of this act, lawfully hold and enjoy the said lands and tenements, in the said lease mentioned, for his, her, or their own proper use, against the owner or owners thereof, and all claiming under him, her, or them, until such purchaser's term therein shall be fully complete and ended; and the said purchaser or purchasers, his, her, or their executors, administrators, and assigns, shall be at liberty to remove all the buildings and materials which he, she, or they shall erect or place thereon, during the said term, within one month after the expiration of the said term, but leaving the lands and tenements, with the streets fronting the same, in the order required by the regulations of the Common Council.

Provided always, that no such proceedings by advertisement and sale as aforesaid shall take place under any such assessment heretofore made and confirmed, unless in cases where the same now is a lien or charge on the lots assessed. Proviso.

III. *And be it further enacted*, that the above-mentioned proceedings by advertisement and sale, may take place in any case of such unpaid tax, as is above mentioned, notwithstanding a warrant of distress may have been issued for the collection thereof, in the manner above mentioned, in case the whole or any part of such tax shall be uncollected thereupon. Sale may be made, notwithstanding a warrant of distress issued.

IV. *And be it further enacted*, that this act shall not be construed to prevent the collection of any assessment or assessments by distress and sale of the goods and chattels of the owner or owners, occupant or occupants of any lands or tenements therein or thereby assessed. This Act not to prevent the sale of goods, &c.

V. *And be it further enacted*, that all the provisions herein before made, relative to the sale of lands and tenements within the city of New York, for unpaid taxes, shall apply to all such taxes charged on lands and tenements within the said city as shall appear by the returns of the respective collectors, at any time heretofore to have been in arrear. Former provisions shall apply to arrears of taxes.

How to be credited.

VI. *And be it fnrther enacted*, that whenever the arrearages of any tax shall be collected, in manner aforesaid, the same shall be carried to the credit of the ward in which it shall be charged.

Certain sections of a former law repealed.

VII. *And be it further enacted*, that the one hundred and fifty-sixth, one hundred and fifty-seventh, one hundred and fifty-eighth, two hundred and fifty-ninth, and two hundred and sixtieth sections of the act, entitled "An act to reduce several laws relating particularly to the city of New York, into one act," passed April 9th, 1813, be, and the same are hereby repealed.

Provided however, that such repeal shall not affect any act done, or proceeding had or commenced under the said sections hereby repealed; but every such act and proceeding shall remain as valid as if the said sections had remained in full force: *And provided* particularly, that the proceedings for the sale of certain lands and tenements for certain unpaid assessments, which are now pending, shall and may proceed, be continued, and completed in the same manner as if this act had not been passed, but the said two hundred and fifty-ninth section of the said act had remained in full force.

Proviso.

1816.—CHAPTER CLX.

AN ACT *further to extend the Powers and Duties of Commissioners of Estimate and Assessment on opening and improving of Streets, in the City of New York.* Passed, April 16, 1816.

Preamble.

Whereas, the Mayor, Aldermen, and Commonalty of New York, have, by their memorial, represented to the Legislature, that the opening and improving of streets in the compactly built part of the said city, will not unfrequently render it necessary that a new regulation should take place in the elevation or depression of streets already regulated previous to such improvement, that by such new regulation the buildings erected upon such streets in conformity with the previous regulation thereof may be essentially damaged; and that no provision is made by the existing laws to afford indemnity to the owners of property thus injured, for the loss and damage which may be sustained by them in the premises, and have prayed legislative aid for the purpose of such indemnity: Therefore,

Profiles and plans of streets, &c., to be furnished by the Corporation.

I. *Be it enacted by the People of the State of New York, represented in Senate and Assembly*, that whenever, and as often as Commissioners of estimate and assessment shall hereafter be appointed under and by virtue of the act, entitled, "An act to reduce several laws relating particularly to the city of New York into one act," passed April 9th, 1813, to perform the duties prescribed by the said act, and the acts amending the same, relative to the opening, extending, enlarging, straightening, altering, or otherwise improving any street or streets, or part of a street, or public place or places, in any part of the said city, not laid out into streets, avenues, squares, and public places, by the Commissioners of Streets and Roads in the said city, under and by virtue of the act, entitled, "An act relative to improvements touching the laying out of streets and roads in the city of New York, and for other purposes," passed April 3d, 1807; and also in all and every case and cases where such Commissioners of estimate and assessment have been heretofore appointed under the first above-mentioned act, to perform the said duties, and have not yet made their report of estimate and assessment to the Supreme Court of this State, and it shall be the duty of the said Commissioners, in each case before the completion of their estimate and assessments in the premises, to obtain from the Corporation of the City of New York a profile or plan, showing the intended regulation of such street or part of a street, or public place, as to the elevation or depression thereof, after the same shall be opened, extended, enlarged, straightened, altered, or otherwise improved, as the case may be; and also profiles or plans, if they shall deem the same useful, showing the intended regulation of the adjacent street or streets, as to the elevation or depression thereof, after such improvement: and if the said Commissioners of estimate and assessment shall judge that such intended regulation will injure any building or buildings not required to be taken for the purpose of opening, extending, enlarging, straightening, altering, or improving such street, or part of a street, or public place, they shall proceed to make (together with the other estimates and assessments required by the first above-mentioned act to be made by them) a just and equitable estimate and assessment of the loss and damage which shall accrue by and in consequence of such intended regulation to the respective owners, lessees, parties, and persons, respectively, entitled unto or interested in the said building or buildings so to be injured by the said intended regulation; and the sums or estimates of compensation or recompense for such loss and damage, shall be included by the said Commissioners in their general report of estimate and assessment, which they shall make in relation to the intended improvement of the street or public place so to be opened, extended, enlarged, straightened, altered, or improved; and the report of the said Commissioners, as to such damage and loss, and as to the person or parties who are to receive the compensation or recompense reported, shall be made in the manner directed by the first above-mentioned act, as to other damages reported by the said Commissioners.

Equitable estimate and assessment to be made.

Compensation for damages, &c., how to be made.

II. *And be it further enacted*, That the sums or estimates of compensation or recompense for the damages aforesaid, reported by the said Commissioners, shall be paid by the said Mayor, Aldermen, and Commonalty of the City of New York, at the time and in the manner prescribed by the first above-mentioned act, for the payment of the damages reported by Commissioners of estimate and assessment, in favor of the persons and parties whom they deem entitled thereto; and the said sums or estimates of compensation and recompense shall be borne and reimbursed to the said Mayor, Aldermen, and Commonalty by the persons and parties interested and entitled, as owners or otherwise, unto or in the lands, tenements, hereditaments, and premises, deemed to be benefited by the opening, extending, enlarging, straightening, altering, or improving the street or public place; the opening, extending, enlarging, straightening, altering, or improving of which, and the subsequent regulation of the same, or of the adjacent street, shall or may produce such damage or loss; and the said Commissioners, or the assessors to be appointed by the said Mayor, Aldermen, and Commonalty, under and by virtue of the said first above-mentioned act, shall assess the said sums upon and among the said persons and parties interested and entitled, as owners or otherwise, unto or in the said lands, tenements, hereditaments, and premises deemed to be benefited by the opening, extending, enlarging, straightening, altering, or improving such street or public place, in the same manner as though the said sums had been awarded for damages for lands or premises required for the purpose of opening, extending, enlarging, straightening, altering, or improving the said street or public place.

1817.—CHAPTER XXV.

AN ACT *relative to Cisterns in the streets of the City of New York.*

Passed January 31st, 1817.

Be it enacted by the People of the State of New York, represented in Senate and Assembly, that whenever, in the opinion of the Mayor, Aldermen, and Commonalty of the City of New York, in Common Council convened, it shall be expedient to make a public cistern in any of the public streets, roads, or places in the said city, it shall be lawful for the said Common Council to order the same to be done accordingly, in such manner and at such places as they shall think most advisable, and the expense thereof shall be estimated and assessed among all the owners or occupants of the houses and lots of ground intended to be benefited thereby, in the manner directed in and by the one hundred and seventy-fifth section of the act entitled "An act to reduce several laws relating to the city of New York into one act," passed April 9th, 1813, and shall be binding and conclusive, in the manner therein prescribed, and shall be collected in the manner therein directed, or in the manner directed in the two hundred and fifty-ninth section of the said act.

1817.—CHAPTER LXXV.

AN ACT *authorizing the Mayor, Aldermen, and Commonalty of the City of New York, to take possession of certain lands.*

Passed March 14th, 1817.

Preamble. *Whereas,* the Mayor, Aldermen, and Commonalty of the City of New York have represented to the Legislature, that the convenience of the said city requires that they should become possessed, in fee simple, of the lands, tenements, and hereditaments, in the Second Ward in the city of New York, bounded south-westerly by Fulton street, lately called Beekman's slip, north-westerly by Front street, north-easterly by Crane wharf, and south-easterly by a line running north-easterly, in the direction of the north-westerly side of South street; and also of the wharves and piers fronting the south-easterly side of the above-described premises, and contiguous to South street, together with the right and title to all and all manner of wharfage, cranage, benefits, and advantages, growing and arising, or which may accrue by or for the same, or by or from that part of South street, which lies fronting the said first-described premises: Therefore

Commissioners of estimate to be appointed.

I. *Be it enacted by the People of the State of New York, represented in Senate and Assembly*, that it shall be lawful for the Mayor, Aldermen, and Commonalty of the City of New York, whenever they shall judge proper, to cause application to be made to the Supreme Court of Judicature of this State, or to either of the justices thereof, for the appointment of Commissioners for the purpose of performing the duties hereinafter prescribed: and upon such application, it shall be lawful for the said court, or justice, to whom such application shall be made, to nominate and appoint three discreet and disinterested persons, being citizens of said city, Commissioners of estimate, for the purpose of performing the duties hereinafter prescribed; which said Commissioners, before they enter upon the duties of their appointment, shall severally take and subscribe an oath or affirmation, before some person authorized to administer oaths, faithfully to perform the trust and duties required of them by this act; which oath or affirmation shall be filed

Oath.

in the Clerk's Office of the city of New York; and it shall be the duty of the said Commissioners, as soon as conveniently may be after their appointment, to make a just and true estimate of the loss and damage to the respective owners, lessees, parties, and persons, respectively, entitled unto, or interested in the said lands, tenements, hereditaments, and premises, or in the appurtenances, privileges, or advantages, to the same belonging, or in any wise appertaining, by and in consequence of relinquishing the same to the said Mayor, Aldermen, and Commonalty of the City of New York, and to report thereon to the said Supreme Court of Judicature without unnecessary delay; and in the said report the Commissioners who shall make the same shall set forth the names of the respective owners, lessees, parties, and persons entitled unto, or interested in, the lands, tenements, hereditaments, and premises, before-mentioned, or in the appurtenances, privileges, or advantages to the same belonging, or in any wise appertaining, and each and every part and parcel thereof, as far forth as the same shall be ascertained by them; and an apt and sufficient designation or description of the said lots or parcels of land, tenements, hereditaments, and premises, or in the appurtenances, privileges, or advantages to the same belonging, or in any wise appertaining; but in each and every case and cases where the owners and parties interested, or their respective estates and interests, are unknown, or not fully known, to the said Commissioners, it shall be sufficient for them to estimate and to set forth and state in their said report, in general terms, the respective sums to be allowed and paid to the owners and proprietors, generally, of such lands, tenements, hereditaments, and premises, or in the appurtenances, privileges, and advantages to the same belonging, or in any wise appertaining, for the loss and damage to

Duty.

such owners, proprietors, and parties interested in respect to the whole estate and interest of whomsoever may be entitled unto, or interested in, the said lands, tenements, hereditaments, and premises, respectively, or in the appurtenances, privileges, or advantages to the same belonging, or in any wise appertaining, by and in consequence of relinquishing the same to the said Mayor, Aldermen, and Commonalty of the City of New York, without specifying the names of the estates or interests of such owners, proprietors, and parties interested, or of any or either of them ; and upon the coming in of the said report, signed by the said Commissioners, or any two of them, the said court shall, by rule or order, after hearing any matter which may be alleged against the same, either confirm the said report, or refer the same to the same Commissioners for revisal and correction, or to new Commissioners, to be appointed by the said court, to reconsider the subject-matter thereof; and the said Commissioners, to whom the said report shall be so referred, shall return the said report corrected and revised, or a new report to be made by them, in the premises, to the said court, without unnecessary delay ; and the same being so returned shall be confirmed or again referred to the said court, in manner aforesaid, as right and justice shall require, and so, from time to time, until a report shall be made or returned in the premises which the said court shall confirm ; and such report, when so confirmed by the said court, shall be final and conclusive, as well upon the said Mayor, Aldermen, and Commonalty of the City of New York, as upon the owners, lessees, and persons and parties interested in, and entitled unto, the lands, tenements, hereditaments, and premises before mentioned, or in the appurtenances, privileges, or advantages to the same belonging, or in any wise appertaining, and also upon all other persons whomsoever ; and on such final confirmation of such report, by the said court, the Mayor, Aldermen, and Commonalty of the City of New York shall become and be seized, in fee simple absolute, of all the said lands, tenements, hereditaments, and premises before mentioned, and of the appurtenances, privileges, and advantages to the same belonging, or in any wise appertaining; and thereupon the said Mayor, Aldermen, and Commonalty, or any person or persons acting under their authority, may immediately, or at any time or times thereafter, take possession of so much of the same as is now covered with water, and of the residue thereof at any time after the first of May, in the year eighteen hundred and eighteen.

Provided, the said report shall be then confirmed; and if it shall not be then confirmed, then as soon thereafter as the same shall be confirmed as aforesaid, or any part or parts thereof, without any suit or proceeding at law for that purpose.

Lease land, how to be taken.

II. *And be it further enacted*, that in all cases where any lot or parcel of lands, tenements, hereditaments, or other premises, or the appurtenances, privileges, or advantages to the same belonging, or in any wise appertaining, under lease or other contract, shall be taken by virtue of this act, all the covenants, agreements, contracts, and agreements, between landlord and tenant, or any other contracting parties, touching the same or any part thereof, shall, upon the confirmation of such report in the premises, as shall be confirmed by the court aforesaid, respectively, cease and determine, and be absolutely discharged.

Copy of estimate to be filed.

And be it further enacted, that the said Commissioners of estimate, to be appointed under and by virtue of this act, after completing their said estimate, and at least twenty-four days before they make their report to the said court, shall deposit a true copy of transcript of such estimate in the

Clerk's Office of the city of New York, for the inspection of whomsoever it may concern, and shall give notice, by advertisements, to be published in at least two of the publip newspapers printed in the said city of New York, of the said deposit thereof in the said office, and of the day on which their report will be presented to the said court; and any person and persons, whose rights may be affected thereby, and who shall object to the same, or any part thereof, may, within twenty days after the first publication of the said notice, state his, her, or their objections to the same in writing, to the said Commissioners; and the said Commissioners, or such of them as shall make such estimate, in case any objections shall be made to the same, and stated in writing, as aforesaid, shall reconsider their said estimate, or the part or parts thereof, so objected to; and in case the same shall appear to them to require correction, but not otherwise, they shall and may correct the same accordingly.

Possession, when to be taken.

IV. *And be it further enacted*, that the said Mayor, Aldermen, and Commonalty shall, within four months after they shall take possession of the before-mentioned lands, tenements, hereditaments, and premises, and on or before the first day of September, eighteen hundred and eighteen, provided the said report shall be then confirmed, and if the same shall not be then confirmed, then within four months after it shall be confirmed by the court, pay to the respective persons and parties mentioned or referred to in the said report, in whose favor any sum or sums of money shall be estimated and reported by the said Commissioners, the respective sum or sums so estimated and reported in their favor, respectively; and in case of neglect or default in the payment of the same, within the time aforesaid, the respective person or persons or party or parties, in whose favor the same shall be so reported, his, her, or their executors, administrators, or successors, at any time or times, after application first made by him, her, or them, to the said Mayor, Aldermen, and Commonalty, in Common Council convened, for payment thereof, may sue for and recover the same with lawful interest, from and after the said application therefor, and the costs of suit, in proper form of action, against the said Mayor, Aldermen, and Commonalty, in any court having cognizance thereof, and in which it shall be sufficient to declare generally, for so much money due to the plaintiff or plaintiffs therein, by virtue of this act, for premises taken by virtue thereof, and it shall be lawful for the plaintiff or plaintiffs to give any special matter in evidence under such general declaration; and this act and the report of the said Commissioners, with proof of the right and title of the plaintiff and plaintiffs to the sum or sums demanded, shall be conclusive evidence in such suit or action.

Proviso. *Provided, and be it further enacted,* That whenever the owners and proprietors of any such lands, tenements, hereditaments, and premises, to be taken by virtue of this act, or of the appurtenances, privileges, or advantages to the same belonging or in any wise appertaining, or the party or parties, person or persons, interested therein, or any or either of them, the said owners, proprietors, parties, or persons in whose favor any such sum or sums, or compensation, shall be so reported, shall be under the age of twenty-one years, *non compos mentis*, feme, covert, or absent from the city of New York; and also in all cases where the name or names of the owner or owners, party or persons, entitled unto or interested in any lands, tenements, hereditaments, or premises that may be so taken, or the appurtenances, privileges, and advantages to the same belonging, or in any wise appertaining, shall not be set forth or mentioned in the said report, or where the said owners, parties, or persons respectively being named therein, cannot, upon diligent inquiry, be found, it shall be lawful for the said Mayor, Aldermen, and Commonalty to pay the sum or sums mentioned in the said report, payable, or that would be coming to such owners, proprietors, parties, or persons respectively, into the said Supreme Court of Judicature, to be secured, disposed of, and improved as the said court shall direct; and such payment shall be as valid and effectual, in all respects, as if made to the said owners, proprietors, parties, and persons, respectively, themselves, according to their just rights, if they had been known, and had all been present, of full age, discovert, and *compos mentis*.

And provided also, That in all, and each, and every case and cases, where any such sum or sums, or compensation, so to be reported by the said Commissioners in favor of any person or persons, or party or parties whatsoever, whether named or not named in the said report, shall be paid to any person or persons, or party or parties whomsoever, when the same shall of right belong, and ought to have been paid, to some other person or persons, or party or parties, it shall be lawful for the said person or persons, or party or parties to whom the same ought to have been paid, to sue for and recover the same, with lawful interest and costs of suit, from the person or persons, party or parties to whom the same shall have been paid, as so much money had and received, to the use of the said plaintiff or plaintiffs, by the person or persons, party or parties, respectively, to whom the same shall have been so paid. Proviso.

V. *And be it further enacted*, That in case of the death, resignation, or refusal to act, of the Commissioners of estimate to be appointed under and by virtue of this act, or either Vacancies to be filled.

of them, it shall and may be lawful for the court aforesaid, or any one of the justices thereof, on the application of the Mayor, Aldermen, and Commonalty of the City of New York, as often as such event shall happen, to appoint a discreet and disinterested person, being a citizen of the said city of New York, in the place and stead of such Commissioner so dying, resigning, or refusing to act, and that the surviving or acting Commissioners, as the case may be, shall have full power to proceed in the execution of the duties of their appointment, until a successor of the Commissioner so dying, resigning, or refusing to act, shall be appointed.

Two Commissioners may act.

VI. *And be it further enacted*, that in all and every case of the appointment of Commissioners under this act, it shall be competent and lawful for any two of said Commissioners, so to be appointed, to proceed to and execute and perform the trust and duties of their said appointment, and their acts shall be as valid and effectual as the acts of all the Commissioners so to be appointed, if they had acted therein, would have been.

And further, that in all cases, the acts, proceedings, and decisions of a major part of such of the Commissioners as shall be acting in the premises, shall be as binding, valid, and effectual, as if the said Commissioners, named and appointed for such purpose, had all concurred and joined therein.

Their pay.

VII. *And be it further enacted*, that the Commissioners to be appointed under and by virtue of this act, who shall enter upon the duties of their appointment, shall each be entitled to receive the sum of not less than four dollars, besides all reasonable expenses for maps, surveys, clerk hire, and other necessary expenses and disbursements, for each day they shall respectively be actually employed in the duties of their appointment, and the same shall be paid by the Mayor, Aldermen, and Commonalty of the City of New York.

Value and benefit to be estimated.

VIII. *And be it further enacted*, That it shall be lawful for the said Mayor, Aldermen, and Commonalty, in Common Council convened, in their discretion, to order and direct the Commissioners who may be appointed as aforesaid, to make a just and equitable estimate of the value of the benefit and advantage to the respective owners, lessees, parties, and persons, respectively, entitled unto, or interested in the lands, tenements, hereditaments, and premises which the said Commissioners may deem to be benefited by, and in consequence of erecting upon the before-mentioned and described premises, a public market, or by and in consequence of removing the Fly Market, so called, in the said city, and appropriating the ground upon which the same is now situated for a public street, deducting from the amount of such estimates the amount which the respective owners, lessees, parties, and persons, respectively, entitled unto, or interested in the lands, tenements, and premises, may have been induced to give for the same, subsequently to the 29th day of March, one thousand eight hundred and sixteen ; and prior to the passing of this act, in consequence of the said Mayor, Aldermen, and Commonalty having contemplated the erection of a public market upon the premises aforesaid, and the removal of the said Fly Market, and appropriating the ground upon which the same is erected for a public street, over and above what would otherwise have been the value of the same ; and it shall thereupon be the duty of the said Commissioners to proceed accordingly, and to include in the report which they shall make, as aforesaid, a statement of the respective owners, lessees, parties, and persons entitled unto, or interested in the said lands, tenements, hereditaments, and premises, as far forth as the same shall be ascertained by them, and an apt and sufficient designation or description of the said respective lots, or parcels of land, tenements, hereditaments, and premises, which may be deemed to be benefited as aforesaid, and also the several and respective sums so to be estimated and reported, shall, upon the said report being confirmed, as aforesaid, be a lien or charge on the lands, tenements, hereditaments, and premises in the said report mentioned; or the said respective sums may be recovered, with the lawful interest which may accrue thereon, from and after thirty days from the date and confirmation of said report, and all costs and charges, by the said Mayor, Aldermen, and Commonalty, from and against the parties aforesaid, respectively, or the owner or owners, respectively, of the respective lands, tenements, hereditaments, and premises deemed to be benefited, as aforesaid, by action of debt or assumpsit, in which it shall be sufficient to declare generally for so much money due by virtue of this act, to the said Mayor, Aldermen, and Commonalty, and any matter may be given in evidence under such general declaration,

Provided, that nothing herein contained shall affect any agreement between landlord and tenant, or any other contracting parties, respecting the payment of any such sums so estimated, but they shall be answerable to each other in the same manner as if the provision of this act concerning the same had not been made.

1819.—CHAPTER LXIX.

AN ACT *authorizing the Mayor, Aldermen, and Commonalty of the City of New York, to take possession of certain unclaimed lands.* Passed March 26, 1819.

I. *Be it enacted by the People of the State of New York, represented in Senate and Assembly,* that it shall be lawful for the Mayor, Aldermen, and Commonalty of the City of New York, and they are hereby authorized and empowered, to take peaceable possession of, or sue for and recover, and to hold, occupy, and enjoy all lots or pieces or parcels of land situate, lying, and being in the said city which have or which may be sold for a term of time for the payment of any taxes or assessments in the said city, after the expiration of the term for which the same may have been or shall be so sold. Un laimed lands.

Provided, The rightful owner of the same shall not then claim possession of the same, and to have, hold, and oocupy the same until the rightful owner shall claim possession of the same, shall pay all sums which may be due thereon for taxes, assessments, and also the value of the improvements which may be made or erected upon the same by the Mayor, Aldermen, and Commonalty of the City of New York, over and above all the rents, issues, and profits which may be received by the Mayor, Aldermen, and Commonalty of the City of New York, for or on account of the rents, issues, and profits of any such premises. Rightful owner.

Provided always, That the said Mayor, Aldermen, and Commonalty of the City of New York, shall not be entitled to demand any sum of money for any such improvements, unless they shall have caused to be published in at least two of the public newspapers printed in the said city, Advertise.

for at least three months previous to the making of such improvements, a notification to the owners of the said lots, to appear and take possession of their said premises.

And further, That in no case shall the owners of the said premises be compelled to pay for any such improvements, a sum exceeding two-thirds of the value of their said lots of land.

And provided also, That nothing herein contained shall interfere with or repeal the provisions of an act entitled "An act authorizing the Mayor, Aldermen, and Commonalty of the City of New York to close streets and roads," passed April 20th, 1818.

II. *And be it further enacted,* that the Mayor, Aldermen, and Commonalty of the City of New York shall account for and pay over to the rightful owner of any such lots of land, all the rents, issues, and profits which they may receive on account of such premises, over and above the amount of all taxes and assessments due for or on account of the said premises, and over and above the value of all such improvements thereon, as shall be made after the notification mentioned in the first section of this act, and as shall not exceed two thirds of the value of said lots of land.

1821.—CHAPTER CXLIX.

AN ACT *to amend an act, entitled "An act for the more effectual collection of Taxes and Assessments in the City of New York."* Passed March 23d, 1821.

Provision in cases where lands taxed, are held by more than one owner.

I. *Be it enacted by the People of the State of New York, represented in Senate and Assembly,* that if a sum of money, in gross, has been or shall be assessed or taxed, upon any lands or premises in the city of New York, by virtue of any law of this State, any person or persons claiming any divided or undivided part thereof, may pay such part of the sum of money, so assessed or taxed, and also of the interest and charges due or charged thereon, as the Mayor, Aldermen, and Commonalty of the City of New York, in Common Council convened, may deem to be just and equitable, and the remainder of the sum of money so assessed or taxed, together with the interest and charges, shall be a lien on the residue of the land only, which may be sold in pursuance of the provisions of the act, entitled "An act for the more effectual collection of taxes and assessments in the city of New York," to satisfy the residue of such assessments or tax, interest and charges, in the same manner which it could have been, provided the residue of said assessment or tax had been imposed upon the residue of said lands and tenements.

Provided always, That nothing herein contained shall be so construed as to release the occupant of any such premises from his liability to pay assessments and taxes upon the whole of the premises which he is or shall be in the occupation of.

Redemption of lands sold.

II. *And be it further enacted*, That the proprietor of any lands sold or which shall be sold for taxes or assessments in the city of New York, in pursuance of the provisions of said act, shall not be permitted to redeem the same within the two years mentioned in said act, unless he shall pay to the Street Commissioner of the City of New York, for the use of the purchaser, his executors, administrators, or assigns, in addition to the sum which such purchaser shall have paid for the same, at the time of sale, by virtue of said act, all such sums of money which the said purchaser shall have paid since the sale of said lands, for taxes or assessments on the same, and also for the costs and charges attending the advertising of the same, and all other costs and charges thereon, together with the interest thereof, at the rate of fourteen per centum per annum, from the time of making such payments.

Interest, when chargeable on a tax.

III. *And be it further enacted*, That the owner of any lands or tenements in the city of New York, upon whom, or on whose lands, any assessment has been or shall be made or imposed, who shall neglect, or has neglected, to pay the same, for the space of sixty days, after the said assessment was or shall be confirmed according to law, shall be liable to pay interest thereon, at the rate of seven per cent. per annum, to be calculated from the time of the confirmation of said assessment.

1824.—CHAPTER XLIX.

AN ACT *to amend an act entitled "An act to reduce several Laws, relating particularly to the City of New York, into one Act," passed April* 9, 1813. Passed February 21, 1824.

Preamble.

Whereas, doubts have arisen whether the two hundred and seventieth section of the act above mentioned applies to all the laws and ordinances of the Mayor, Aldermen, and Commonalty of the City of New York, in Common Council convened, touching any acts, works, or labor to be done and performed, and improvements to be made in the said city, which under that act, or any other act or acts of the Legislature, they are authorized to pass, order, and direct, and the expenses of which may be estimated and assessed on the owner or occupants of all the houses and lots intended to be benefited thereby, by skillful and competent disinterested persons appointed by the said Common Council: Therefore,

A certain section extended.

I. *Be it enacted by the People of the State of New York, represented in Senate and Assembly*, That the provisions of the above section shall apply to all and every of the laws, ordinances, orders, and directions which the said Corporation are authorized to make, under and by virtue of any part or section of the aforesaid act, or of any other act or acts of the Legislature; and that the two hundred and seventy-first section shall in like manner apply thereto, and that assessments for any such expenses, with interest, may be made or directed in and by the one hundred and seventy-fifth section of said act, and shall be a real incumbrance upon the houses and lots, lands and tenements therein mentioned, which may be sold for any such assessment thereon, and every remedy and proceeding had for the collection thereof, according to the provisions of an act entitled "An act for the more effectual collection of taxes and assessments in the city of New York," passed April 12, 1816, and any act amendatory thereof.

Assessments declared a lien, etc.

Regulations as to raising or filling up lots, etc.

II. *And be it further enacted*, that it shall and may be lawful for the said Mayor, Aldermen, and Commonalty, in all cases where they may deem it necessary for the more speedy execution of any by-law or ordinance requiring the owner or joint owners, agent or joint agents, lessee or joint lessees, and occupant or joint occupants of any lot or lots, to fill up or raise such lot or lots forthwith, upon the passage of such by-law or ordinance, or at any time thereafter when they may deem it expedient to cause such lot or lots to be filled up or raised at their own expense, on account of such owner or owners, agent or agents, lessee or lessees, and occupant or occupants, respectively; and the said Mayor, Aldermen, and Commonalty shall have full power, and are hereby authorized to levy the same, with lawful interest, and all reasonable costs and expenditures attending such proceedings, by distress and sale of the goods and chattels of such owners, agents, lessees, or occupants, or to recover the amount of every such expense, by action of debt, in any court of record, from the persons, respectively, on whose account the same shall have been incurred, their respective heirs, executors, or administrators; in all which actions they shall also recover lawful interest upon said amount, with full costs of suit.

Amount declared a lien, etc.

And further, that the amount of the moneys which the said Mayor, Aldermen, and Commonalty shall have advanced for the above purposes, with lawful interest for the same, shall be deemed a lien on such lot or lots, and that such lot or lots may be sold therefor, according to the provisions of the said act for the more effectual collection of taxes and assessments in the city of New York, or any act amendatory thereof, in the same manner as if the said amount and interest had been charged on the said lot or lots, by virtue of an assessment.

1830.—CHAPTER II.

AN ACT *to amend an act, passed April 12th*, 1816, *entitled "An Act for the more effectual Collection of Taxes and Assessments in the City of New York."* Passed January 15, 1830.

The People of the State of New York, represented in Senate and Assembly, do enact as follows:

Sales may be postponed fifteen months

Sec. 1. It shall be lawful for the Mayor, Aldermen, and Commonalty of the City of New York, whenever they shall deem it expedient, by a resolution to be passed in

Common Council, to suspend or postpone any sale or sales of lands and tenements, or any portion thereof, which shall have been advertised for sale in pursuance of the second section of the act hereby amended, to any time not exceeding fifteen months from the day specified in any such advertisement.

Sec. 2. All sales which shall be postponed or suspended by virtue of this act, shall be made without further advertisement, other than a general notice of such postponement, to be published in two or more of the public newspapers in the city of New York, at least once a week until the time of sale, and such sales, when made, shall be as valid and effectual as if the same had taken place at the time for that purpose first advertised. Notice thereof.

Sec. 3. All sales of lands and tenements for assessments under and by virtue of this act, or of the act hereby amended, may hereafter be conducted by the Street Commissioner of the city of New York, or by his assistant or deputy; and all such sales for taxes may hereafter be conducted by the Comptroller of the said city, or by his assistant or deputy; and it shall not be necessary to employ a public auctioneer for any such sales. Sales, how and by whom to be made.

Sec. 4. All advertisements hereafter to be published, prior to any sale of lands and tenements, for taxes or assessments, in pursuance of the provisions of the second section of the act hereby amended, shall require the owner of such lands and tenements to pay the amount of such tax or assessment, with interest and charges, as specified in the said act, to such person or persons, to be named in such advertisements, as may be appointed by the Common Council, to collect the same, instead of the Treasurer or Chamberlain of the said city, as by the said act hereby amended is directed. Payments.

Act, when to take effect. Sec. 5. The provisions of this act shall be in force, and take effect from and immediately after the passing thereof.

1840.—CHAPTER CCCXXVI.

AN ACT *in relation to the Collection of Assessments and Taxes in the City and County of New York, and for other purposes.* Passed May 14, 1840.

The People of the State of New York, represented in Senate and Assembly, do enact as follows:

Duty of Assessors. Sec. 1. In all cases where Commissioners or assessors shall describe the houses and lots assessed for any improvement, the assessment shall describe and particularize all such houses and lots by the known street number, as well as the ward number, and shall also state the names of the owner or owners, and occupant or occupants; and it shall be the duty of the surveyors who shall make out the assessment list, to ascertain, by inquiry to be made of the collector of taxes of the ward in which the property assessed is situate, and by inquiry of the person who collected the taxes of such ward the previous year, as to such ownership; and such collectors shall afford the requisite information.

And surveyors.

Sec. 2. [This section repealed by section 2, chapter 171, laws of 1841.]

Lots, etc., how advertised. Sec. 3. In advertising houses and lots, improved or unimproved lands, to be sold for the non-payment of assessments, it shall be the duty of the Street Commissioner to advertise all the houses and lots, or other lands lying contiguous to each other, and belonging to the same owner, in one parcel, unless otherwise requested by such owner.

Sec. 4. It shall not be lawful for any Commissioner or

Charges for assessments, etc.

assessor to charge for any services in making estimates and assessments for any improvements, authorized by law to be assessed upon the owners or occupants of houses and lots, or improved or unimproved lands, not actually rendered by him, nor for any part of days as whole days, where the time occupied was less than six hours of such day.

Certificates of sale.

Sec. 5. Certificates of sale shall be made and delivered to the purchasers without charge, and no charge shall be made in the sale for the second advertisement and lease; but the expense of the former shall be paid by the owner at the time of redeeming, or by the purchaser when he shall receive a lease. The expense of drawing and executing a lease shall be paid by the purchaser at the time of receiving the same, and shall not exceed fifty cents.

Leases.

Interest on purchase money.

Sec. 6. The rate of interest allowed by law to the purchaser, at the time of redemption, on the amount of the purchase-money, shall be reduced to fourteen per cent. per annum; but no interest shall be calculated on a less portion or time than one quarter of a year; and in all cases where the property shall be redeemed during any fractional part of a year, the interest shall be calculated so as to include the quarter in which such redemption shall be made, the time to be computed from the day of sale.

Amount which property is to be assessed.

Sec. 7. Commissioners or assessors for making estimates and assessments for any improvements authorized by law to be assessed upon the owners or occupants of houses and lots, or improved or unimproved lands, shall in no case assess any house, lot, improved or unimproved land, more than one half the value of such house, lot, improved or unimproved land, as valued by the assessors of the ward in which the same shall be situate.

Sec. 8. [This section obsolete. Office of collector of taxes abolished by section 1, chap. 230, Laws of 1843.]

Notice of sale for assessments on taxes.

Sec. 9. No houses and lots, or improved or unimproved lands in the city and county of New York, shall be hereafter sold or leased at public auction for the non-payment of any assessment or tax which may be due thereon, unless notice of such sale shall have been published once in each week for three months, in at least ten of the daily newspapers printed and published in the city of New York; one of which shall contain a particular and detailed statement of the property to be sold for assessments, and such as is now published by the Street Commissioner, in two of the daily newspapers in the city of New York, or the said detailed statement or description shall be printed in a pamphlet in the discretion of the Street Commissioner, in which case the pamphlet shall be deposited in the Street Commissioner's Office in the city of New York, and with the collectors of taxes of the different wards of the said city, and shall be delivered to any person applying therefor; and the notice provided for in this section, of the sale of houses and lots, and improved or unimproved lands, shall also state that the detailed statement of the assessment, or tax and ownership of the property assessed or taxed, is published in one of the daily newspapers, naming the same, or in a pamphlet, as the case may be, and where the pamphlets are deposited, to be delivered to any person applying for the same.

Notice of sale for assessments on taxes.

Sec. 10. It shall not be necessary to give any further publicity of any intended sale of property for unpaid assessments and taxes, than is contemplated by the last preceding section; and in giving the further notice required by section two of the act entitled "An act for the more effectual collection of taxes and assessments in the city of New York," passed April 12, 1816, of the sale of property six months previous to the expiration of the time for redemption, it shall only be necessary to publish the same in one daily newspaper printed and published in the city of New York, twice in each week for six weeks successively: and so much of the said section as is inconsistent with this act, is hereby repealed.

And not of redemption.

Sec. 11. In all cases where pieces, parcels, or lots of lands shall have been sold for assessments, and any person shall claim to redeem any portion of the same within the time limited for redemption, he shall be permitted to do so on paying the apportionment of the assessment for which the property was sold, together with the interest on the same, and an equitable proportion of the expenses.

Redemption of portions of land sold.

The apportionment to be made by the Street Commissioner.

Sec. 12. Nothing contained in the ninth section of this act shall be construed to postpone the sale now advertised to take place in June next.

Pending notice not affected.

1840—CHAPTER CCCLXXXVII.

AN ACT *authorizing Mortgagees to redeem Real Estate sold for Taxes and Assessments.* Passed May 14, 1840.

The People of the State of New York, represented in Senate and Assembly, do enact as follows:

Sec. 1. No sale of real estate hereafter made for the non-payment on any tax or assessment, shall destroy or in any

Mortgage not affected by sale of

land for taxes, etc. manner affect the lien of any mortgage thereon, duly recorded or registered at the time of such sale, except as hereinafter provided.

Purchasers to give notice to mortgagee. Sec. 2. It shall be the duty of the purchaser at such sale, to give to the mortgagee a written notice of such sale, requiring him to pay the amount of the purchase-money, with the interest at the rate allowed by law thereon, within six months after the giving of such notice.

Effect of redemption by mortgagee. Sec. 3. If such payment shall be made, the sale shall be of no further effect, and the mortgagee shall have a lien on the premises for the amount paid, with the interest which may thereafter accrue thereon, at the rate of seven per cent. per annum, in like manner as if the same had been included in this mortgage.

Failure to redeem. Sec. 4. In case the mortgagee shall fail to make such within the time so limited, he shall not be entitled to the benefit of the first section of this act.

Construction of certain terms. Sec. 5. The term "mortgagee," as used in this act, shall not be construed to include assignees whose assignment shall be duly recorded, and personal representatives; and the term "purchaser" shall be construed to include assignees, and real or personal representatives, as the case may be.

Notice, how given. Sec. 6. The notice required by this act may be given either personally or in the manner required by law, in respect to notices of non-acceptance or non-payment of notes or bills of exchange; and a notarial certificate thereof shall be presumptive evidence of the fact of such notice; such certificates may be recorded in the county in which the mortgage was recorded, in the same manner, and with the same effect, as is by law prescribed in respect to deeds or other evidences of title of real estate. Evidence of notice.

1841.—CHAPTER CLXX.

AN ACT *in relation to the Redemption of Land sold for Taxes or Assessments in the City of New York.* Passed May 7, 1841.

The People of the State of New York, represented in Senate and Assembly, do enact as follows:

Street Commissioner to notify mortgagees.

Sec. 1. In cases of sales of real estate for the non-payment of taxes and assessments in the city of New York, it shall be the duty of the Street Commissioner of the said city, sixty days before the time limited by law for the redemption of any real estate from the effect of such sales, to cause notice to be given to all mortgagees of real estate so sold, their assignees or personal representatives, who shall at any time, at least one month before the time for the giving of such notice, have filed in the office of the Register of the City and County of New York, a memorandum of such mortgage, containing a brief abstract, designating the property, with street number, if there be any, or such definite description or diagram, as will enable the said Street Commissioner to designate the said premises upon the city maps, and the name and residence of such mortgagee, assignee, or personal representatives.

Notice, how to be served.

Sec. 2. Such notice shall be given by putting the same in the post office of the city of New York, to such mortgagee, assignee, or personal representatives, with such description and place of residence as shall be contained in such memorandum, and such notice shall require such mortgagee, assignee, or personal representatives, to pay the amount of such tax or assessment, with all interest and expenses allowed by law, before the time limited for the redemption, as aforesaid.

Proof of such service. Sec. 3. An affidavit of the service of such notice as is above required, before any officer authorized to take affidavits, to be read in a court of record and filed in the office of the said Register of Deeds, or a certified copy thereof, under the signature of such Register, shall be evidence of the fact of such notice.

Register to record memorandums. Sec. 4. It shall be the duty of the said Register of Deeds to keep in his office a book, alphabetically arranged, for the registering of all such memorandums as aforesaid, which book shall be open to the inspection of any person desiring to examine the same.

His fees. Sec. 5. The said Register shall be entitled to receive twenty-five cents for registering the memorandum of each mortgage as above provided.

Right to redeem lands within two years. Sec. 6. Such mortgagees, or their assignees or personal representatives, shall be entitled to redeem the property sold from the effect of such sale, at any time within two years from the date of such sale, and shall have a lien on the property for the amount paid, with the interest which may thereafter accrue thereon, at the rate of seven per cent. per annum, in like manner as if the same had been included in such mortgage.

Act of May 14, 1840, not to apply to N. Y. City. Sec. 7. The act entitled "An act authorizing mortgagees to redeem real estate sold for taxes and assessments," passed May 14, 1840, shall not apply to the city and county of New York, in any case in which the notice and affidavit herein provided for shall have been given and filed, as in this act required.

Sec. 8. This act shall take effect immediately.

1841.—CHAPTER CLXXI.

AN ACT *to amend an act entitled, "An act in relation to the Collection of Assessments and Taxes in the City and County of New York, and for other purposes," passed May* 14, 1840. Passed May 7, 1841.

The People of the State of New York, represented in Senate and Assembly, do enact as follows:

Notice to be given of completion of estimate and assessment.

Sec. 1. It shall be the duty of all Commissioners and assessors authorized to make any estimate and assessment for any improvement, to give notice to the owner or owners, and to the occupant or occupants of all houses and lots, and improved or unimproved lands affected thereby, that they have completed the estimate and assessment; such notice shall be published daily in at least two of the daily newspapers, for ten days successively, which shall be annually designated by the Common Council. The notice shall describe the limits embraced by such assessment, and shall contain a request for all persons whose interest may be affected thereby, and who may be opposed to the same, to present their objections in writing to the chairman of Commissioners or assessors within thirty days from the date of such notice; and if, after examining such objections, the Commissioners or assessors shall not deem it proper to alter their assessment, or, having altered it, there shall still be objections to the same, it shall be their duty to present such objections, with the assessment, to the court or persons authorized to confirm the same; but nothing herein contained shall conflict with or render invalid the act entitled "An act to reduce several laws relating to the city of New York into one act," passed April 20, 1839.

Repeal

Sec. 2. The second section of the "Act in relation to the collection of assessments and taxes in the city and county of New York into one act, and for other purposes," passed May 14, 1840, is hereby repealed.

Lots lying contiguous, owned by one person, may be sold separately.

Sec. 3. Nothing contained in the third section of the act last above mentioned shall be construed to prevent the Street Commissioner from selling separately any houses and lots or other lands lying contiguous to each other, and belonging to the same owner, which shall have been advertised in one parcel, and he is hereby authorized to sell the same separately as the same may have been assessed.

Sec. 4. This act shall take effect immediately.

1841.—CHAPTER CCXXX.

AN ACT *in addition to the acts respecting the Collection of Taxes and Assessments in the City and County of New York.* Passed May 25, 1841.

The People of the State of New York, represented in Senate and Assembly, do enact as follows:

Owners and lessees, how to be notified.

Sec. 1. All owners, lessees, or persons otherwise interested in any lands or tenements sold for taxes or assessments in the city of New York, who shall file in the manner and within the time specified in the act entitled "An act in relation to the redemption of land sold for taxes or assessments in the city of New York," passed May 6th, 1841, a memorandum containing a like description of such lands and tenements, and of the name and residence of such owners, lessee, or persons otherwise interested therein, or their legal representatives, as is required in and by the said last-mentioned act with regard to mortgagees, assignees, or their personal representatives, shall be notified in the same manner as such mortgagees, assignees, or their personal representatives are required to be notified, in and by the provisions of the said last-mentioned act.

Persons entitled to the benefits of the Act of 1846.

Sec. 2. No person shall be entitled to the benefit of the provisions of the first, second, and sixth sections of the act entitled "An act authorizing mortgagees to redeem real estate sold for taxes and assessment," passed May 14, 1840, or of the act entitled "An act in relation to the redemption of land sold for taxes or assessments in the city of New York," passed May 6, 1841, for any land or tenements in the city of New York sold for assessments, unless the memorandum required by the first section of the act last mentioned shall have been filed as therein required, and in such case it shall only be necessary to give the notice mentioned in the manner designated in the last-mentioned act.

Purchaser to serve notice on occupant, of land sold.

Sec. 3. Whenever any land or tenements sold for assessments or taxes in the city of New York, and conveyed in the manner provided by law, shall, at the time of conveyance, be in the actual occupancy of any person, the grantee to whom the same shall have been conveyed, or the person claiming under him, shall serve a written notice on the person occupying such land or tenements, and the person last assessed as owner, stating in substance the sale and conveyance, the person to whom made, and the amount of consideration-money mentioned in the conveyance, with the addition of forty-two per cent. on such amount as the said lands or tenements were struck off for at the time of the sale, and the further addition of the sum paid for the lease and advertisements, and stating also, that unless such consideration-money, and the said forty-two per cent., together with the sum paid for the lease, shall be paid to the Street Commissioner for the benefit of the grantee, in case the said premises shall have been sold for assessments, or to the Comptroller, if the same shall have been sold for taxes within six months after the service of such notice, that the said conveyance will become absolute, and the occupant and all others interested in the land or tenements be barred from all right or title thereto, during the term of years for which such lands or tenements shall have been conveyed.

Notice, how to be served.

Sec. 4. Such notice shall be served personally, or by leaving the same at the dwelling-house of the occupant or person last assessed as owner, with any person of suitable age or discretion belonging to his family.

Land may be redeemed within six months.

Sec. 5. The occupant, or any other person, may at any time, within the six months mentioned in such notice, redeem the said land or tenements in the same manner as now provided by law, for the redemption of lands sold for taxes and assessments in the city of New York, by paying such purchase-money, with the addition of forty-two per cent. thereon, and the amount that shall have been paid for the lease, and every such redemption shall be as effectual as if made before the conveyance of the lands or tenements sold.

Affidavit to be filed with Street Commissioner or Comptroller.

Sec. 6. In every such case of actual occupancy, the grantee or the person claiming under him, in order to complete his title to the land conveyed, shall file with the Street Commissioner, if sold for assessments, and with the Comptroller, if sold for taxes, the affidavit of some person who shall be certified as creditable by the officer before whom such affidavit shall be taken, that such notice as is above required was duly served, specifying the mode of service, and a copy of such notice shall be attached thereto.

Sec. 7. If the Street Commissioner, in case of a conveyance on account of assessments, or the Comptroller, in a case of conveyance on the account of taxes, shall be satisfied by such affidavit that the notice has been duly served, and if the moneys required to be paid for the redemption of such land or tenements shall not have been paid as hereinbefore provided, they shall, respectively, certify to the fact, and the conveyance shall thereupon become absolute, and the occupant and all others interested in the land or tenements shall be barred of all right and title thereto, during the term of years for which the same shall have been conveyed.

Conveyance, when to become obsolete.

Sec. 8. In cases of sales of any lands, tenements, or real estate for taxes, in the city of New York, the Comptroller of said city shall do and perform all the acts and duties required by law of the Street Commissioner of said city, in cases of the sale of any lands for assessments in the said city.

Duty of the City Comptroller in cases of tax sales.

Sec. 9. This act shall be construed to authorize the computing of the forty-two per cent. named therein on the amount of sale and expenses authorized by law, and not to be in addition to or upon the interest accruing after the sale.

Computation of interest.

1841.—CHAPTER CCCXLI.

AN ACT *to authorize the Sale of Real Estate in certain cases to pay Assessments, and for other purposes.* Passed May 26, 1841.

The People of the State of New York, represented in Senate and Assembly, do enact as follows:

Apportionment of tax or assessment on lands held by several persons in cities.

Sec. 1. In all cases where any real estate situated within the bounds of any city or village in this State, is owned by several persons having estates therein, in possession, reversion, or remainder, and such real estate or any part thereof, has been sold, or shall hereafter be sold, or is liable to be sold for any term of years to satisfy any tax or assessment imposed thereon by the authorities of any such city or village, upon a bill filed by any person interested in such estate against other persons interested therein, for the purpose of compelling a just and equitable apportionment of such tax or assessment amongst those liable to contribute to the payment thereof, or the redemption of the premises so sold, the Court of Chancery shall have power, at any time, on the application of any party to such suit, to extend the time of redemption of any such land sold, or to be hereafter sold, by authority of such city or village, to a period not exceeding six months from the entry of the final decree to be made in such cause, or to order a sale in fee of any part or parts of such real estate to pay such tax or assessment, or to redeem such parts thereof as may hereafter be sold at any time during the progress of such cause, and to direct the proceeds of such sale to be applied to the payment of such tax or assessment, or to the redemption of the lands sold for the satisfaction of such tax or assessment.

Powers of Court of Chancery.

Proceedings in cases of unknown owners of future estates.

Sec. 2. Whenever the person entitled to a future estate in such lands as are mentioned in the preceding section, cannot be ascertained, the Court of Chancery shall have and exercise all the powers and authority conferred in that section, whenever the persons having vested estates shall be made parties to a bill filed for the purposes therein specified.

Contributions by owners, how compelled.

Sec. 3. In any final decree made in a cause instituted in the Court of Chancery for the purposes mentioned in this act, such Court shall compel a just and equitable apportionment to be made by all persons having different estates in such lands as are hereinbefore specified, and liable to contribute to the payment of such tax or assessment, or to the redemption of such parts thereof as may have been sold by the authority of any city or village ; and if any portions thereof have been sold by virtue of any order made during the progress of the cause, or by the authority of such city or village, whereby the interest or estate of one party has been charged with or made to contribute more than a just and equitable proportion of such tax or assessment, such excess shall be deemed and decreed to be a lien upon the interest and estate of the other parties in such proportions as shall be equitable and just.

Contracts for payment of taxes, &c., not affected, nor liability of persons to payments.

Sec. 4. Nothing in this act contained shall be construed to affect or impair any contract or covenant heretofore or hereafter made respecting the payment of any such taxes or assessments, on real estate ; or to change the relative rights of the several persons having any estate therein, as to their liability to such payments.

Sec. 5. This act shall take effect immediately.

1842.—CHAPTER CLIV.

AN ACT *in relation to the sale of Real Estate to pay assessments.* Passed April 11, 1842.

The People of the State of New York, represented in Senate and Assembly, do enact as follows:

Sales, by whom and where made.

Sec. 1. All sales made on an order of the Court of Chancery for the payment of assessments, pursuant to any law of this State, shall be made by or under the direction of one of the masters of said court, in the county where the premises, or some part thereof, are situated.

Effect of deeds to purchasers.

Sec. 2. Deeds shall thereupon be executed by such master, which shall vest in the purchaser the entire estate, as well present as future, of each and every of the parties to such suit or suits.

Feigned issue may be ordered.

Sec. 3. In case any person or party in any such suit in the Court of Chancery, shall question the validity of the assessment or assessments which are to be paid out of the proceeds of sale, it shall be the duty of the Court to order a feigned issue, to be tried in the Circuit Court, to determine the validity thereof, or in some other manner ascertain the same.

1843.—CHAPTER CCXXXV.

AN ACT *to authorize the Mayor, Aldermen, and Commonalty of the City of New York, to purchase lands for taxes and assessments in certain cases, and for other purposes.* Passed April 18, 1843, by a two-third vote.

The People of the State of New York, represented in Senate and Assembly, do enact as follows:

Lands may be bid in for city, at sales for taxes or assessments.

Sec. 1. It shall be lawful for the Comptroller of the city of New York, at any sale of lands for taxes in the said city, and for the Street Commissioner of the said city, at any sale of lands for assessments in the said city, held pursuant to law, to bid in, for the Mayor, Aldermen, and Commonalty of the said city, every lot of land and premises by them put up, for which no person shall offer to bid; and certificates of such sale shall be made by the said Comptroller, and the Street Commissioner, in the several cases of such sale for taxes or assessments, which shall describe the lands purchased, and specify the term of years for which the same shall have been sold, and the time when the said Mayor, Aldermen, and Commonalty will be entitled to a lease of such lands and premises. Such purchases shall be subject to the same right of redemption as purchases by individuals, and if the lands sold shall not be redeemed, or shall not have been assigned as hereinafter provided, the said Comptroller, in sales for taxes, and the said Street Commissioner, in sales for assessments, shall execute a lease therefor, by virtue of the authority in them vested by this act, to the said Mayor, Aldermen, and Commonalty, in the same form and with the same effect as in the cases of leases to individuals, as now authorized by law.

Comptroller and Street Commissioner to bid in lands.

Sec. 2. It shall be the duty of the said Comptroller, in all cases of purchases of land by the said Mayor, Aldermen, and Commonalty, for taxes, and of the said Street Commissioner, in all cases of purchases of land by the said Mayor, Aldermen, and Commonalty, for assessments, to assign any and all of such purchases to any person who shall at any time within one year, from the time when such purchases were made, offer to take the same, upon their paying to the said Comptroller and Street Commissioner respectively, for the use of the said Mayor, Aldermen, and Commonalty, the purchase-money, with seven per cent. interest thereon.

Lands, how and on what terms redeemed.

Sec. 3. The persons receiving the assignments mentioned in the next preceding section, shall be entitled, upon the redemption of the property, to receive the amount paid by them to the said Mayor, Aldermen, and Commonalty, with interest from the time of such payment, at the same rate and in the same manner as if they had purchased the property at a sale for taxes or assessments.

Time for redemption.

Sec. 4. In all cases of lands and premises purchased by the Mayor, Aldermen, and Commonalty, for taxes or assessments, in which the same shall not have been assigned as provided in the second section of this act, any person may redeem the same previous to the time when the Mayor, Aldermen, and Commonalty shall be entitled to a lease of such lands and premises; by paying in the manner provided by law, for the use of the said Mayor, Aldermen, and Commonalty, the purchase-money, with seven per cent. interest thereon, together with any expense which shall have accrued since the sale.

Rights of Mortgagees and lessees.

Sec. 5. In all cases where mortgagees of real estate sold for taxes and assessments, in the city of New York, their personal representatives or owners, lessees, or persons otherwise interested in any lands or tenements so sold, shall file in the Register's office of the said city a memorandum of such mortgage or property, pursuant to the act entitled "An act in relation to the redemption of lands sold for taxes or assessments in the city of New York," passed May 6, 1841, and the act entitled "An act in addition to the acts respecting the collection of taxes and assessments in the city and county of New York," passed May 25, 1841, the Street Commissioner shall cause the notice of such sale required by said acts to be given by such persons, by sending to them, in the manner therein provided, a printed list, describing all the property sold for assessment or taxes, and remaining unredeemed; such description shall name the street or avenue on which the property may be situated, the side of the street or avenue, and between what streets or avenues, with the map or street numbers of the property, and in whose name assessed, together with the term of years and amount for which the same shall have been sold, and the day or days on which the time limited for the redemption of the property will expire, with a notice that unless the property shall be redeemed on or by such days, by the payment of the sums for which the same was sold, with all interest and expenses allowed by law, leases will be given to the purchasers in accordance with the statute in such case made and provided, and it shall not be necessary for the Street Commissioner to give any other or further notice to the person aforesaid, than is herein contained.

Notice to occupant of property sold.

Sec. 6. The notice required to be given to the occupant of property sold for taxes and assessments in the city of New York, and the person last assessed as owner, by the grantees of such property, in accordance with the third and fourth sections of the last-mentioned act, shall be extended in all cases to the person last assessed as owner, whether the property be in occupancy or not; such person so to be notified, shall be the person who shall have been last assessed as owner, by the assessors of the ward in which the property shall be situate, at the time when such notice shall be actually given by such grantee; but such notice, shall only apply to the persons assessed, who have a residence, or who actually reside, in the city and county of New York.

1851.—CHAPTER CCLXXVI.

AN ACT *to increase the Powers and Duties of the Deputy Collectors of Assessments in the City of New York.* Passed June 23, 1851.

The People of the State of New York, represented in Senate and Assembly, do enact as follows:

Sec. 1. All duties or acts, which are by section second of the act entitled, "An act for the more effectual collection of taxes and assessments in the city of New York," passed April twelfth, eighteen hundred and sixteen, required to be performed by the Collector of Assessments in the city of New York, may be performed and discharged by any Deputy Collector of Assessments in said city.

Sec. 2. This act shall take effect immediately.

1851.—CHAPTER CCCCXXX.

AN ACT *to regulate the compensation of the Assessors of the Street Department of the City of New York.* Passed July 9, 1851.

The People of the State of New York, represented in Senate and Assembly, do enact as follows:

Sec. 2. (Amended by section 1, chap. 508, Laws of 1853, to read as follows): The officers of the Bureau of Assessments in the Street Department of the City of New York, known as the Assessors of the Street Department, shall include in every assessment-list an amount equal to two per cent. on the total amount of such assessment, as a compensation to said assessors, for their services in making such assessment, and shall be advanced and paid to the said assessors by the Common Council of the City of New York, on the confirmation of such assessment-lists, to be equally divided between them.

Duty of Assesors in making Assessment List.

Sec. 3. The said assessors shall, quarter-yearly, viz., on the first days of January, April, July, and October, make a written and detailed statement, under oath, of all assessments made by them during the previous three months, together with the amount of each assessment; which statement shall be filed in the Comptroller's office of the city of New York. They shall also enter at length, in a book to be kept by them for that purpose, the names of each and every person included in each assessment list, together with the amount that each person is assessed; which book shall be opened for inspection at all reasonable hours.

Quarterly statement by Assessors.

Sec. 4. This act shall take effect immediately.

1852.—CHAPTER CCCXCVII.

AN ACT *to authorize the Mayor, Aldermen, and Commonalty of the City of New York, to issue Assessment Bonds.* Passed April 16, 1852, three-fifths being present.

The People of the State of New York, represented in Senate and Assembly, do enact as follows:

Amount that may be issued, and rate of interest.

Sec. 1. It shall be lawful for the Mayor, Aldermen, and Commonalty of the City of New York, to borrow, from time to time, by the issue of bonds, bearing such rates of interest as they may deem proper, not exceeding seven per cent. per annum, such sums as may be necessary to pay all expenses incurred, or to be incurred, on account of regulating and paving streets, building sewers, and all other work ordered to be done by contract under and by virtue of ordinances passed by the said Mayor, Aldermen, and Commonalty; the expense whereof is to be afterwards collected by assessment from the property benefited by said work or works; but no money shall be paid out of the proceeds of said bonds, on account of any such contract, until a copy of said contract has been filed with the Comptroller of said city, by the head of the department having such work in charge; also, a certificate, in writing, from the head of such department, stating that a payment is due, and the amount of such payment.

Duty of Common Council.

Sec. 2. Immediately upon the passage of this act, it shall be the duty of the Common Council of said city to pass such ordinances or laws as may be necessary to carry the same into effect.

Sec. 3. This act shall take effect immediately.

CHAPTER DVIII.

AN ACT *to amend an act entitled "An act to regulate the compensation of the Assessors of the Street Department of the city of New York."* Passed June 30, 1853, three-fifths being present.

The People of the State of New York, represented in Senate and Assembly, do enact as follows:

Amendment.

§ 1. The law to regulate the compensation of the Assessors of the Street Department of the city of New York, passed July 9, 1851, is hereby amended so as to read as follows:

Duty of Assessors in making Assessment Lists.

§ 2. The officers of the Bureau of Assessments in the Street Department of the city of New York, known as the Assessors of the Street Department, shall include in every assessment-list an amount equal to two per cent. on the total amount of such assessment, as a compensation to said Assessors for their services in making such assessment, and shall be advanced and paid to the said Assessors by the Common Council of the City of New York, on the confirmation of such assessment-lists, to be equally divided between them.

Quarterly statement by Assessors.

§ 3. The said Assessors shall, quarter-yearly, viz., on the first days of January, April, July, and October, make a written and detailed statement, under oath, of all assessments made by them during the previous three months, together with the amount of each assessment, which statement shall be filed in the Comptroller's office of the city of New York; they shall also enter at length in a book to be kept by them for that purpose, the names of each and every person included in each assessment-list, together with the amount that each person is assessed, which book shall be opened for inspection at all reasonable hours.

§ 4. This act shall take effect immediately.

1853.—CHAPTER DLXXIX.

AN ACT *to simplify the manner of collecting Arrears of Taxes and Assessments, and Regular Rents of Croton Water, in the city and county of New York.* Passed July 20, 1853, three-fifths being present.

The People of the State of New York, represented in Senate and Assembly, do enact as follows:

Confirming of assessment.

Sec. 6. No assessment for any improvement shall hereafter be deemed to be fully confirmed, so as to be due and be a lien upon the property included in it, until the title thereof, with the date of confirmation, shall have been entered, with the date of such entry, in a record of the titles of assessments to be kept in the Street Commissioner's office, and which may be used as an index to a record of assessments, and until the title of the said assessments shall have been also entered, with the date of confirmation, and the date of such entry, in a record of the titles of assessments confirmed, to be kept in the office of the Clerk of Arrears,

CHAPTER CCCXCIII.

AN ACT *to amend an act entitled "An act to authorize the sale of real estate in certain cases to pay Assessments, and for other purposes," passed May* 26, 1841. Passed April 17, 1854, three-fifths being present.

The People of the State of New York, represented in Senate and Assembly, do enact as follows:

Lots remaining unsold may be sold for subsequent taxes and assessments.

§ 1. In case any order or decree heretofore made or entered, or hereafter to be made or entered, under or by virtue of the power or authority contained in said act, shall embrace or direct to be sold, a greater quantity or number of portions or lots of land, than shall, on the sale under the said order or decree, be found necessary to be sold in order to raise or produce an amount of money sufficient to meet and satisfy the requirements of the said order or decree; and if, after such sale, any tax or assessment shall be levied or imposed on the parcels or lots of land embraced in the order or decree remaining unsold as aforesaid, it shall be lawful and competent for the court in which such order or decree was entered, from time to time, upon the petition of either of the parties of the suit in which such order or decree was entered, to direct a sale of so many of the said lots so remaining unsold, and subsequently taxed or assessed as aforesaid, as shall be necessary to pay and satisfy such subsequent taxes or assessments, and the costs and expenses of the application and proceeding thereupon.

Validity of such sale.

§ 2. All sales or conveyances, made under or by virtue of an order made or granted on such petition, shall be as valid and effectual, to pass the estate in the land conveyed, as the sales and conveyances first made under or by virtue of the original order or decree.

Notice. § 3. The court shall, on presenting such petition, direct notice to be published for six successive weeks, and once at least in each week, in two or more public newspapers printed in the county where the said lands are situated and in the State paper, setting forth the general objects of the petition, and the time and place at which it will be again presented to the court, and shall also direct such notice and a copy of such petition, to be served personally upon all persons who have become interested by transfer or assignment in such lots of land or portions thereof remaining unsold since the making of such order or decree, and who shall have recorded such assignment in the office provided by law for the record of deeds in the county where said lots are situated, at such time, or as soon thereafter as the court can hear the same, and upon due proof of such publication and service, said petition may be presented and a motion made for said order; any party in interest may show cause (if any there be) why the order prayed for should not be granted. The said publication of notice shall be deemed and held to be sufficient service upon all the parties to the suit and their representatives, of the petition and the notice of motion for the order.

§ 4. This act shall take effect immediately.

CHAPTER CCCXXVII.

AN ACT *to provide for the due apportionment of taxes and assessments, and for the sale of real estate to pay the same.* Passed April 12, 1855, three-fifths being present.

The People of the State of New York, represented in Senate and Assembly, do enact as follows:

Court may order sale in certain cases.

§ 1. In all cases where there are several persons interested, at law or in equity, in a real estate situate within the bounds of any city or village in this State, either as owning estates therein, in possession, reversion, or remainder, or as being presumptively entitled by virtue of any deed or will to such estates, on the death of any person or persons in being, or upon the happening of any contingency in such deed or will specified, and such real estate, or any part thereof, has been sold, or shall hereafter be sold, or is or shall become liable, in case of default, to be sold for any term of years, to satisfy any tax or assessment imposed thereon, then and in every such case, upon any action brought by any person so interested therein for the purpose of compelling a just and equitable apportionment of such tax or assessment upon the several present future, and presumptive interests, as aforesaid, in such real estate, and the payment thereof, or the redemption of the real estate so sold accordingly, the Supreme Court shall have power, at any time, on the application of any party to such action, to extend the time of redemption of any such real estate sold or to be hereafter sold, by authority of such city or village, to a period not exceeding six months from the entry of the final judgment to be given in such action, and to order a sale in fee simple absolute for such real estate, or any part or parts thereof, to pay such tax or assessment, or to redeem the same, or any part thereof, as aforesaid, and to direct the proceeds of such sale to be applied to the payment of such tax or assessment, or to the redemption of the real estate sold for such tax or assessment, after defraying the costs, charges and expenses of the action, and the proceedings connected therewith.

Redemption by agreement.

§ 2. Like proceedings may be had to redeem, by agreement with the purchaser of any real estate so sold, or hereafter sold, as aforesaid, after the time allowed by law for redemption shall have expired; but every such agreement shall be ratified and approved by the court, and the redemption thereof shall be evidenced by the deed of the purchaser, his heirs or assigns, granting the property to some party in the action expressed, to be made in the extinguishment of the tax or assessment title, pursuant to this act.

Proceedings in case of unknown owners.

§ 3. If any person so interested as aforesaid in said real estate, is unknown, or if either of the known parties to such action, whether minors or of full age, reside out of the State, or cannot, on inquiry had, be found therein, and that fact made to appear to the satisfaction of the court by affidavit, an order made by the court containing a sufficient description of the premises, of which, or of part whereof, a sale is sought, and requiring all parties interested therein, to appear and answer the action by a day in said order specified, which order shall be published for three months, once at least in each week successively, in the State paper, and in a newspaper printed in the county where the premises are situated, if there be any, and if there is none, then in a newspaper printed in the city of New York.

The publication of such order shall authorize a judgment, as by default, against all such unknown persons and parties not resident in this State, or not found therein, as shall not appear and answer accordingly, and all such unknown persons as may appear on such notice may be made parties to the action, and the complaint may be amended for that purpose.

§ 4. The court, in its discretion, may direct any person not already made a party to such action, who shall seem to be presumptively entitled as in the first section of this act specified, to be so made a party thereto, and whenever, in any action to which all persons having vested estates at law or in equity, shall have been made parties, or shall have been so proceeded against as unknown owners, a sale shall be had as aforesaid by order of the Court; such sale shall vest in the purchaser a fee simple, absolute at law and in equity, in the property so sold.

Presumptive owners may be made parties.

§ 5. All sales to be directed as aforesaid, shall be made by or under the direction of a referee, to be for that purpose appointed by the Court, who shall have power to perfect every such sale by executing under his hand and seal a deed to the purchaser.

Sales, how made.

§ 6. The third and fourth sections of the act, entitled, "An act to authorize the sale of real estate in certain cases to pay assessments, and for other purposes," passed May twenty-sixth, eighteen hundred and forty-one, and the third section of the act, entitled, "An act in relation to the sale of real estate to pay assessments," passed April eleventh, eighteen hundred and forty-two, shall apply to actions under this act.

CHAPTER DCLXXVII.

AN ACT *in relation to Assessments in the City of New York, and to amend the several Acts in relation thereto.* Passed April 16, 1857, three-fifths being present.

The People of the State of New York, represented in Senate and Assembly, do enact as follows:

Commissioners of taxes.

§ 1. There shall be in the city of New York, three Tax Commissioners, as now provided for by law, but they shall hereafter be designated Commissioners of Taxes and Assessments, and the persons now holding such offices shall continue to hold the same until the first Monday of July eighteen hundred and fifty-nine, when their several terms shall expire.

Election by Supervisors.

§ 2. The Supervisors of said county shall, on the first Monday of June eighteen hundred and fifty-nine, and every third year thereafter, meet in the City Hall of said city, and proceed to elect, by ballot, three Commissioners of Taxes and Assessments for the full term of three years; not more than two names shall be written or printed upon any ballot, and the two persons receiving the highest number of votes, shall be declared appointed, and the said Supervisors shall immediately thereafter select from the two persons having the next highest number of votes, the third Commissioner of Taxes and Assessments; any vacancy in said Board of Commissioners, from death, resignation, or otherwise, shall be filled by said Supervisors for the balance of the term for which such Commissioner was appointed; the said Commissioners so appointed shall enter upon their duties on the first Monday of July next ensuing; the annual compensation for each Commissioner shall be three thousand five hundred dollars, to be paid as a county charge. Compensation.

§ 3. In addition to the duties now prescribed by law, or hereinafter imposed by this act, the said Commissioners, by three of their deputies especially by them selected and designated for this purpose, shall perform the duties now discharged by the officers of the Bureau of Assessments, which bureau of the Street Department is hereby abolished. Duties.

§ 4. The offices of Ward Assessors in the City of New York, as heretofore existing, are hereby abolished, and the powers and duties now vested in and performed by those officers relative to the assessment of real and personal estate, shall hereafter be vested in and performed by the officers provided for by this act and in the manner hereinafter provided; and the provisions of law now existing in respect to the mode and manner of making assessments by the Ward Assessors in the city of New York, as far as the same are conformable to the supervision of the Commissioners of Taxes and Assessments, are hereby made applicable to the officers provided for in this act. Ward Assessors.

§ 5. The Commissioners of Taxes and Assessments shall appoint twelve persons, to be known as Deputy Tax Commissioners, who shall perform under their direction and supervision the duties now performed by the Assessors of the several wards of said city, and such other duties as they shall prescribe; they shall hold office during the pleasure of the Commissioners, and shall receive such annual compensation as may be determined by the Board of Supervisors, not to exceed two thousand dollars per annum. Deputies.

§ 6. It shall be the duty of the Deputy Tax Commissioners, under the direction of the Commissioners of Taxes and As- Duties.

sessments, to assess all the taxable property in the several districts that may be assigned to them for that purpose by said Commissioners, and shall furnish to them, under oath, a detailed statement of all such property, that said deputies have personally examined each and every house, building, lot, pier, or other assessable property, giving the street and ward map number of such real estate embraced within said districts, together with the name of the owner or occupant, if known; also, in their judgment, the sum for which such property, under ordinary circumstances, would sell, with such other information in detail, relative to personal property, or otherwise, as the said Commissioners may, from time to time, require; such Deputies shall commence to assess real and personal estate on the first Monday of September, in each and every year.

Offices. § 7. The Board of Supervisors shall assign the said Commissioners and their deputies a suitable office or offices in the city of New York, which shall be kept open during the usual days and hours as the other city offices are by law required to be kept open for the transaction of business. The books, maps, assessment rolls, and other papers now pertaining to the office of Tax Commissioner and the Bureau of Assessment of the Street Department, shall be transferred to the custody and control of the Commissioners of Taxes and Assessments, and shall continue to be public records, and at all reasonable times shall be open to public inspection.

Clerks. § 8. The said Commissioners shall appoint such number of clerks as the Supervisors, by resolution, shall prescribe, who shall hold office during the pleasure of the Commissioners, and receive for their services such compensation as may be fixed by said Supervisors, to be paid as a county charge.

§ 9. The said Commissioners shall also appoint, by and with the consent of the Supervisors, a City Surveyor, whose duty it shall be to make the necessary surveys and corrections of the ward maps, and also all new maps which may be required for the more accurate assessment of real estate. He shall hold office at the pleasure of the Commissioners, and shall receive for his services an annual compensation, not to exceed the sum of three thousand dollars, to be fixed by the Supervisors and paid as a county charge. City Surveyor.

§ 10. The said Commissioners shall keep in their office books, to be provided for that purpose by the Board of Supervisors, to be called "the Annual Record of the Assessed Valuation of Real and Personal Estate," in which shall be entered in detail the assessed valuations of such property within the city and county of New York, and which said books shall be open for examination and correction from the second Monday of January until the first day of May in each and every year, but on said last-mentioned day the same shall be closed, to enable the Commissioners to prepare assessment-rolls of the several wards for delivery to the Supervisors, as hereinafter provided. Office books.

§ 11. The said Commissioners, previous to and during the time said books are open for inspection, shall advertise the fact in the several newspapers, or in such manner as they may deem most advisable, and the charges therefor, certified by the Commissioners, shall be awarded and allowed by the Supervisors as a county charge.

§ 12. During the time the books shall be open to public inspection, as hereinbefore provided, application may be made by any person considering himself aggrieved by the assessed valuation of his real or personal estate, to have the same corrected; if such application be made in relation Applications.

to the assessed valuation of real estate, it must be made in writing, stating the ground of objection thereto, and thereupon the Commissioners shall examine into the complaint, and if in their judgment the assessment is erroneous, they shall cause the same to be corrected; if such application be made in relation to the assessed valuation of personal estate, the applicant shall be examined under oath by the said Commissioners, or any of them, and if in their judgment the assessment is erroneous, they shall cause the same to be corrected, and declare their decision thereon within thirty days after such application shall have been made to them. No reduction shall be made by the Board of Supervisors of any assessment on real or personal estate imposed under this act, unless it shall appear under oath or affirmation, that the party aggrieved was unable to attend within the period prescribed for the correction of taxes, by reason of sickness or absence from the city.

Increase of valuation.

§ 13. It being the intention of this act to provide for the better equalization of the taxation in the city and county of New York, the Commissioners may, at any time before the second day of April in each year, increase at any time before the closing of the books of annual record, on the first day of May in each year, diminish the assessed valuation of any real or personal estate in said city, as in their judgment may be necessary for such equalization, but they shall not increase such valuations after said books are open for correction and review, except upon notice being given to the party affected by such increase, twenty days before the closing of said books.

Assessment rolls.

§ 14. On the first day of May in each year the Commissioners shall cause to be prepared, from the books of annual record of assessed valuations of real and personal estate in the city of New York, assessment rolls for each of the several wards of said city, in the same form as the same are now by law directed to be prepared, and shall annex to each of said rolls their certificate that the same is correct, in accordance with the entries in said books of record.

§ 15. The rolls thus certified must, on the first Monday of July in each year, be delivered by the said Commissioners to the Supervisors of the City and County of New York, who shall meet at noon on that day, at the City Hall in said city, for the purpose of receiving the same, and for the purpose of performing such other duties in relation thereto as are prescribed by law. Delivery to Supervisors.

§ 16. Whenever any permit shall be granted by the proper officer of the city government, for the erection of any building, pier or bulkhead within said city, a copy of such permit shall be furnished by the said officer to the Commissioner of Taxes and Assessments. Permits.

§ 17. All assessments directed by ordinance of the Common Council of the City of New York shall be made in accordance with existing laws, by the persons selected and designated as Deputies; the said Commissioners, with any one of said Deputies, shall together form a Board and select a President, who shall give all notices now required by law to be given by assessors, or the chairman thereof, for assessments directed by Corporation ordinances, and all objections shall be heard before said Board, until the first day of January, eighteen hundred and fifty-nine; the persons now in office, known as the Assessors of the Street Department, shall be designated by said Commissioners as their Deputies for making the assessments so directed by Corporation ordinances, and shall exercise the powers, perform the duties, and receive the compensation, as provided Board of Assessors.

by law, before the passage of this act, but at the expiration of the said term, the Deputies designated for such duty shall receive an annual salary, as provided for in section five of this act.

Wells, pumps, &c

§ 18. The said Deputies, or a majority thereof, shall make the estimates and assessments, required by law for building wells, erecting pumps, pitching, paving, and repairing streets and sidewalks, constructing sewers, fencing lots, filling public slips, or any other improvement directed by an ordinance of the Common Council.

Notices of completion of assessments.

§ 19. The said Commissioners shall, on the completion by said Deputies of any assessment mentioned in the last section, publish, for ten days, in the Corporation papers, a notice that the same is completed, and will remain in their office thirty days for examination by all parties interested therein, and that at the end of that time the said Commissioners, or a majority of them, shall certify the same, in writing, to the Common Council for confirmation; their notices shall also contain a general description of the limits within which the property is affected by the assessment; if objections be presented within the time then mentioned in the notice, upon which they shall refuse to alter their assessment-list, or if, notwithstanding its alteration, objections shall be made, they shall present the assessment-list, with such objections, to the Common Council.

Description of houses, &c.

§ 20. The Commissioners shall describe in the assessment-list the several houses and lots assessed by the known street numbers, and the ward map numbers, and shall also state therein the names of the owner or owners and occupant or occupants thereof, respectively; in making their assessment, the Commissioners shall in no case assess upon a house or lot, or upon land, whether improved or unimproved, more than one-third the value, as fixed by them on the annual record of assessments for taxes last confirmed by the Board of Supervisors.

§ 21. They shall enter in books to be provided for that purpose, a full and complete record in detail of all assessments confirmed by the Supreme Court, or by the Common Council, which shall, at all convenient times, be open to public inspection. Entry of Assessments.

§ 22. All the powers and duties now possessed by the Street Commissioner of the City of New York, or by his department, in regard to making and perfecting assessments, shall devolve upon the Commissioners of Taxes and Assessments. Powers and duties.

§ 23. All acts and parts of acts of the Legislature of this State, not inconsistent with the provisions of this law, shall continue to remain in full force and effect.

§ 24. A certiorari to review and correct on the merits any decision or action of the said Commissioners, under section twelve or thirteen of this act, shall be allowed by the Supreme Court, or any judge thereof, directed to the said Commissioners, on the petition of the party aggrieved, and shall, with the return, be heard and decided forthwith by said court, in preference to all other matters, actions, or proceedings. Certiorari.

§ 25. This act shall take effect immediately.

CHAPTER CCCXXXVIII.

AN ACT *in relation to frauds in assessments for local improvements in the city of New York.* Passed April 17, 1858, three-fifths being present.

The People of the State of New York, represented in Senate and Assembly, do enact as follows:

Sec. 1. If, in the proceedings relative to any assessment or assessments for local improvements in the city of New York, or in the proceedings to collect the same, any fraud or legal irregularity shall be alleged to have been committed, the party aggrieved thereby may apply to a judge of the Supreme Court, in special term or in vacation, who shall thereupon, upon due notice to the Counsel of the Corporation of the city in which the lands so assessed are situated, proceed forthwith to hear the proofs and allegations of the parties.

§ 2. If upon such hearing, it shall appear that the alleged fraud or irregularity has been committed, the said assessments shall be vacated, and the lien created thereby, or by any subsequent proceedings, shall cease.

§ 3. On the production of the certificate of the judge, before whom the proceedings shall be had, that a judgment vacating any assessment has been made by him, it shall be the duty of the officer having charge of the assessment lists to cancel thereon the assessments so vacated, and all proceedings under the same.

§ 4. Any person applying for relief under the provisions of this act, may embrace in one proceeding any or all assessments for local improvements in which he is interested.

§ 5. Any lands which may be discharged from any lien for an assessment for any local improvement, may be again assessed in the manner now provided by law, for such amount as would have been justly chargeable, if fraud or irregularity had not been committed; but the amount so assessed shall be a lien on said lands until paid, and shall be collectable in the manner now provided by law for the collection of assessments, but all proceedings to make a new assessment shall be at the expense of the Corporation of the city in which the lands may be situated.

§ 6. This act shall take effect immediately.

CHAPTER CCXCV.

AN ACT *to amend the several acts relating to assessments in the city of New York, for the opening, widening, altering, or amending the streets, avenues, and public places in said city.* Passed April 13, 1859.

The People of the State of New York, represented in Senate and Assembly, do enact as follows:

Reports may not be altered in certain cases.

Sec. 1. It shall not be lawful for Commissioners of Estimate and Assessment to alter or amend any report, or supplemental or amended report, after the same shall have been deposited for inspection, as now required by law, by increasing the amount of any assessment for benefit, or diminishing any award for damage, unless the person or persons, party or parties, affected by such increase or diminution shall have had notice thereof, and an opportunity of being heard before said Commissioners, before their report shall be presented to the court for confirmation.

Sec. 2. This act shall take effect immediately.

CHAPTER CCCII.

AN ACT *in relation to taxes and assessments in the city of New York, and to amend the several acts in relation thereto.* Passed April 14, 1859, three-fifths being present.

The People of the State of New York, represented in Senate and Assembly, do enact as follows:

Commissioners to be appointed.

Sec. 1. Immediately upon the passage of this act, there shall be appointed by the Comptroller of the City of New York, three Commissioners, who shall form a board, and be designated Commissioners of Taxes and Assessments for the City and County of New York, who shall hold their office for the term of five years, and until others are appointed in their places; any vacancy in said Board of Commissioners, from death or resignation, or otherwise, shall be filled by said Comptroller for the balance of the term for which such Commissioners are appointed. The annual compensation for each Commissioner shall be three thousand five hundred dollars, to be paid monthly by the Comptroller, out of the county treasury.

Ward Assessors abolished.

Sec. 2. The offices of Ward Assessors in the city of New York, and Commissioners of Taxes and Assessments, as heretofore existing, are hereby abolished, and the powers and duties now or heretofore vested in and performed by the officers thereof, relative to the assessment of real and personal estate, shall hereafter be vested in and performed by the officers provided by this act, and in the manner hereinafter provided, and the provisions now existing in respect to the mode and manner of making assessments in the city of New York, as far as the same are conformable to the supervision of the Commissioners of Taxes and Assessments, are hereby made applicable to the officers provided for by this act.

§ 3. The Board of Commissioners of Taxes and Assessments shall appoint not to exceed twelve persons, to be known as Deputy Tax Commissioners, who shall perform, under their direction and supervision, the duties heretofore performed by the Assessors of the several wards of said city, or such other duties as they shall prescribe; they shall hold their office during the pleasure of the said Commissioners, and shall receive such compensation as may be determined by the said Comptroller and Board of Commissioners, not to exceed the sum of two thousand dollars per annum, to each of said deputies, to be paid by the Comptroller out of the county treasury. Deputy Tax Commissioners.

§ 4. The said Board of Commissioners may appoint such number of regular and extra clerks as in their judgment may be necessary to perform such duties as may be prescribed by said Commissioners, who shall hold their office during the pleasure of said Commissioners, and shall receive for their services such compensation as may be fixed by the Comptroller and the Board of Commissioners, not exceeding at the rate of twelve hundred dollars per annum for the time employed, to be paid by the Comptroller out of the county treasury. Clerks.

§ 5. The said Board of Commissioners shall appoint a Surveyor from one of the City Surveyors, whose duty it shall be to make the necessary surveys and corrections of the ward maps, and also all new maps which may be required for the more accurate assessment of real estate. He shall hold his office at the pleasure of the Commissioners, and shall receive for his services three thousand dollars per annum. Surveyor.

Offices to be assigned.

§ 6. The Board of Supervisors of the City and County of New York shall provide for and assign to the Commissioners and their deputies, a suitable and convenient office or offices, in any of the public buildings in the city of New York, or elsewhere in the city of New York, together with the requisite and necessary books, stationery, lights and fuel, and which said office or offices shall be kept open during the usual days and hours, as the other offices are by law required to be kept open for the transaction of business; the books, maps, assessment rolls, and other papers now pertaining to the office of Commissioners of Taxes and Assessments, shall be transferred to the custody and control of the Commissioners of Taxes and Assessments, appointed under this act, and shall continue to be public records, and at all reasonable times shall be open to public inspection.

Duty of Deputy Tax Commissioners.

§ 7. It shall be the duty of the Deputy Tax Commissioners, under the direction of the Commissioners of Taxes and Assessments, to assess all the taxable property in the several districts that may be assigned to them for that purpose by said Commissioners, and shall furnish to them, under oath, a detailed statement of all such property, that said Deputies have personally examined each and every house, building, lot, pier, and other assessable property, giving the street and ward map number of such real estate, embraced within said districts, together with the name of the owner or occupant, if known; also, in their judgment, the sum for which such property, under ordinary circumstances, would sell, with such other information, in detail, relative to personal property, or otherwise, as the said Commissioners may, from time to time, require; such deputies shall commence to assess real and personal estate on the first Monday of September in each and every year.

§ 8. The said Commissioners shall keep in their office books, to be provided for that purpose by the Comptroller, to be called "The Annual Record of the Assessed Valuation of Real and Personal Estate," in which shall be entered in detail the assessed valuations of such property within the city and county of New York, and which said books shall be open for examination and correction from the second Monday of January until the first day of May in each and every year, but on said last-mentioned day the same shall be closed, to enable the Commissioners to prepare assessment rolls of the several wards, for delivery to the Supervisors, as hereinafter provided. Annual record to be kept.

§ 9. The said Commissioners, previous to and during the time said books are open for inspection, shall advertise the fact in the several newspapers, or in such manner as they may deem most advisable, and the charges therefor, certified by the Commissioners, shall be audited and allowed by the Supervisors as a county charge. Advertising by Commissioners.

§ 10. During the time the books shall be open to public inspection, as hereinbefore provided, application may be made by any person considering himself aggrieved by the assessed valuation of his real or personal estate, to have the same corrected. If such application be made in relation to the assessed valuation of real estate, it must be made in writing, stating the ground of objection thereto; and thereupon the Commissioners shall examine into the complaint, and if, in their judgment, the assessment is erroneous, they shall cause the same to be corrected. If such application be made in relation to the assessed valuation of personal estate, the applicant shall be examined under oath by the said Commissioners, who shall be authorized to administer such oath, or any of them, and if in his or their judgment Books to be kept open, &c.

the assessment is erroneous, they shall cause the same to be corrected, and fix the amount of such assessment as they may believe to be just, and declare their decision thereon within thirty days after such application shall have been made to them. No reduction shall be made by the Board of Supervisors, of any assessment on real or personal estate, imposed under this act, unless it shall appear under oath or affirmation, that the party aggrieved was unable to attend within the period prescribed for the correction of taxes, by reason of sickness or absence from the city.

Intention of Act.

§ 11. It being the intention of this act to provide for the better equalization of the taxation in the city and county of New York, the Commissioners may at any time before the second day of April, in each year, increase or diminish at any time before the closing of the books of annual record on the first day of May, in each year, the assessed valuation of any real or personal estate in said city, as in their judgment may be necessary for such equalization, but they shall not increase such valuations after said books are open for correction and review, except upon notice being given to the party affected by such increase twenty days before the closing of said books.

Valuations.

Assessment rolls to be made.

§ 12. On the first day of May, in each year, the Commissioner shall cause to be prepared from the books of annual record of assessed valuations of real and personal estate in the city of New York, assessment-rolls for each of the several wards of said city, in the same form as the same are now by law directed to be prepared, and shall annex to each of said rolls their certificate that the same is correct in accordance with the entries in said books of record.

§ 13. The rolls thus certified must on the first Monday

of July in each year be delivered by the said Commissioners to the Supervisors of the City and County of New York, who shall meet at noon on that day, at the City Hall in said city, for the purpose of receiving the same, and for the purpose of performing such other duties in relation thereto as are prescribed by law. Rolls to be delivered to the Supervisors.

§ 14. Whenever any permit shall be granted by the proper officer of the city government, for the erection of any building, pier, or bulkhead within said city, a copy of such permit shall be furnished by the said officer to the Commissioners of Taxes and Assessments. Erection of buildings, piers, &c.,

§ 15. The said Commissioners of Taxes and Assessments shall appoint three skillful and competent disinterested persons, citizens of the United States and residents of the city of New York, who shall constitute a board, to be known as the Board of Assessors, and who shall be charged with the duty of making the estimates and assessments required by law for building wells, erecting pumps, pitching, paving, regulating, and repairing streets, constructing sewers, fencing vacant lots and public slips, and all other improvements directed by Corporation ordinance for which an assessment may be made. Assessors.

§ 16. The said Board of Assessors, or a majority thereof, shall make all estimates and assessments, give all notices, receive and pass upon all objections, and certify to the Common Council, in accordance with the existing laws relative to all such matters. The said Assessors shall each receive an annual compensation of two thousand dollars, to be paid by the Comptroller of the City of New York, from the city treasury, and which shall be in lieu of all other compensation. The said Assessors shall hold their office during the pleasure of the appointing power, and no Board of Assessors.

longer. The Common Council of the City of New York shall provide for and assign to said Assessors a suitable and convenient room or rooms, for the transaction of their business, and shall provide the said Assessors with the requisite and necessary stationery, lights, and fuel; it shall be lawful for the said Commissioners of Taxes and Assessments to appoint a clerk to assist said Assessors in the performance of their duties, and who shall receive an annual compensation, to be fixed by said Commissioners, not exceeding the sum of twelve hundred dollars, to be paid by the Comptroller out of the city treasury.

Assessment list, and duty of Common Council.

§ 17. Whenever any assessment list shall be certified by the Assessors to the Common Council of the City of New York, for confirmation, as provided by law, it shall be the duty of the Common Council to proceed forthwith to confirm such assessment, or refer the same back to the said Board of Assessors, if necessary, for revisal and correction and all such matters shall have precedence to all other matters before the Common Council, or in either Board thereof.

Record

§ 18. The said Board of Assessors shall cause to be entered in books to be provided for that purpose by the Common Council, a full and complete record in detail, of all assessments confirmed by the Supreme Court, or by the Common Council, which shall, at all convenient times, be open to public inspection.

Duties of Assessors.

§ 19. All the powers and duties now possessed by the Street Commissioner of the City of New York, or by his department, in regard to making and perfecting assessments, shall devolve upon the Assessors appointed under the provisions of this act.

§ 20. A certiorari to review and correct on the merits, any decision or action of the said Commissioners, under section ten or eleven of this act, shall be allowed by the Supreme Court, or any judge thereof, directed to the said Commissioners, on the petition of the party aggrieved, and shall, with the return, be heard and decided forthwith by said Court, in preference to all other matters, actions, or proceedings.

§ 21. The act entitled "An act in relation to assessments in the city of New York, and to amend the several acts in relation thereto," passed April sixteenth, eighteen hundred and fifty-seven, is hereby repealed; and also all laws, and acts, and parts of acts, so far as the same are inconsistent with this act, are hereby repealed: provided, however, that nothing contained in this act shall be so construed as to repeal any act or law now exempting real or personal estate from taxation.

§ 22. This act shall take effect immediately.

APPENDIX.

A COMPILATION

OF THE

LAWS

OF THE

STATE OF NEW YORK,

RELATIVE TO THE

ASSESSMENT AND COLLECTION OF TAXES IN THE CITY AND COUNTY OF NEW YORK:

CONTAINING SUCH PORTIONS OF THE GENERAL PROVISIONS OF THE REVISED STATUTES, AND THE AMENDMENTS THERETO, AS ARE APPLICABLE TO THE CITY AND COUNTY OF NEW YORK; THE LAWS RELATING EXCLUSIVELY TO THE CITY AND COUNTY OF NEW YORK; AND NOTES OF CASES RELATING TO THE SUBJECT OF TAXATION.

BY A. R. LAWRENCE, JR.,

COUNSELLOR AT LAW.

PREFACE.

THIS Compilation has been prepared by the direction of the Board of Supervisors of the County of New York.

For the purpose of convenient reference, it has been divided into three parts.

PART I.—Contains, principally, those provisions of the Revised Statutes, and the amendments thereto, relative to the assessment and collection of taxes, which are applicable to the city and county of New York.

PART II.—Includes the laws which relate exclusively to the assessment, imposition, and collection of taxes, in the city and county of New York.

PART III.—Embraces notes of cases, in which decisions have been made, upon the subject of taxation.

In making the collection of notes, the following Reports of this State have been consulted: Caine's Cases, 2 volumes; Caine's Reports, 3 volumes; Johnson's Cases, 3 volumes; Johnson's Reports, 20 volumes; Cowen's Reports, 9 volumes; Wendell's Reports, 26 volumes; Hill's Reports, 7 volumes; Denio's Reports, 5 volumes; Barbour's Reports, 27 volumes; Comstock's Reports, 4 volumes; Selden's Reports, 5 volumes; Kernan's Reports, 4 volumes; New York (E. P. Smith's) Reports, 3 volumes; Sandford's Superior Court Reports, 5 volumes; Duer's Reports, 6 volumes; Bosworth's Reports, 1 volume; E. D. Smith's Reports, 4 volumes; Lalor's Supplement to Hill and Denio, 1 volume; Johnson's Chancery Reports, 7 volumes; Edward's Chancery Reports, 4 volumes; Paige's Reports, 11 volumes; Barbour's Chancery Reports, 3 volumes; Sandford's Chancery Reports, 4 volumes; Hopkins' Chancery Reports, 1 volume; Hoffman's Chancery Reports, 1 volume; Abbott's Practice Reports, 7 volumes, and Howard's Practice Reports, 17 volumes.

Reference has also been made to several cases contained in Wheaton's, Peters', and Howard's Reports of decisions by the Supreme Court of the United States.

The provisions of the Revised Statutes, which have been inserted at length, have been taken from the fifth edition, which embraces all alterations and amendments up to and including the year 1858; but the numbers of the pages of the first edition have been retained in the margin.

To the section mark of each new section which has been incorporated into the Revised Statutes, an asterisk is prefixed, as in the fifth edition, and where the number of a section has been changed, the original number has been printed in brackets.

The Compiler has examined the amendatory law, in every case where an amendment or alteration has been incorporated into the Revised Statutes.

A table of reference to the Annual Tax Bills for the City and County of New York, from 1813 to 1859, inclusive, has been appended to Part III, and to avoid confusion, each part has been separately indexed.

The Compiler submits the result of his labors to the Supervisors, with the hope that it may aid them in the discharge of their official duties.

NEW YORK, JUNE, 1859.

A. R. LAWRENCE, JR.

PART I.

GENERAL LAWS

OF THE

STATE OF NEW YORK,

IN RELATION TO THE

Assessment and Collection of Taxes.

PROPERTY LIABLE TO TAXATION.

[Revised Statutes, Part I, Chapter 13, Title I, vol. 1, 5th ed., p. 905.]

Of the property liable to taxation.

SEC. 1. Property subject to taxation.

2. Non-residents doing business in this State taxed on sums invested in said business.

3. Meaning of terms "land," "real estate," and "real property."

4. Meaning of terms "personal estate" and "personal property."

5. Property exempt from taxation.

6. Exemption of buildings for worship and school purposes, not to apply to such buildings in New York City, unless used for such purposes, &c.

7 and 8. Branch Mint and Assay Office of United States in New York City exempt from tax.

9. Lands held and used by agricultural societies for shows, exempt from taxation.

10 and 11. * * * * * *

12. If property of ministers exceed $1,500, that sum to be deducted, and residue taxed.

13. Lands sold by State to be assessed, though not conveyed.

14. When owners of stock are not to be taxed therefor as individuals.

Land and personal estate.

§ 1. All lands and all personal estate within this State, whether owned by individuals or by corporations, shall be liable to taxation, subject to the exemptions hereinafter specified.[1]

Non residents, doing business in this State, to be taxed.

*§ 2. All persons and associations doing business in the State of New York, as merchants, bankers, or otherwise, either as principals or partners, whether special or otherwise, and not residents of this State, shall be assessed and taxed on all sums invested in any manner in said business, the same as if they were residents of this State; and said taxes shall be collected from the property of the firms, persons, or associations to which they severally belong. [*Laws* 1855, *chap.* 37, *page* 44.]

"Land" defined.

§ 3. [Sec. 2.] The term "land," as used in this chapter, shall be construed to include the land itself, all buildings, and other articles erected upon or affixed to the same, all trees and underwood growing thereon, and all mines, minerals, quarries, and fossils, in and under the same, except mines belonging to the State; and the terms "real estate,"
[388.] and "real property," whenever they occur in this chapter, shall be construed as having the same meaning as the term "land," thus defined.

---

1 This chapter was compiled, with various alterations and additions, from the following statutes: Laws of 1823, p. 389; 1824, pp. 16, 112; 1825, pp. 282, 330, 355, 373; 1826, pp. 45, 94, 135, § 4; 327, § 6 and 7; 1827, p. 4, § 4.

§ 4. [Sec. 3.] The terms "personal estate" and "personal property," whenever they occur in this chapter, shall be construed to include all household furniture, moneys, goods, chattels, debts due from solvent debtors, whether on account, contract, note, bond or mortgage, public stocks, and stocks in moneyed corporations. They shall also be construed to include such portion of the capital of incorporated companies, liable to taxation on their capital, as shall not be invested in real estate. "Personal estate" defined.

PROPERTY EXEMPT.

§ 5. [Sec. 4.] The following property shall be exempt from taxation: Property exempt.

1. All property, real or personal, exempted from taxation by the constitution of this State, or under the Constitution of the United States:

2. All lands belonging to this State, or the United States:

3. Every building erected for the use of a college, incorporated academy, or other seminary of learning; every building for public worship; every school-house, court-house, and jail; and the several lots whereon such buildings are situated, and the furniture belonging to each of them:

4. Every poor-house, alms-house, house of industry, and every house belonging to a company incorporated for the reformation of offenders, and the real and personal property belonging to, or connected with the same:

5. The real and personal property of every public library:

6. All stocks owned by the State, or by literary or charitable institutions:[1]

7. The personal estate of every incorporated company not made liable to taxation on its capital, in the fourth title of this chapter:

8. The personal property of every minister of the gospel, or priest of any denomination; and the real estate of such minister, or priest, when occupied by him, provided such real and personal estate do not exceed the value of one thousand five hundred dollars: and,

9. All property exempted by law from execution.

Buildings for public worship, school houses, &c., exempt.

*§ 6. The exemption from taxation of every building for public worship, and every school-house or other seminary of learning, under the provisions of subdivision three of section four, title one, chapter thirteen, of part first of the Revised Statutes, or amendments thereof, shall not apply to any such building or premises in the city of New York, unless the same shall be exclusively used for such purposes, and exclusively the property of a religious society, or of the New York Public School Society. (*a*) [*Laws of* 1852, *chap.* 282, *page* 417.]

---

[1] By chap. 195, p. 224, of Laws of 1845, the exemption from taxation under this subdivision is declared to be for the benefit of the State, or the literary or charitable institutions, and the amount of the exemption is to be added to the dividends on such stock.

(*a*) This provision was made in consequence of the *dictum* of Judge Ruggles in the case of Chegary vs. Jenkins, 1 Selden, p. 376. It had previously been determined in the same case in the Superior Court, 3 Sanford, S. C. R. 409, that the act of April 6th, 1825 [Laws of 1825, p. 123, sec. 3], respecting the collection of taxes in the city of New York, which limited the meaning of the act for the assessment and collection of taxes, passed on the 23d of April,

*§ 7. No tax or assessment shall at any time be imposed, assessed, or collected upon the mint or branch mint of the United States, which may be authorized by act of Congress to be established in the city of New York, neither upon the land on which the buildings used or to be used therefor, shall or may be erected, nor upon the buildings used, or to be used therefor, nor upon the machinery used or to be used therein, nor upon bullion or metal deposited for coinage, nor upon coin deposited for re-coinage, nor upon the coin stamped at said mint or branch mint, while in the custody of the officers of said mint or branch mint of the United States in the city of New York. [*Laws of* 1852, *chap.* 46, *page* 40.]

Certain property in New York City exempt from tax:

*§ 8. No assessment or tax of any description, general or local, shall be imposed, assessed, or collected upon the assay office of the United States, which by act of Congress of March, 1853, it is provided shall be established in the city of New York; neither upon the land owned by the United States on which the building or buildings used or

No assessment or tax to be imposed on the Assay Office in New York City.

1823 [Laws of 1823, p. 390], by providing that "the exemption from taxation of any building for public worship, or any school, under and by virtue of the third section of the said act of the 23d of April, 1823, &c., shall not extend or apply to any such buildings or premises in the said city, unless the same shall be exclusively used for such purposes, and exclusively the property of a religious society, or the New York Free School Society," was still in force and not affected by the general repealing act. [3 R. S., p. 161, 3d ed.] See 3 R. S., p. 1108, 5th ed.

The *dictum* of Judge Ruggles was, that the exemption contained in the Revised Statutes applied to private as well as public schools. In Chegary vs. Mayor, &c., 3 Kernan, p. 220, this dictum was disapproved. The decision of the Superior Court in Chegary vs. Jenkins, on this point, is therefore unreversed.

It has therefore been deemed proper to insert the act of 1823 in this compilation. [For the acts of 1823 and 1825, see post, pages 174 and 175, part 2, of this compilation.]

to be used therefor, shall or may be erected, nor upon the buildings used or to be used therefor, nor upon the machinery used or to be used therein, nor upon the metal, bullion, or coin deposited for melting, remelting, or assaying, nor upon the bars or ingots after melting, remelting, or assaying, while the same is in the custody, possession, or under the control of the officers of the assay office of the United States in the city of New York. [*Laws of* 1853, *chap.* 406, *page* 803.]

Land held by agricultural societies exempt.

*§ 9. All lands now held, or which may hereafter be held by any agricultural society in this State, and permanently used for show grounds by any such society, shall be exempt from taxation during the time so used. [*Laws of* 1856, *chap.* 183, *page* 304.] (*a*)

* * * * * *

Minister or priest.

§ 12. [Sec. 5.] If the real and personal estate, or either of them, of any minister or priest, exceed the value of one thousand five hundred dollars, that sum shall be deducted from the valuation of his property, and the residue shall be liable to taxation.

Lands sold by the State.

§ 13. [Sec. 6.] Lands sold by the State, though not granted or conveyed, shall be assessed in the same manner as if actually conveyed.

Owner of stock.

§ 14. [Sec. 7.] The owner or holder of stock in any incorporated company liable to taxation on its capital, shall not be taxed as an individual for such stock.

(*a*) §§ 10 and 11 exempt certain Indian reservations, and Sackett's Harbor, and Saratoga Railroad Company lands from taxation, and are therefore omitted.

ADDITIONAL EXEMPTIONS.

[Chapter 10, part 1, title 10, article 2, Revised Statutes, 5th ed., vol. 1, pp. 803, 804.]

Of the first division of militia [and fifth brigade.]

*§ 168. Every officer, non-commissioned officer, musician. and private, actually and faithfully serving in such division, shall be entitled to a reduction of five hundred dollars, from the amount assessed upon him by the assessors, as the value of his property, and the residue shall be the sum for which he shall be assessed. [1855, *chap.* 536, *sec.* 75.] duction of assessment.

*§ 169. Every officer, non-commissioned officer, musician, and private, in any troop or company of light artillery in such division, shall be entitled to a similar reduction, to the amount of one thousand dollars. [1855, *chap* 536, *sec.* 76.] $1,000, ib.

PERSONS OF COLOR.

No persons of color shall be subject to direct taxation, unless he shall be seized and possessed of a freehold estate entitling him to vote. [*Constitution, art.* 2, *sec.* 1.]

[389.] **ASSESSMENTS.**

TITLE II.

[Revised Statutes, vol. 1, 5th ed., p. 908.]

Of the place and manner in which property is to be assessed.

ARTICLE FIRST.

Of the place in which property is to be assessed.

Lands where taxed.

§ 1. Every person shall be assessed in the town or ward where he resides when the assessment is made for all lands then owned by him within such town or ward, and occupied by him, or wholly unoccupied.

§ 2. Land occupied by a person other than the owner,

may be assessed to the owner or occupant, or as non-resident lands. [*As amended by chapter* 176 *of* 1851, *sec.* 1.]

Assessment of land not occupied by owner.

§ 3. Unoccupied lands, not owned by a person residing in the ward or town where the same are situated, shall be denominated "lands of non-residents," and shall be assessed as hereinafter provided.

Ib.

§ 4. When the line between two towns or wards divides a farm or lot, the same shall be taxed, if occupied, in the town or ward where the occupant resides; if unoccupied, each part shall be assessed in the town in which the same shall lie; and this, whether such division line be a town line only, or be also a county line.

How, if divided by town line.

§ 5. Every person shall be assessed in the town or ward where he resides when the assessment is made, for all personal estate owned by him, including all personal estate in his possession, or under his control as agent, trustee, guardian, executor, or administrator; and in no case shall property so held, under either of these trusts, be assessed against any other person; and in case any person possessed of such personal estate shall reside, during any year in which taxes may be levied, in two or more counties, towns, or wards, his residence for the purposes and within the meaning of this section, shall be deemed and held to be in the county, town, or ward in which his principal business shall have been transacted, but the products of any State of the United States, consigned to agents in any town or ward of this State, for sale on commission, for the benefit of the owner thereof, shall not be assessed to such agent, nor shall such agents of moneyed corporations or capitalists be liable to taxation under this section, for any moneys in their possession or under their control, transmitted to them

Personal estate, how assessed.

for the purposes of investment or otherwise. [*As amended by chap.* 176, *sec.* 2 *of laws of* 1851.]

Property of corporations

§ 6. The real estate of all incorporated companies liable to taxation, shall be assessed in the town or ward in which the same shall lie, in the same manner as the real estate of individuals. All the personal estate of every incorporated company liable to taxation on its capital, shall be assessed in the town or ward where the principal office or place for transacting the financial concerns of the company shall be;
[390.] or if such company have no principal office or place for transacting its financial concerns, then in the town or ward where the operations of such company shall be carried on. In the case of toll-bridges, the company owning such bridge shall be assessed in the town or ward in which the tolls are collected; and where the tolls of any bridge, turnpike, or canal company, are collected in several towns or wards, the company shall be assessed in the town or ward in which the treasurer or other officer authorized to pay the last preceding dividend resides.

ARTICLE SECOND.

Of the manner in which assessments are to be made, and the duties of the assessors.

SEC. 7. Assessors may divide their town or ward into districts.

8. To ascertain number of taxable inhabitants, and amount of taxable property.

9. Form of assessment-roll.

10. Manner in which persons are to be assessed as trustees, &c.

11, 12, and 13. Manner in which lands of non-residents are to be designated in assessment-roll.

14. When necessary, assessors to have survey made of non-resident lands.

15. Property to be assessed at its true value.

§7. The assessors chosen in each town or ward may divide the same, by mutual agreement, into convenient assessment districts, not exceeding the number of assessors in such town or ward. Assessment districts.

(a) NOTE.—By the act, entitled, "An act in relation to taxes and assessments in the city of New York, and to amend the several acts in relation thereto," passed April 14th, 1859 [Laws of 1859, chap. 302, p. 679], the offices of ward assessors are abolished, but the powers and duties vested in those officers relative to the assessment of real and personal estate, are vested by said act in the officers thereby created; and the provisions of law then existing in relation to the mode and manner of making assessments, so far as conformable to the supervision of the Commissioners of Taxes and Assessments, are made applicable to said officers.

It has, therefore, been deemed proper to insert the foregoing article. See post, p. 226.

(b) NOTE.—For act relative to State assessors, see post p. 169, at the end of this part of the compilation, and Laws of 1859, ch. 312, p. 702.

Inquiry to be made.

§ 8. Between the first days of May and July, in each year, they shall proceed to ascertain, by diligent inquiry, the names of all the taxable inhabitants in their respective towns or wards, and also all the taxable property, real or personal, within the same.

Assessment roll.

§ 9. They shall prepare an assessment-roll, in which they shall set down, in four separate columns, and according to the best information in their power:

1. In the first column the names of all the taxable inhabitants in the town or ward, as the case may be.

2. In the second column the quantity of land to be taxed to each person.

3. In the third column the full value of such land, ac-
[391.] cording to the definition of the term land, as given in the first title of this chapter.

4. In the fourth column the full value of all the taxable personal property owned by such person, after deducting the just debts owing by him.

Trustee, guardian, &c.

§ 10. Where a person is assessed as trustee, guardian, executor, or administrator, he shall be assessed as such, with the addition to his name of his representative character, and such assessment shall be carried out in a separate line from his individual assessment; and he shall be assessed for the value of the real estate held by him in such representative character, at the full value thereof, and for the personal property held by him in such representative character, deducting from such personal property the just debts due from him in such representative character.

Lands of non-residents.

§ 11. The lands of non-residents shall be designated in the same assessment-roll, but in a part thereof separate from the other assessments, and in the manner prescribed in the two following sections.

§12. If the land to be assessed be a tract which is subdivided into lots, or be part of a tract which is so subdivided, the assessors shall proceed as follows : Lands o non-residents.

1. They shall designate it by its name, if known by one, or if it be not distinguished by a name, or the name be unknown, they shall state by what other lands it is bounded.

2. If they can obtain correct information of the subdivisions, they shall put down in their assessment-rolls, and in a first column, all the unoccupied lots in their town or ward, owned by non-residents, by their numbers alone, and without the names of their owners, beginning at the lowest number, and proceeding in numerical order to the highest.

3. In a second column, and opposite to the number of each lot, they shall set down the quantity of land therein, liable to taxation.

4. In a third column, and opposite to the quantity, they shall set down the valuation of such quantity.

5. If such quantity be a full lot, it shall be designated by the number alone; if it be a part of a lot, the part must be designated by boundaries, or in some other way, by which it may be known.

§ 13. If the land so to be assessed be a tract which is not subdivided, or if its subdivisions cannot be ascertained by the assessors, they shall proceed as follows : Ib.

1. They shall enter in their roll the name or boundaries thereof, as above directed, and certify in the roll that such tract is not subdivided, or that they cannot obtain correct information of the subdivisions, as the case may be :

[392.] 2. They shall set down in the proper column, the quan tity and valuation as above directed:

3. If the quantity to be assessed be the whole tract, such a description, by its name or boundaries, will be sufficient; but if a part only is liable to taxation, that part, or the part not liable, must be particularly described:

4. If any part of such tract be settled and occupied by a resident of the town or ward, the assessors shall except such part from their assessment of the whole tract, and shall assess it as other occupied lands are assessed; and if they cannot otherwise designate such parts, they shall notify the supervisor of the town, who shall cause a survey and two manuscript maps to be made, for the purpose of ascertaining the situation and quantity of every such occupied part.*

5. One of those maps shall be delivered by the supervisor to the county treasurer, to be by him transmitted to the comptroller, and the other shall be delivered in like manner to the assessors:*

6. The assessors shall then complete the assessment of the tract, and shall deposit the map in the town clerk's office, for the information of future assessors. And the expense of making such survey and maps shall be immediately repaid to the supervisor, out of the county treasury; and it shall be added by the board of supervisors to the tax on the tract, distinguishing it from the ordinary tax.*

NOTE.—Subdivisions 4, 5, and 6, must be read with reference to section 5 of Laws of 1859, chapter 302, relative to the powers of the commissioners of taxes and assessments. Vide that act, post p. 226, et seq., and Laws of 1859, page 680.

§ 14. Whenever it shall be deemed necessary by the assessors of any town to have an actual survey made, to ascertain the quantity of any lot or tract of non-resident lands which is divided by the town line, they shall notify the supervisor, who shall cause the necessary surveys to be made at the expense of the town. [393.]

Survey of non resident lands.

§ 15. [Sec. 17.] All real and personal estate liable to taxation, shall be estimated and assessed by the assessors at its full and true value, as they would appraise the same in payment of a just debt due from a solvent debtor. [*As amended* 1851, *chap.* 176, *sec.* 3.]

Property, how valued.

§ 16. [Sec. 18.] The preceding section shall be followed in all assessments made under this chapter, except where the assessors shall be specially required by law to observe a different rule.

Qualification.

§ 17. [Sec. 19.] The assessors shall complete the assessment rolls on or before the first day of August in every year, and shall make out one fair copy thereof, to be left with one of their number. They shall forthwith cause notices thereof to be left with one of their number. They shall forthwith cause notices thereof to be put up at three or more public places in their town or ward. [*As amended* 1857, *chap.* 536, *sec.* 2, *and* 1858, *chap.* 110.]

Assessment rolls.

§ 18. [Sec. 20.] Such notices shall set forth that the assessors have completed their assessment-roll, and that a copy thereof is left with one of their number at a place to be specified therein, where the same may be seen and examined by any person interested, until the third Tuesday of August, and that on that day the assessors will meet at a time and place also to be specified in such notice, to review their assessments. On the application of any person

Assessors' notice of completion of roll.

9

conceiving himself aggrieved, it shall be the duty of the said assessors on such day to meet at the time and place specified, and hear and examine all complaints in relation to such assessments that may be brought before them, and they are hereby empowered, and it shall be their duty, to adjourn, from time to time, as may be necessary to hear and determine such complaints; but in the several cities of this State, the notices required by this section may conform to the requirements of the respective laws regulating the time, place, and manner for revising the assessments in said cities, in all cases where a different time, place, and manner are prescribed by said laws from that mentioned in this act. [*As amended* 1851, *chap.* 176, *sec.* 4.]—See note.

Penalty for neglect.

*§ 19. If the assessors shall willfully neglect to hold the meeting specified in the last preceding section, each assessor so neglecting shall be liable to a penalty of twenty dollars, to be sued for and recovered before any court having jurisdiction thereof, by the supervisor of the town, for the use of the poor of the same town; and in case of such neglect to meet for review, any person aggrieved by the assessment of the assessors may appeal to the board of supervisors at their next meeting, who shall have power to review and correct such assessment. [1851, *chap.* 176, *sec.* 5.]

Inspection of roll.

§ 20. [Sec. 21.] The assessor with whom such assessment roll is left, shall submit the same, during the twenty days specified in such notice, to the inspection of all persons who shall apply for that purpose.

*§ 21. Whenever any person, on his own behalf, or on

Note.—Application in the city of New York by persons aggrieved by assessments, is to be made to the commissioners of taxes and assessments. Laws of 1859, chap. 302, sec. 10, p. 681. See post, pp. 230 and 231.

behalf of those whom he may represent, shall apply to the assessors of any town or ward to reduce the value of his real and personal estate, as set down in the assessment roll, it shall be the duty of such assessors to examine such person under oath touching the value of his or their said real or personal estate; and after such examination and such other supplementary evidence under oath, as shall be presented by the party or person aggrieved, they shall fix the value thereof at such sum as they may deem just under the rule prescribed by section ** of this title; but if such person shall refuse to answer any question as to the value of his real or personal estate, or the amount thereof, or present sufficient supplementary evidence under oath to justify a reduction, the said assessors shall not reduce the value of such real or personal estate. The examination so taken shall be written, and shall be subscribed by the person examined, and shall be filed in the office of the town clerk of the town or city in which such assessment shall be made, and any person who shall willfully swear false on such examination, before the assessors, shall be deemed guilty of willful and corrupt perjury. It shall also be the duty of the assessors whenever the value affixed to * them after such examination shall exceed that sworn to by the aggrieved party or person, to indorse on the written examination the words, "Disagreed to by the undersigned assessors, under the rule prescribed for making assessments by section fifteen, article two, title two, chapter thirteen, part one of the Revised Statutes, and in view of the obligations imposed by the deposition and oath subscribed and made on the completion of the assessment roll to which this disagreement refers." It shall be the duty of the assessors on the same occasion to furnish the aggrieved party

Manner of reducing valuation, examination of person applying.

Duty of assessors.

* Probable omission, so in original.

or person a duplicate copy of the beforementioned written examination, together with the indorsement of disagreement aforesaid, duly signed. [1851, *chap.* 176, *sec.* 6, *as amended* 1857, *chap.* 536, *sec.* 5.]

Oaths.

*§ 22. The assessors of the several towns and wards of this State shall have power to administer oaths to any person applying to them under the provisions of the sixth section of this act. [*Same chap., sec.* 7.]

Term "person" construed to include corporation.

*§ 23. Where the term "person" or "persons" is used in sections eighteen and twenty of said title two, and in sections five, six, and seven of chapter one hundred and seventy-six of the laws of eighteen hundred and fifty-one, such terms shall be construed to include corporations as well as individuals. [1857, *chap.* 536, *sec.* 3.]

Amendment of section 18, of title 2.

*§ 24. Section eighteen of said title is amended by adding after the words "hear and determine" the words "in accordance with the rule prescribed by section fifteen of said title two." [1857, *chap.* 536, *sec.* 4.]

Assessment roll to be sworn to.

*§ 25. When the assessors, or a majority of them, shall have completed their roll, they shall severally appear before one of the justices of the town or city in which they shall reside, and shall severally make and subscribe before such justice, an oath, in the following form :

We, the undersigned, do severally depose and swear, that we have set down in the foregoing assessment roll, all the real estate situated in the (town or ward, as the case may be), according to our best information; and that, with the exception of those cases in which the value of the said real estate has been changed by reason of proof produced before us, we have estimated the value of the said real estate, at the sums which a majority of the assessors have decided to be the full and true value thereof, and at which they would appraise the same in payment of a just debt due from a solvent debtor; and also that the said assessment roll contains a true statement of the aggregate amount of the taxable personal estate of each and every person named in such roll, over and above the amount of debts due from such persons respectively, and excluding such stocks as are otherwise taxable, and such other property as is exempt by law from taxation, at the full and true value thereof, according to our best judgment and belief. Which oath shall be written on said roll, signed by the assessors, and certified by the justice, and shall be in place of the official certificate now required by law; and every assessor who shall willfully swear false, in taking and subscribing said oath, shall be deemed guilty of, and liable to the penalties of willful and corrupt perjury. [*Laws* 1851, *chap.* 176, *sec.* 8].*

Roll to be delivered.

§ 26. [Sec. 27.] The roll, thus certified, shall, on or before the first day of September in every year, be delivered by the assessors of each ward in the city of New York, to [394.] the clerk of the city, and by the assessors of every other town or ward, to the supervisor thereof, who shall deliver the same to the board of supervisors at their next meeting.†

* NOTE.—Sections 17, 18, 19, 20, 21, 22, 23, 24, 25, *supra*, it is conceived are rendered inapplicable to the deputy tax commissioners created by laws of 1859, chap. 302, p. 678, *et seq.*, but in the absence of any judicial determination of the fact, it has been deemed more prudent to insert them.

† By laws of 1850, chap. 121, p. 191, sec. 17, as amended by sec. 1, chap. 319, p. 611, laws of 1851, the assessors were to deliver the assessment rolls to the tax commissioners on or before the first day of April in each year. By section 22 of the act of 1850, aforesaid, the certified rolls were to be delivered by the tax commissioners to the comptroller, on the first day of July in each year, to be by him delivered to the supervisors. By laws of 1859, chap. 302,

Duty of assessors. § 27. [Sec. 28.] The assessors, in the execution of their duties, shall use the forms, and pursue the instructions, which shall from time to time be transmitted to them by the comptroller.

Ib. § 28. [Sec. 29.] If any assessor shall willfully refuse or neglect to perform any of the duties required of him by this chapter, he shall forfeit to the people of this State, the sum of fifty dollars.

Ib. § 29. [Sec. 30.] If any assessor shall neglect, or from any cause omit to perform his duties, the other assessors, or either of them, of the town or ward, shall perform such duties, and shall certify to the supervisors with their assessment roll, the name of such delinquent assessor, stating therein the cause of such omission.

[395.] ARTICLE THIRD.

[Revised Statutes, 5th edition, vol. 1, p. 914.]

Of the equalization of the assessments, and the correction of the assessment rolls.

§ 30. [Sec. 31.] The board of supervisors of each

---

p. 682, sec. 13, the certified rolls are to be delivered by the commissioners of taxes and assessments to the supervisors, on the first Monday of July in each year.

county in this State, at their annual meeting, shall examine the assessment rolls of the several towns in their county, for the purpose of ascertaining whether the valuations in one town or ward bear a just relation to the valuations in all the towns and wards in the county; and they may increase or diminish the aggregate valuations of real estates, in any town or ward, by adding or deducting such sum upon the hundred, as may, in their opinion, be necessary to produce a just relation between all the valuations of real estates in the county; but they shall, in no instance, reduce the aggregate valuations of all the towns and wards, below the aggregate valuation thereof, as made by the assessors.

Supervisors to examine assessment roll.

§ 31. [Sec. 32.] The board of supervisors shall also make such alterations in the descriptions of the lands of non-residents, as may be necessary to render such descriptions conformable to the provisions of this chapter; and if such alterations cannot be made, they shall expunge the descriptions of such lands, and the assessments thereon, from the assessment rolls.

Land of non-residents.

§ 32. [Sec. 33.] They shall also estimate and set down, in a fifth column, to be prepared for that purpose, in the assessment rolls, opposite to the several sums set down as the valuations of real and personal estates, the respective sums in dollars and cents, rejecting the fractions of a cent, to be paid as a tax thereon.

Tax to be set down.

§ 33. [Sec. 34.] They shall also add up, and set down, the aggregate valuations of the real and personal estates in the several towns and wards, as corrected by them; and shall cause their clerk to transmit to the comptroller, by mail, a certificate of such aggregate valuations, showing separately the aggregate amount of real and personal es-

Aggregate valuations.

[396.] tate in each town or ward, as corrected by the board.—See notes 1, 2, 3, and 4.

Account to be transmitted to county treasurer.

§ 37. [Sec. 38.] As soon as the board of supervisors shall have sent or delivered the rolls, with such warrants annexed, to the collectors, they shall transmit to the treasurer of the county an account thereof, stating the names of the several collectors, the amount of money they are respectively to collect, the purposes for which the same are to be collected, and the persons to whom, and the time when, the same are to be paid; and the county treasurers,

---

1 NOTE.—(Sec. 34.) Refers to the delivery of the corrected assessment roll, or a copy thereof, of each town or ward, by the board of supervisors, to each of the supervisors of the several towns or wards, to be delivered to city or county clerk.

The supervisors of the county of New York are to deliver the corrected assessment rolls to the receiver of taxes in the city of New York, on or before the first day of September in each year. Laws of 1850, chap. 121, sec. 27, p. 193. See post p. 217. Sec. 34 is therefore omitted.

2 NOTE.—§ 35 (Sec. 36), § 36 (Sec. 37), refer to the delivery of the corrected assessment rolls by the board of supervisors to the collectors, and to the form of the warrants issued to the collectors. The act in relation to the collection of taxes in the city of New York, passed April 18, 1843, abolishes the office of collector of taxes in the city of New York, and abrogates all provisions by charter, statute, ordinance, resolution, or otherwise, creating such offices, and imposing or defining the duties thereof. Laws of 1843, chap. 230, art. 1, sec. 1, p. 314.

The act of March 30, 1850, provides that the rolls shall be delivered to the receiver of taxes. Laws of 1850, chap. 121, sec. 27, p. 192. And the act of 1843, aforesaid, art. 2, sec. 2, p. 317, prescribes the form and contents of the warrant to be issued to the receiver of taxes. See post, p. 201.

The above sections of the Revised Statutes are therefore omitted.

3 NOTE.—§ 37 (Sec. 38), § 38 (Sec. 39), may possibly be considered as applicable to the supervisors, and to the officers who are now intrusted by law with the collection of taxes, and are therefore inserted above.

4 NOTE.—§ 39 is taken from chapter 180 of the laws of 1845, Sec. 31, p. 190, and is inapplicable to the city of New York.

on receiving such account, shall charge to each collector the sums to be collected by him.

§38. [Sec. 39.] Wherever the laws respecting cities shall have directed the moneys assessed for any local purpose, to be paid to any person or officer other than those named in the preceding thirty-seventh section, the collector's warrant may be varied accordingly, so as to conform to such alteration.—See note 4. Cities.

PAYMENTS AND RETURNS BY COUNTY TREASURERS.

TITLE III.

ARTICLE SECOND. *(a) (b)* [402.]

[Part 1, chapter 13, title three, Revised Statutes, 5th edition, vol. 1, p. 924.]

Of the payments and returns to be made by the county treasurers, and the duty of the comptroller and other officers thereupon.

* * * * * *

* * * * * *

(a) NOTE.—Article 1 of this title refers to the manner in which taxes are to be collected, and the duties of the collector, and is made inapplicable to the city and county of New York, by sec. 1, of art. 4, of act of April 18, 1843. Laws of 1843, chap. 230, p. 328. See post, p. 205.

(b) NOTE.—This article is taken from chap. 427, Laws of 1855, p. 781, and only the second, third, eighth, twelfth, thirteenth, and fourteenth sections are made applicable to the city of New York.

The other sections are therefore omitted.

See Laws of 1855, pp. 781–799, sec. 91, vol. 1, Revised Statutes, p. 939, 5th edition, sec. 127.

State tax, when to be paid.

*§38. [Sec. 2.] The several county treasurers shall, on or before the first day of March, in each year, pay to the Treasurer of this State, the amount of the State tax, if any, raised and paid over to them respectively, retaining the compensation to which they may be entitled.

How paid.

*§39. [Sec. 3.] Such payment may also be made by depositing such money, to the credit of the Treasurer of this State, in such banks in the city of New York or Albany, as shall have been designated by the Comptroller, and shall then be entitled to receive the State deposits, and in case of such payment to either of those banks, the county treasurer making it shall forthwith transmit a certificate of deposit to the Comptroller, who shall thereupon certify such payment to the State Treasurer, and charge him with the amount thereof.

* * * * * *

Apportionment of State tax.

*§44. [Sec. 8.] The Comptroller shall, from the annual returns made to him of the valuations of real and personal estates in the several counties in the State, charge the several county treasurers with the amount of the State taxes, if any, to be raised in their respective counties, crediting them with their own fees; but no fees shall be allowed by the Comptroller to the county treasurers, in adjusting the accounts of the county treasurers, for such portion of the

State tax as is paid by credit given for taxes on non-resident property returned to him.

* * * * * *

*§48. [Sec. 12.] If any county treasurer shall refuse or neglect to pay such balance within such time, the Comptroller shall forthwith (unless he shall be satisfied, by due proof, that such treasurer has not received such balance, and has taken all proper steps to collect the same) deliver a copy of such county treasurer's account to the Attorney General, who shall prosecute forthwith; and the State shall be entitled to recover the balance due, with interest thereon from the first day of May, in the year when the same ought to have been paid. Suits for neglect to pay.

*§49. [Sec. 13.] The Comptroller may also, in his discretion, direct the board of supervisors of the proper county, to institute one or more suits on the bond of such treasurer and his sureties. Bond to be sued.

*§50. [Sec. 14.] If the defendants in any suit to be brought under either of the two last preceding sections, shall, at any time before judgment is obtained therein, pay the balance due the State, with interest, into the treasury, or account for the same to the Comptroller, it shall be his duty, on payment of costs of suit, to direct such suits to be discontinued. Suits, when to be discontinued.

TAXES ON RENTS RESERVED, AND DEBTS DUE NON-RESIDENTS.

TITLE III.

ARTICLE FOURTH. *(a) (b)*

Of taxes upon rents reserved on certain leases, and on debts owing non-residents of the United States.

(a) NOTE.—This article contains the "act to equalize taxation," chap. 327 of 1846, p. 466; and "an act to subject certain debts owing to non-residents to taxation," chap. 371 of 1851, p. 721.

(b) NOTE.—Article 3 of this title refers to sales for unpaid taxes, and to the conveyance and redemption of land sold, and is made inapplicable to the city and county of New York, by sec. 2 of art. 4 of act of April 18, 1843.—Laws of 1843, chap. 230, p. 328. See post, p. 205.

*§ 129. It shall be the duty of the assessors of each town and ward, while engaged in ascertaining the taxable property therein, by diligent inquiry to ascertain the amount of rents reserved in any leases in fee, or for one or more lives, or for a term of years exceeding twenty-one years, and chargeable upon lands within such town or ward, which rents shall be assessed to the person or persons entitled to receive the same, as personal estate, which is hereby declared to be, for the purpose of taxation under this act, at a principal sum, the interest of which at the legal rate per annum shall produce a sum equal to such annual rents; and in case such rents are payable in any other thing except money, the value of such annual rents in money shall be ascertained by the assessors, and the same shall be assessed in manner aforesaid. [1846, *chap.* 327, *sec.* 1.] Duty of assessors.

*§ 130. The Board of Supervisors in each county shall assess the taxes to be raised for town, county, and State purposes, upon the person or persons entitled to receive such rents within the town or ward where the lands upon which such rents are reserved and situated, in the same Duty of boards of supervisors.

manner and to the same extent as any personal estate of the inhabitants of such town. [*Same chap.*, *sec.* 2.]

Tax may be levied by distress.

*§ 131. If such tax shall not be paid, the collector shall levy the same by distress and sale of the goods and chattels of the person against whom the same is assessed, within the town or ward of such collector, in the same manner as if such person was an inhabitant of such town or ward. [*Same chap.*, *sec.* 3.]

Duty of county treasurer.

*§ 132. When it shall appear by the return of any collector, made according to law, to a county treasurer, that any tax imposed under the provisions of this act, remains unpaid, such county treasurer shall issue his warrant to the sheriff of any county where any real or personal estate of the person upon whom such tax is imposed may be found, commanding him to make of the goods and chattels and real estate of such person, the amount of such tax, together with one dollar for the expense of issuing such warrant, and to return the said warrant to the treasurer issuing the same, and to pay to him the money which shall be collected by virtue thereof, by a certain time therein to be specified, not less than sixty days from the date of such warrant. [1846, *chap.* 327, *sec.* 4.]

Warrant to be a lien on real and personal estate.

*§ 133. Such warrant shall be a lien upon, and shall bind the real and personal estate of the person against whom the same shall be issued, from the time an actual levy shall be made by virtue thereof; and the sheriff to whom such warrant shall be directed, shall proceed upon the same in all respects with the like effect, and in the same manner as prescribed by law in respect to executions against property, issued by a county clerk upon judgments rendered by a justice of the peace, and shall be entitled

to the same fees for his services in executing the same, to be collected in the same manner. [*Same chap., sec.* 5.]

Sheriff to be proceeded against in case of neglect.

*§ 134. In case of the neglect of any sheriff to return such warrant according to the directions therein, or to pay over any money collected by him in pursuance thereof, he shall be proceeded against in the Supreme Court by attachment, in the same manner and with the like effect as for similar neglects in reference to an execution issued out of the Supreme Court in a civil suit, and the proceedings thereon shall be the same in all respects. [*Same chap., sec.* 6.]

When returned unsatisfied.

*§ 135. If any such warrant shall be returned unsatisfied, in whole or in part, the county treasurer, under the direction of the board of supervisors of his county, may file a bill in his name of office in the Supreme Court,[1] whatever may be the amount so remaining unsatisfied against the person against whom such warrant was issued, and any other person having the possession of his property, for the discovery and sequestration of such property; and on the filing of such bill, the court shall order such part of the property of the person upon whom the tax specified in the said warrant was imposed, as shall be necessary for the purpose of satisfying the taxes in arrear and imposed as aforesaid, with the cost of prosecution, to be sequestered; and may order and direct such other proceedings as may be necessary to compel the payment of such tax and costs. [*Same chap., sec.* 7.]

Debts owing for the purchase of real estate taxable.

*§ 136. All debts owing by inhabitants of this State to persons not residing within the United States, for the purchase of any real estate, shall be deemed personal property, within the town or county where the debtor resides, and

1 "Court of Chancery" in the original.

as such shall be liable to taxation in the same manner and to the same extent as the personal estate of citizens of this State. [1851, *chap.* 371, *sec.* 1.]

Agents of non-resident creditors to report to county treasurer.

*§ 137. If there shall reside in any county of this State an agent of any non-resident creditor having debts owing to him of the description mentioned in the first section of this act, he shall, on or before the twenty-fifth day of July in such year, furnish to the county treasurer of each county where such debtor resides, the true and accurate amount of debts of the description mentioned in the first section of this act, which were owing on the first day of January preceding, to the principal of such agent, in each town in such county, which shall be verified by the oath of such agent, taken before any officer authorized to administer oaths. [1851, *chap.* 371, *sec.* 2.]

Penalty for not making report.

*§ 138. Any such agent who shall refuse or neglect, without good and sufficient cause, to furnish such list, shall forfeit the sum of five hundred dollars to the use of each county in which such debtor resides, to be sued for by the treasurer of such county in his name of office, and to be recovered upon proof that the principal of such agent had debts owing to him by the inhabitants of such county, of the description mentioned in the first section of this act, and that the existence of such debts was known to such agent. [*Same chap., sec.* 3.]

Abstract to be sent to assessors.

*§ 139. The county treasurer, on receiving such statement, shall immediately make out and transmit to the assessors of the several towns of his county in which any such debtor resides, an abstract or copy of so much of such statement as relates to the town of such assessor, with the name of such creditor. [*Same chap., sec.* 4.]

*§ 140. The assessors, on receiving such abstract or statement from the county treasurer, shall, within the time in which they are now required by law to complete their assessment roll, enter thereon the name of such non-resident debtor,[1] and the aggregate amount due him in such town, on the first day of January preceding, in the same manner other personal property is entered on said roll. [*Same chap., sec.* 5.]

Name and amount due to be entered on assessment roll.

*§ 141. When it shall appear by the return of any collector, made according to law to a county treasurer, that any tax imposed on a debt owing to a person not residing in the United States, remains unpaid, such county treasurer shall, after the expiration of twenty days from the return of such collector, issue his warrant to the sheriff of any county in this State, where any debtor of such non-resident creditor may reside, commanding him to make of the goods and chattels and real estate of such non-resident, the amount of such tax, to be specified in a schedule annexed to the said warrant, together with his fees and the sum of one dollar for the expense of issuing such warrant, and to return the said warrant to the treasurer issuing the same, and to pay over to him the money which shall be collected by virtue thereof, except the said sheriff's fees, by a certain day therein to be specified, within sixty days from the date of such warrant. [*Same chap., sec.* 6.]

Unpaid taxes, how collected.

*§ 142. The taxes upon several debts owing to the non-resident shall be included in one warrant, and the taxes upon several debts owing to different non-residents may be included in the same warrant, and where several non-residents are included in the same warrant, the sheriff shall be directed to levy the sums specified in the schedule thereto

Warrants, how made out.

---

1 So in the original.

annexed, upon the personal and real property of the non-residents respectively, opposite to whose names, respectively, such sums shall be written, together with the sum of fifty cents upon each non-resident, for the expense of such warrant. [*Same chap., sec.* 7.]

Lien of warrant.

*§ 143. Such warrant shall be a lien upon, and shall bind the real and personal estate of the non-residents against whom the same shall be issued, from the time an actual levy shall be made upon any property by virtue thereof; and the sheriff to whom such warrant shall be directed, shall proceed upon the same, in all respects, with the like effect and in the same manner as prescribed by law in respect to executions against property, issued upon judgments rendered in the Supreme Court, and shall be entitled to the same fees for his services in executing the same, to be collected in the same manner. [*Same chap., sec.* 8.]

Sheriff, how proceeded against for neglect to return warrant.

*§ 144. In case of the neglect of any sheriff to return such warrant according to the direction therein, or to pay over any money collected by him in pursuance thereof, he shall be proceeded against in the Supreme Court, by attachment, in the same manner and with the like effect, as for similar neglects in reference to an execution issued out of the Supreme Court in a civil suit, and the proceedings thereon shall be the same in all respects. [1851, *chap.* 371, *sec.* 9.]

Proceedings when warrant returned unsatisfied.

*§ 145. If any such warrant shall be returned unsatisfied in whole or in part, the county treasurer, or, in the city and county of New York, the comptroller therein, under the direction of the board of supervisors, may obtain an order from a judge of the Supreme Court, or a county judge of the county to which said warrant was issued, requiring such non-resident, or any person having property

of such non-resident, or indebted to him, to appear and answer concerning the property of such non-resident, and the same remedies and proceedings may be had in the name of the county treasurer or comptroller, before the officer granting such order, and with the like effect as are provided by the statute in case of a judgment debtor after the return of an execution against him, unsatisfied in whole or in part. [*Same chap.*, *sec.* 10.]

Expenses of treasurer and assessors, how paid.

*§ 146. The expenses of county treasurers, and such compensation as their boards of supervisors shall allow them for their services in executing this act, shall be county charges; and the expenses and charges for the services of assessors under this act, shall be town charges, and audited and paid as such. [*Same chap.*, *sec.* 11.]

Assessments made against persons in town in which he does not reside, may be corrected by board of supervisors, &c.

*§ 147. The assessor shall, in all cases of assessments under chapter three hundred and twenty-seven of the laws of eighteen hundred and forty-six, specify in the assessment rolls each rent so assessed, and the value fixed upon articles other than money, in which such rents are payable, and whenever assessments are made against any person in any town or ward in which he does not reside, the board of supervisors of the county to which such assessments are returned, shall have in all respects as full power and authority, and it shall be their duty to correct such assessments as to the valuation of the rents, and as to the gross amount for which such person shall be assessed, as the assessors have as to a resident of the town; and such board of supervisors may reduce the amount of such assessments in the respective towns or wards of the county, in proportion or otherwise, as the nature of the corrections require, to make such assessments just. [1858, *chap.* 357.]

CORPORATIONS.

[414.]

TITLE IV.

Chapter 13, part 1, 5th edition of Revised Statutes, page 944.

Regulations concerning the assessment of taxes on incorporated companies, and the commutation or collec tion thereof.

Companies liable to taxation.

§ 1. All moneyed or stock corporations, deriving an income or profit from their capital, or otherwise, shall be liable to taxation on their capital, in the manner hereinafter prescribed.

Certain life insurance companies to be subject to taxation.

*§ 2. Any mutual life insurance company in this State, incorporated previously to the passage of the general insurance law, on the tenth day of April, eighteen hundred and forty-nine, shall be subject to taxation in the same manner as if it were incorporated under said general law, with a capital of one hundred thousand dollars, as required by the sixth section of the said general law. [1853, chap. 469.] *(a) (b)*

(*a*) NOTE.—Any mutual life insurance company incorporated in this State previous to the passage of the general insurance law on the tenth day of April, eighteen hundred and forty-nine, shall be subject to taxation on the sum of one hundred thousand dollars for personal property, and no more. And it is hereby declared that such was the intention, and it is the true construction of said act of June twenty-ninth, eighteen hundred and fifty-three, in regard to any taxes imposed on said companies after said act took effect. Laws of 1855, chap. 83, p. 122.

(*b*) NOTE.—All individual bankers, and all banking associations, which are now, or shall be hereafter engaged in the business of banking, under the provisions of the act, entitled "An act to authorize the business of banking," shall be subject to taxation on the full amount of actual capital paid in or secured to be paid in, as such capital by them severally, at the actual market value of such securities, to be estimated by the comptroller, without any reduction for the debts of such individual banker, or banking association. But in no case shall the capital of any such banking association, or individual banker, be estimated at a less sum than the amount of circulating notes delivered to such banking association or individual banker, and not returned to the comptroller; and in case the capital of such banking association has been reduced by the surrender of any securities to the stockholders thereof, and the certificates of stock held on account of such securities being surren-

Officers to to deliver statements to assessors.

§ 3. [Sec. 2.] The president, cashier, secretary, treasurer, or other proper officer of every such incorporated company, shall, on or before the first day of July in each year, make and deliver to the assessors, or one of them, of the town or ward in which such company is liable to be taxed, according to the provisions of the sixth section of the second title of this chapter, a written statement, specifying—

1. The real estate, if any, owned by such company; the towns or wards in which the same is situated, and the sums actually paid therefor:

2. The capital stock actually paid in, and secured to be paid in, excepting therefrom the sums paid for real estate, and the amount of such capital stock held by the State, and by any incorporated literary or charitable institution: And,

3. The town or ward in which the principal office or place of transacting the financial business of such company
[415.] is situated; or if there be no such principal office, the town or ward in which its operations are carried on, or in which it is liable to be taxed, under the provisions of this chapter.

Statement to comptroller

§ 4. [Sec. 3.] The president, or other proper officer, of every such company, shall also deliver to the comptroller, on or before the first day of July in each year, a written statement, containing the same matters required by the foregoing section to be specified in the statement to be delivered to the assessors. The statements required by this

---

dered to such banking association and cancelled, such banking association shall not be subject to taxation upon such part of its capital. Laws of 1847, chap. 419, vol. 2, p. 521, sec. 4.

and the preceding section of this title, shall be certified under the oath of the said president or other proper officer, to be in all respects just and true.

§ 5. [Sec. 4.] If the statements above required, or either of them, shall not be furnished by any company to the assessors, and to the comptroller, within thirty days after the time above provided, the company neglecting to furnish such statements, or either of them, shall forfeit to the people of this State, for each statement omitted to be furnished, the sum of two hundred and fifty dollars; and it shall be the duty of the comptroller to furnish the attorney-general with an account of all companies that shall neglect to render such lists, that he may prosecute for the penalties hereby imposed. Penalty.

§ 6. [Sec. 5.] If any company that shall be prosecuted for any such penalty, shall pay the costs of prosecution, and furnish the statement required, the comptroller, if he shall be satisfied that the omission was not willful, may, in his discretion, discontinue such suit. Suit therefor.

§ 7. [Sec. 6.] The assessors shall enter all incorporated companies from which such statements shall have been received by them, and the property of such companies, and the property of all other incorporated companies, liable to taxation in their respective towns, in their assessment rolls, in the following manner: Companies, how assessed.

1. They shall insert in the first column of their assessment rolls, the name of each incorporated company in their respective towns or wards, liable to taxation on its capital or otherwise, and under its name they shall specify the amount of its capital stock paid in, and secured to be paid in; the amount paid by such company for real estate then First column of assessment roll. Taxes on incorporated companies.

belonging to such company, wherever the same may be situated; the amount of all surplus profits or reserved funds exceeding ten per cent. of their capital, after deducting therefrom the said amount of said real estate, and the amount of its stock, if any, belonging to the State, and to incorporated literary and charitable institutions. [*As amended, chap.* 654, *sec.* 1, *laws* 1853, *p.* 1240.] (*a*)

2. In the second column they shall enter the quantity of real estate owned by such company, and situated within their town or ward; and in the third column, the actual value thereof, estimated as in other cases.

Fourth column, what to be inserted in.

3. In the fourth column they shall enter the amount of the capital stock of every incorporated company paid in, and secured to be paid in, and of all such surplus profits or reserved funds as aforesaid, after deducting the sums paid out for all the real estate of such company, wherever the
[416.] same may be situated, and then belonging to it, and the amount of stock, if any, belonging to the people of this State, and to incorporated literary and charitable institutions. [*As amended, chap.* 654, *sec.* 1, *laws of* 1853, *p.* 1240.]

Preceding section extended.

§ 8. The provisions of the fifteenth section of the second title of this chapter, shall be, and are hereby extended to

---

(*a*) NOTE.—Any moneyed or stock corporation deriving profit or income from its capital or otherwise, shall add to the dividend which shall be declared upon any stock owned by the State or by any literary or charitable society or institution a sum equal to the assessment for taxes paid upon an equal amount of the stock of such corporation not exempt from taxation. Laws of 1845, ch. 195, § 1, page 224.

The provisions of the sixth subdivision of the fourth section of the first title of chapter thirteen of the first part of the Revised Statutes, whereby all stocks owned by the State or by literary or charitable institutions in moneyed or stock corporations are exempted from taxation, are hereby declared to be for the benefit of the State or the institutions owning such stocks, and not for the benefit of the said corporations. Laws of 1845, ch. 195, § 2, p. 224.

the incorporated companies in the two preceding sections named; and the president, secretary, or other proper officer, may make the affidavit required by said section. (*a*)

§ 9. [Sec. 15.] The amount of taxes assessed on all incorporated companies, liable to taxation, shall be set down by the board of supervisors in the fifth column of the corrected assessment roll, and shall form a part of the moneys to be collected by the collector. [*As amended*, 1857, *chap.* 456, *sec.* 2, vol. 2, p. 2.]

Capital stock, with certain exceptions, to be taxed at its actual value.

*§ 10. The capital stock of every company liable to taxation, except such part of it as shall have been excepted in the assessment roll, or as shall have been exempted by law, together with the surplus profits or reserved funds exceeding ten per cent. of its capital, after deducting the assessed value of its real estate, and all shares of stock in other corporations actually owned by such company, which are taxable upon their capital stock under the laws of this State, shall be assessed at its actual value, and taxed in the same manner as the other personal and real estate of the county. [1857, *chap.* 456, *sec.* 3, *vol.* 2, *p.* 2.]

Deposits in savings banks, etc., not liable to be taxed other than real estate, etc., of bank.

*§ 11. The deposits in any bank for savings which are due to depositors, and the accumulations in any life insurance company organized under the laws of this State, so far as the said accumulations are held for the exclusive benefit of the assured, shall not be liable to taxation, other than the real estate and stocks which may be owned by such bank or company, and which are now liable to taxation under the laws of this State. [*Same chap.*, *sec.* 4, *laws of* 1857, *vol.* 2, *p.* 2.]

(*a*) NOTE.—The fifteenth section of title 2, chapter 13, in this section referred to, was repealed by section three of laws of 1851, chap. 176, p. 333.

Duty of supervisors.

§ 12. [Sec. 16.] The board of supervisors having completed the assessment, shall transmit to the comptroller, with the aggregate valuations of the real and personal estate in their county, a statement showing the names of the several incorporated companies liable to taxation in such county; the amount of the capital stock paid in, and secured to be paid in by each; the amount of real and personal property of each, as put down by the assessors, or by them; and the amount of taxes assessed on each. In those counties in which there is no such company, the boards of supervisors shall certify such fact to the comptroller, with their returns of the aggregate valuations of real and personal estate.

Duty of collector.

§ 13. [Sec. 17.] The collector shall demand payment of all taxes assessed on incorporated companies, from the president, or other proper officer, of such companies; and if not paid, shall proceed in the collection and payment thereof, in the same manner as in other cases, and shall be liable to the same penalties for the non-payment of moneys collected by him. And the collector's receipt shall be evidence of the payment of such tax. (*a*)

Taxes, how paid.

§ 14. [Sec. 18.] Such taxes shall be paid out of the funds of the company, and shall be ratably deducted from the dividends of those stockholders whose stock was taxed, or shall be charged upon such stock, if no dividends be afterwards declared.

Proceedings if taxes cannot be collected.

§ 15. [Sec. 19.] If the collector shall not be able to collect any tax assessed upon an incorporated company, he shall return the same to the county treasurer, and at the same time time make affidavit before the county treasurer,

---

(*a*) NOTE.—The office of collector of taxes was abolished in the city of New York, by laws of 1843, chap. 230, p. 314. See post, p. 181.

or some other officer authorized to administer oaths, that he had demanded payment thereof from the president, or [418.] other proper officer of the company, and that such officer had refused to pay the same, or that he had not been able to make such demand, as the case may be; and that such company had no personal property from which he could levy such tax.

§ 16. [Sec. 20.] The county treasurer shall thereupon certify such facts to the comptroller, who shall pass to the credit of such county treasurer the amount of all taxes so returned and certified, as in the cases of taxes on the lands of non-residents. Ibid.

§ 17. [Sec. 21.] The comptroller shall furnish the attorney-general with the names of all the companies and banks refusing or neglecting to pay the taxes imposed on them, with the amount due from them respectively; and the attorney-general shall thereupon file a petition in the supreme court against every such company or bank, for the discovery and sequestration of its property. [*As amended* 1857, *ch.* 456, *sec.* 5, *laws of* 1857, *vol.* 2, *p.* 2.]

Attorney General to file petition in Supreme Court.

Companies and banks refusing to pay.

*§ 18. The supreme court, on the filing of such petition, or on the coming in of the answer thereto, may order such part of the property of such company or bank to be sequestrated, as shall be deemed necessary, for the purpose of satisfying the taxes in arrear, with the costs of prosecution. And the court may also, at its discretion, enjoin such company or bank, and the officers thereof, from any further proceedings under their charter or act of incorporation, and may order and direct such other proceedings as shall be deemed necessary to compel the payment of such taxes and costs. [1857, *ch.* 456, *sec.* 6, *laws of* 1857, *vol.* 2, *p.* 2.]

Sequestration of property.

§ 19. [Sec. 22.] The [court, on the commencement of

Powers of Court. the action], or on the coming in of the answer thereto, shall order such part of the property of such company to be sequestered, as [it] shall deem necessary, for the purpose of satisfying the taxes in arrear, with the costs of prosecution; and may also, at discretion, enjoin such company, and the officers thereof, from any further proceedings under their act of incorporation, and may order and direct such other proceedings as [it] shall deem necessary, to compel the payment of such tax and costs.*

Further remedy. § 20. [Sec. 23.] The attorney-general may also recover such tax, with costs, from such delinquent company, by action in any court of record in this State.

---

* The section modified to render it conformable to the code of procedure, by substituting the words in brackets in section 22, for "chancellor, on the filing of such bill," and also "it" for "he," where necessary.

NOTE.—By Laws of 1849, chap. 178, p. 239, sec. 1, it was provided that there should be paid to the Treasurer of the Fire Department of the City of New York, for the use and benefit of said Fire Department, on the first day of February in each year, by every person who shall act in the city and county of New York as agent for or on behalf of any individual, or association of individuals not incorporated by the laws of this State, to effect insurances against losses or injury by fire in the city and county of New York, &c., the sum of two dollars upon the hundred dollars, and at that rate, upon the amount of all premiums, which during the year or part of a year ending on the next preceding first day of September, shall have been received by such agent or person, or received by any other person for him, or shall have been agreed to be paid for any insurance effected, or agreed to be paid for any insurance effected, or agreed to be effected, or promised by him as such agent or otherwise, against loss or injury by fire in the city and county of New York.

By Section 1 of Act of April 16, 1857, chap. 548, vol. 2, p. 171, the first section of the Act of 1849 aforesaid is, among others, repealed so far as it relates to the city and county of New York, and the following provision was made by the first section of the latter Act:

Provided, however, that any corporation or association, created by or organized under the laws of any government other than the States of this Union, and having assets, funds, or capital, not less in amount than three

TITLE V.

Miscellaneous provisions of a general nature.

* * * * *

SEC. 2. Delinquent town clerks and assessors to be reported to comptroller and prosecuted.

3. Bonds, notes, &c., sent to this State for collection, not to be taxed.

4. When tenant paying tax, may sue therefor, or retain out of rent.

* * * * *

12 and 13. Comptroller to send forms, &c., to county treasurers to be distributed by them.

14. Comptroller to cause copies of this chapter to be printed and distributed.

15. Punishment of officers for willfully neglecting the execution of this chapter.

16. Clerks of supervisors to return aggregate valuations in their counties to the Comptroller.

17. When prosecution for crime, &c., transferred from county where same is laid to another county, the mode of paying the expenses, &c.

---

hundred thousand dollars, invested in this State, shall be liable to taxation upon such assets, funds, or invested capital, as the same is levied or assessed yearly by law, which tax shall be paid as follows : such an amount thereof as would be equal to two per cent. upon its gross premiums, received for insurances upon property in the city of New York, shall be paid annually as herein before provided, to the Treasurer of the Fire Department of the City of New York, and the residue of said tax, requisite to make up the full amount of taxation upon its capital as herein before provided, shall be paid to the Mayor, Aldermen, and Commonalty of the City of New York, as in the case of ordinary taxation, and the payments so made as aforesaid, shall exempt such corporation or association making the same, from any and all further taxation upon its premiums, capital, or assets, and whenever such capital shall be reduced below said sum of three hundred thousand dollars, or withdrawn entirely, then, and in either event, such corporation or association shall be liable to pay the tax upon its premiums, as heretofore provided in this Act.

By Act of April 15th, 1858 [Laws of 1858, chap. 255, p. 405], the above section was amended by altering the words "three hundred" to "one hundred and fifty," wherever they occur in said section, or the proviso therein contained.

Duty of Board of Supervisors.

§ 2. The boards of supervisors of the several counties, at every annual meeting, shall transmit to the comptroller the names and places of abode of the town clerks and assessors, in their respective counties, who shall have willfully refused or neglected to perform the duties required of [419.] them in this chapter; and the comptroller shall thereupon give notice to the district attorneys of the proper counties, to the end that they may prosecute such delinquent town clerks and assessors, for the penalties incurred by them.

Bonds, &c., sent to this State for collection, not to be taxed.

§ 3. When any bond, mortgage, note, contract, account, or other demand, belonging to any person not being a resident of this State, shall be sent to this State for collection, or shall be deposited in this State for the same purpose, such property shall be exempt from taxation; and nothing contained in this chapter shall be construed to render any agent of such owner liable to be assessed or taxed for such property; but every such agent shall be entitled to have any such property deducted from his assessment, upon making affidavit before the assessors, at the time appointed by them for reviewing their assessments, that such property belongs to a non-resident owner, and therein specifying his name and residence.[1]

Remedy of tenant for taxes paid.

§ 4. When the tax on any real estate shall have been collected of any occupant or tenant, and any other person, by agreement or otherwise, ought to pay such tax, or any part thereof, such occupant or tenant shall be entitled to recover, by action, the amount which such person ought to have paid; or to retain the same from any rent due, or accruing from him to such person, for the land so taxed.

---

[1] Act concerning the Revised Statutes, passed December 10, 1828, sec. 17.

NOTE.—The provisions contained in this title which have been omitted, are inapplicable to the city of New York.

§12. The comptroller shall, from time to time, at his discretion, transmit blank forms of assessment-rolls, and of returns of unpaid taxes, to the several county treasurers in this State, together with such instructions as he shall think useful for the purpose of enforcing the uniform and proper execution of this chapter. Blank forms and instructions. [420.]

§13. The county treasurers shall distribute such of the said forms and instructions as shall have been intended for the use of assessors, among the town clerks in their respective counties, who shall deliver the same to the assessors in their respective towns. The county treasurer shall also transmit or deliver a copy of such forms and instructions to each of the assessors in any city in his county. *(a)* Distribution thereof.

§14. The comptroller shall, from time to time, whenever he shall find it to be necessary, cause to be printed at the expense of this State a sufficient number of copies of this chapter, to furnish one copy to each county treasurer, supervisor, town clerk, assessor, and collector, within this State, and shall transmit to each county treasurer a sufficient number for his county; every county treasurer receiving such copies shall immediately transmit, at the expense of the county, to the clerk of each town therein, five copies, to be distributed by him among the officers entitled thereto, and he shall also transmit or deliver one such copy to each assessor and collector in every city in his county. Copies of this chapter. [421.]

§15. If any of the officers concerned in the execution of this chapter, shall willfully neglect, or refuse to perform Officers guilty of neglect of duty.

(a) Note.—Office of collector of taxes abolished in the city of New York, by laws of 1843, chap. 230, p. 314. See post, p. 181. Office of ward assessors abolished, and deputy tax commissioners substituted therefor, in said city. laws of 1859, chap. 302, sec. 2, p. 679. See post, p. 230.

the duties assigned them, such officer shall be deemed guilty of a misdemeanor, and on conviction, shall be punished by fine or imprisonment, or both, in the discretion of the court.

Real and personal estate to be reported.

*§16. The clerk of the board of supervisors of the several counties in this State, shall, on or before the second Monday in December in each year, transmit to the comptroller, by mail, in the form which shall be prescribed by the comptroller, a certificate or return of the aggregate valued amount of real and personal estate in each town or ward, as corrected by the board of supervisors. The clerk who shall neglect, or refuse to make such return, shall forfeit to the people of this State the sum of fifty dollars. [1836, ch. 117.]

When prosecution for crime transferred from county where venue laid to another county, expenses, &c. how paid.

*§17. Whenever, under the order of any court of competent jurisdiction, the pleadings and issue in any indictment or prosecution for any crime or misdemeanor, shall have been sent down to any county in this State for trial therein, in consequence of any inability to obtain an unprejudiced or impartial jury in the county in which the venue was originally laid, the expenses of the trial of said indictment or prosecution shall be a charge upon the county from which the same was transferred; and in case they shall have been assessed on any county in which any such issue shall have been determined, the same, with interest thereon, shall be reimbursed to the treasury of such county by the county treasurer in the county from which such proceedings have been sent down, and the board of supervisors of the county liable to pay such expenses as aforesaid, are hereby authorized to include the same in their annual levy of taxes. [*Laws of* 1853, *chap.* 195, *page* 376.]

Provisions of Revised Statutes relative to apportionment of tax by Court of Chancery and Supreme Court.

Revised Statutes, part 3, chap. 1, article 2, vol. 3, pp. 264–268, 5th ed. (*a*)

* * * * * * *

Sec. 46. Power to compel contribution between owners of lands liable to taxes and assessments, and to extend time of redemption, &c.

47. Proceedings when owners of future estates, &c., are unknown.

48. Equitable apportionment to be made in final decree.

49. Contracts for payment of taxes or assessments not affected.

50. Sales in chancery made in the county where the premises lie.

51. Deeds, how executed, and their effect.

52. Feigned issue to be awarded in certain cases.

53. Lots remaining unsold, may be sold for subsequent taxes and assessments.

54. Validity of such sale by virtue of order made.

55. Notice of petition, and on whom to be served, &c.

56. Court may order sale in certain cases.

57. Redemption by agreement with purchaser.

58. Proceedings in case of unknown owners.

59. Presumptive owners may be made parties.

60. Sales, how made and executed.

61. What act shall apply, &c.

Apportionment of tax or assessment on lands held by several persons in cities.

*§ 46. In all cases where any real estate situated within the bounds of any city or village in this State, is owned by

---

(*a*) Note.—It has been deemed proper to insert the provisions of this article, because it is supposed that under the provisions of the constitution of 1846, articles 6 and 14, the Supreme Court is now vested with all the powers conferred by this article on the court of chancery.

Note.—By section 30 of article 7th, of chapter 5, of title 1, of part 2, of the Revised Statutes, it is provided that "all debts and duties to this State, *except taxes*, shall be affected by proceedings under this title in the same manner as debts to individuals." 3 R. S., p. 113, 5th ed.

several persons having estates therein, in possession, reversion, or remainder, and such real estate, or any part thereof, has been sold, or shall hereafter be sold, or is liable to be sold for any term of years to satisfy any tax or assessment imposed thereon by the authorities of any such city or village, upon a bill filed by any person interested in such estate against other persons interested therein, for the purpose of compelling a just and equitable apportionment of such tax or assessment among those liable to contribute to the payment thereof, or the redemption of the premises so sold, the court of chancery shall have power, at any time, on the application of any party to such suit, to extend the time of redemption of any such land sold, or to be hereafter sold, by the authority of such city or village, to a period not exceeding six months from the entry of the final decree to be made in such cause, or to order a sale in fee of any part or parts of such real estate, to pay such tax or assessment, or to redeem such parts thereof as may hereafter be sold at any time during the progress of such cause, and to direct the proceeds of such sale to be applied to the payment of such tax or assessment, or to the redemption of the lands sold for the satisfaction of such tax or assessment. [1841, *ch.* 341, *sec.* 1.]

Powers of court of chancery.

Proceedings in cases of unknown owners of future estates.

*§ 47. Whenever the person entitled to a future estate in such lands as are mentioned in the preceding section, cannot be ascertained, the court of chancery shall have and exercise all the powers and authority conferred in that section, whenever the persons having vested estates shall be made parties to a bill filed for the purposes therein specified. [*Same ch., sec.* 2.]

Contributions by owners, how compelled.

*§ 48. In any final decree made in a cause instituted in the court of chancery, for the purposes mentioned in this

act, such court shall compel a just and equitable apportionment to be made by all persons having different estates in such lands, as are hereinbefore specified, and liable to contribute to the payment of such tax or assessment, or to the redemption of such parts thereof, as may have been sold by the authority of any city or village; and if any portion thereof have been sold by virtue of any order made during the progress of the cause, or by the authority of such city or village, whereby the interest or estate of one party has been charged with, or made to contribute more than a just and equitable proportion of such tax or assessment, such excess shall be deemed and decreed to be a lien upon the interest and estate of the other parties, in such proportions as shall be equitable and just. [*Same ch., sec.* 3.]

Contracts for payment of taxes, &c., not affected, nor liability of persons to payments.

*§ 49. Nothing in this act contained shall be construed to affect or impair any contract or covenant heretofore or hereafter made, respecting the payment of any such taxes or assessments on real estate, or to change the relative rights of the several persons having any estate therein, as to their liability to such payments. [*Same ch., sec.* 4.]

Sales, by whom, and where made.

*§ 50. All sales made on an order of the court of chancery for the payment of assessments, pursuant to any law of this State, shall be made by or under the direction of one of the masters of said court, in the county where the premises, or some part thereof, are situated. [1842, *ch.* 154, *sec.* 1.]

Effect of deeds to purchasers.

*§ 51. Deed shall thereupon be executed by such master, which shall vest in the purchaser the entire estate, as well present as future, of each and every of the parties to such suit or suits. [*Same ch., sec.* 2.]

Feigned issue may be ordered.

*§ 52. In case any person or party in any such suit in the court of chancery, shall question the validity of the

assessment or assessments which are to be paid out of the proceeds of sale, it shall be the duty of the court to order a feigned issue to be tried in the circuit court, to determine the validity thereof, or in some other manner ascertain the same. [1842, *ch.* 154, *sec.* 3.]

Lots remaining unsold, may be sold for subsequent taxes and assessments.

*§ 53. In case any order or decree heretofore made or entered, or hereafter to be made or entered, under or by virtue of the power or authority contained in said act, shall embrace, or direct to be sold, a greater quantity or number of portions or lots of land than shall, on the sale under the said order or decree, be found necessary to be sold in order to raise or produce an amount of money sufficient to meet and satisfy the requirements of the said order or decree; and if after such sale any tax or assessment shall be levied or imposed on the parcels or lots of land embraced in the order or decree remaining unsold as aforesaid, it shall be lawful and competent for the court, in which such order or decree was entered, from time to time, upon the petition of either of the parties to the suit in which such order or decree was entered, to direct a sale of so many of the said lots so remaining unsold, and subsequently taxed or assessed as aforesaid, as shall be necessary to pay and satisfy such subsequent taxes or assessments, and the costs and expenses of the application, and the proceedings thereupon. [1854, *ch.* 393, *sec.* 1.][1]

Validity of such sale by virtue of order made.

*§ 54. All sales or conveyances made under or by virtue of an order made or granted on such petition, shall be as valid and effectual to pass the estate in the land conveyed, as the sales and conveyances first made under or by virtue of the original order or decree. [*Same ch., sec.* 2.]

---

1 NOTE.—"An act to amend an act entitled, An act to authorize the sale of real estate in certain cases, to pay assessments, and for other purposes," passed May 26, 1841.

*§ 55. The court shall, on presenting such petition, direct notice to be published for six successive weeks, and once at least in each week, in two or more public newspapers, printed in the county where the said lands are situated, and in the State paper, setting forth the general objects of the petition, and the time and place at which it will be again presented to the court; and shall also direct such notice, and a copy of such petition, to be served personally upon all persons who have become interested by transfer or assignment in such lots of land, or portions thereof, remaining unsold since the making of such order or decree, and who shall have recorded such assignment in the office provided by law for the record of deeds in the county where said lots are situated. At such time, or as soon thereafter as the court can hear the same, and upon due proof of such publication and service, said petition may be presented, and a motion made for said order; any party in interest may show cause (if any there be), why the order prayed for should not be granted. The said publication of notice shall be deemed and held to be sufficient service, upon all the parties to the suit and their representatives, of the petition and the notice of motion for the order. [*Same ch., sec.* 3.]

Notice of petition, and on whom to be served, &c.

*§ 56. In all cases where there are several persons interested at law or in equity, in any real estate situate within the bounds of any city or village in this State, either as owning estates therein, in possession, reversion, or remainder, or as being presumptively entitled by virtue of any deed or will to such estate, on the death of any person or persons in being, or upon the happening of any contingency in such deed or will specified, and such real estate, or any part thereof, has been sold, or shall hereafter be sold, or is or shall become liable, in case of default, to be sold for any

Court may order sale in certain cases.

term of years, to satisfy any tax or assessment imposed thereon, then and in every such case, upon any action brought by any person so interested therein, for the purpose of compelling a just and equitable apportionment of such tax or assessment upon the several present, future, and presumptive interests as aforesaid, in such real estate, and the payment thereof, or the redemption of the real estate so sold accordingly, the Supreme Court shall have power, at any time, on the application of any party to such action, to extend the time of redemption of any such real estate sold, or to be hereafter sold, by authority of such city or village, to a period not exceeding six months from the entry of the final judgment to be given in such action, and to order a sale in fee simple absolute for such real estate, or any part or parts thereof, to pay such tax or assessment, or to redeem the same, or any part thereof as aforesaid, and to direct the proceeds of such sale to be applied to the payment of such tax or assessment, or to the redemption of the real estate sold for such tax or assessment, after defraying the costs, charges, and expenses of the action, and the proceedings connected therewith. [1855, *ch.* 327, *sec.* 1.]

Redemption by agreement.

*§ 57. Like proceedings may be had to redeem, by agreement with the purchaser of any real estate so sold, or hereafter sold, as aforesaid, after the time allowed by law for redemption shall have expired; but every such agreement shall be ratified and approved by the court, and the redemption thereof shall be evidenced by the deed of the purchaser, his heirs or assigns, granting the property to some party in the action expressed, to be made in the extinguishment of the tax or assessment title pursuant to this act. [*Same chap.*, *sec.* 2.]

*§ 58. If any person, so interested as aforesaid in said

real estate, is unknown, or if either of the known parties to such action, whether minors or of full age, reside out of the State, or cannot, on inquiry had, be found therein, and that fact made to appear to the satisfaction of the court by affidavit, an order may be made by the court, containing a sufficient description of the premises of which, or of part whereof, a sale is sought, and requiring all parties interested therein to appear and answer the action by a day in said order specified, which order shall be published for three months, once at least in each week, successively, in the State paper, and in a newspaper printed in the county where the premises are situated, if there be any, and if there is none, then in a newspaper printed in the city of New York. The publication of such order shall authorize a judgment as by default against all such unknown persons and parties not resident in this State, or not found therein, as shall not appear and answer accordingly, and all such unknown persons as may appear on such notice may be made parties to the action, and the complaint may be amended for that purpose. [*Same chap.*, *sec.* 3.]

Proceedings in case of unknown owners.

*§ 59. The court, in its discretion, may direct any person not already made a party to such action, who shall seem to be presumptively entitled, as in the first section of this act specified, to be so made a party thereto. And whenever in any action to which all persons having vested estates at law or in equity, shall have been made parties, or shall have been so proceeded against as unknown owners, a sale shall be had as aforesaid, by order of the court; such sale shall vest in the purchaser a fee simple absolute at law and in equity, in the property so sold. [1855, *chap.* 327, *sec.* 4.]

Presumptive owners may be made parties.

*§ 60. All sales to be directed as aforesaid, shall be made by or under the direction of a referee, to be for that pur-

Sales, how made.

pose appointed by the court, who shall have power to perfect every such sale, by executing under his hand and seal a deed to the purchaser. [*Same chap., sec.* 5.]

What acts shall apply to actions under this act.

*§ 61. The third and fourth sections of the act entitled "An act to authorize the sale of real estate in certain cases, to pay assessments, and for other purposes," passed May twenty-sixth, eighteen hundred and forty-one, and the third section of the act entitled "An act in relation to the sale of real estate to pay assessments," passed April eleventh, eighteen hundred and forty-two, shall apply to actions under this act. [*Same chap., sec.* 6.]

LAWS OF 1859—CHAP. 312, PAGE 702.

AN ACT *to Equalize the State Tax among the several Counties in this State.*

[Passed April 14, 1859; three-fifths being present.]

The People of the State of New York, represented in Senate and Assembly, do enact as follows:

Board of equalization.

SECTION 1. The commissioners of the land office and three State assessors, whose appointment is herein provided for, shall constitute a board of equalization, whose duty it shall be to equalize the State tax among the several counties of the State, and fix the amount of assessment of real and personal estate on which the State tax shall be levied in each county.

Governor to appoint assessors.

§ 2. There shall be nominated by the governor, and appointed by and with the advice and consent of the Senate, three officers by the name of State assessors, who shall hold their offices for three years, and until their successors shall be duly qualified, except as hereinafter provided.

Term of office.

§ 3. The term of office of one of said State assessors shall expire on the first day of April in each year, commencing with the first day of April, eighteen hundred and sixty; and at the first meeting of the State assessors to be appointed the present year, they shall determine by lot the length of their respective terms, whether one, two, or three years.

Powers of State assessors.

§ 4. The said assessors shall have power to swear witnesses and examine all persons and papers which they shall deem necessary to the proper discharge of their duties, and the State, town, county, and city officers shall furnish them with all information belonging to or connected with their respective offices, and copies of all papers in their various offices which the assessors may require of them in the proper discharge of their duties.

Meeting of.

§ 5. The said assessors shall meet within ten days after their appointment, in the city of Albany, and adopt their plan of action.

Two to transact business.

§ 6. Any two of said assessors shall have authority to transact all business appertaining to their office, but all three must be duly notified of each and every meeting for the transaction of business. In case of the death, resignation, refusal, or inability to serve, of any one or more of said assessors, while the senate is not in session, the governor is hereby authorized to fill such vacancies, and the person so appointed shall hold the office the balance of the term ; provided his appointment shall be confirmed by the senate, on the nomination of the governor, at the next session thereof.

State assessors to visit, &c.

§ 7. The State assessors shall visit, officially, every county in the State, at least once in two years, and they shall prepare a written digest of such facts as they may deem most important for aiding the board of equalization in the discharge of its duties. They shall commence a course of examination and visitation of the counties in the month of May next, or before, and digiently[1] prosecute the same.

Meetings of board of eqalization

§ 8. The board of equalization shall meet in the city of Albany on the first Tuesday in September in each year,

---

[1] So in original.

for the purpose of examining and revising the valuations of the real and personal estate of the several counties as returned to the office of the comptroller, and fixing the aggregate amount of assessment for each county on which the comptroller shall compute the State tax. The board of equalization may increase or diminish the aggregate valuations of real estate in any county by adding or deducting such sum as in their opinion may be just and necessary to produce a just relation between all the valuations of real estate in the State; but they shall in no instance reduce the aggregate valuations of all the counties below the aggregate valuations thereof as returned by the boards of supervisors to the comptroller's office; but the aggregate of the assessed valuation of the whole State shall not for the year eighteen hundred and fifty-nine be increased or diminished by the board ef equalization. A statement of the amount of assessment for each county, as fixed by the board of equalization, shall be certified by said board, and deposited in the office of the comptroller, as soon as completed, and before the tenth day of October in each year. The comptroller shall immediately ascertain from this assessment, the proportion of State tax each county shall pay, and send a statement of the amount by mail, to the county clerk, and the chairman and clerk of the board of supervisors of each county.

Statement to be made.

If the name or residence of the chairman or clerk of the board of supervisors shall be unknown to the comptroller, he may inclose such statement in an envelope addressed to him by his name of office, and directed to the county town of the county. The county clerk shall file the statement received by him in his office, and immediately send a copy thereof to the chairman of the board of supervisors of the county.

State tax. § 9. The amount of State tax which each county is to pay, as so fixed and certified by the comptroller as aforesaid, shall be raised and collected by the annual collection of taxes, in the several counties, in the manner now prescribed by law.

Compensation of State assessors. § 10. Each State assessor shall receive five dollars for every day's service necessarily spent in the performance of his duties, and shall be allowed, in addition thereto, all the travelling expenses, board excepted, necessarily incurred by him, not exceeding three hundred dollars per annum; the bill of such expenses shall be rendered to the comptroller in items, and verified by the affidavit of such assessor; no allowance shall be made to such assessors for railroad fare, unless such affidavit shall specify that such fare has been actually and in good faith expended.

Books, when deposited. § 11. All books and papers pertaining to the duties of the office of State assessor shall be deposited with the comptroller.

Oath of office. § 12. The said assessors, before entering upon the duties of their office, shall take and subscribe the usual oath of office before the Secretary of State or a justice of the supreme court.

Appeals. § 13. Any supervisor may appeal in behalf of the town, city, or ward, which he wholly or in part represents, to the Comptroller of the State of New York, from any act or decision of the board of supervisors in the equalization of assessments, and the correction of the assessment rolls, under the provisions of the first title of chapter thirteen, of the first part of the Revised Statutes. Such appeal shall be brought by serving a notice thereof, within ten days after the corrected assessment rolls shall be completed by the board of supervisors, or the chairman and clerk of said board, and also filing such notice in the office of the clerk of the county, together with the affidavit of the supervisor so appealing, that in his opinion injustice has been done to such town, city, or ward by the act or decision appealed from. The comptroller shall hear the proofs of the parties, which may be presented in the form of affidavit or otherwise, as he shall direct; after hearing such proofs, he shall determine whether any, and if any, what deduction ought to have been made from the corrected valuation of such town, city, or ward; and in the assessment and collection of taxes of the next following year, such town or city shall be credited with the amount of taxes levied from it on such excess of valuation, and the same shall be levied and collected from the other towns and cities of the county.

§ 14. This act shall take effect immediately.

PART II.

LAWS RELATIVE TO TAXATION IN THE CITY AND COUNTY OF NEW YORK.

AN ACT *for the Assessment and Collection of Taxes, passed April* 23*d*, 1823. *Chapter* 262, *Laws of* 1823, *pages* 390 *and* 391.

* * * * * * *

Property exempt from taxation.

§ 3. *And be it further enacted,* That no real estate belonging to the United States, or to this State, nor any college or incorporated academy, nor any building for public worship, school-house, court-house, jail, alms-house, house of industry, and all the real and personal property belonging thereto, nor the lot whereon the buildings of any college or incorporated academy, building for public worship, school-house, court-house, jail, alms-house, nor the furniture belonging to either of them, nor the property belonging to any public library, or any personal property belonging to any minister of the gospel, or to any priest of any denomination, nor any real estate belonging to any such minister or priest, if occupied by him, provided such real and personal estate does not exceed in value one thousand five hundred dollars, shall be liable to taxation within this State. *And provided further,* That all property now exempted by law from execution, shall not be liable to taxation. [*See note to succeeding act.*]

AN ACT *respecting the Collection of Taxes in the City of New York, passed April* 6, 1825. *Laws of* 1825, *chap.* 83, *page* 123.

* * * * * * *

§ 3. *And be it further enacted,* That the exemption from taxation of any building for public worship, or any school, under and by virtue of the third section of the said Act of the 23d of April, 1823, entitled "An Act for the Assessment and Collection of Taxes," shall not extend or apply to any such buildings or premises in the said city, unless the same shall be exclusively used for such purposes, and exclusively the property of a religious society, or the New York Free School Society. (*a*)

Exemption from taxation, &c.

AN ACT *to amend the Act passed April 6th,* 1825, *entitled "An Act respecting the Collection of Taxes in the city of New York," passed April* 20, 1830. [*Laws of* 1830, *p.* 365, *chap.* 307.] *(b)*

The People of the State of New York, represented in Senate and Assembly, do enact as follows:

§ 1. It shall be the duty of the assessors, annually chosen in the several wards of the city of New York, before they proceed to assess the property in their respective wards, to meet together in the City Hall of the said city, at eleven

General board of assessors.

(*a*) It was decided by the Superior Court, in Chegary vs. Jenkins, 3 Sandford, p. 409, that this act was not repealed by the general repealing act in the Revised Statutes. The dictum of Ruggles, *contra*, in 1 Selden, 376, was overruled in Chegary vs. the Mayor, &c., 3 Kernan, 220. It has therefore been deemed proper to insert this and the preceding act. See note to *§ 6 of R. S., chap. 13, art. 1, part. 1, ante, p. 118.

(*b*) The powers and duties of assessors were modified, and in some respects altered, by laws of 1850, chap. 121, p. 188. It has, however, been thought

o'clock in the forenoon, to wit: in the present year, on the first Tuesday of May next, and annually thereafter on the first Tuesday after they shall have been sworn into office, and then and there to appoint from among themselves, a president and secretary, and to organize themselves into a board for the transaction of business, to be called the general board of assessors. *(a)*

Their meetings. § 2. The said general board of assessors shall have power to adjourn to meet again at such time and place, and from time to time, as they may think fit, and the secretary thereof shall keep a regular book of minutes of all the proceedings of the said board.

To make rules. § 3. It shall be the duty of the said general board of assessors, either at their first, or at any subsequent meeting, before the members thereof proceed to assess property in their respective wards, to adopt such rules or by-laws, as may, in their opinion, be best calculated to produce equality and uniformity in the different valuations of property and assessments in the several wards.

Assessment rolls to be compared. § 4. After the several assessment rolls for all the wards of the said city shall have been completed by the assessors for each ward respectively, and before fair copies thereof are made for the inspection of the inhabitants of the said wards respectively, it shall be the duty of the president of

---

proper to insert this act in full, in order that the two acts may be compared. By laws of 1859, chap. 230, sec. 2, p. 679, the office of assessor is abolished, and the deputy tax commissioners are invested with the powers formerly exercised by the assessors. See post, p. 227.

(*a*) The time of meeting of assessors was changed by laws of 1850, chap. 121, sec. 9, p. 189, to the first Tuesday after the assessors were sworn into office. By chap. 302, laws of 1859, sec. 7, p. 680–81, deputy tax commissioners are to commence their assessments on the first Monday of September in each year. See post, p. 230.

the said general board of assessors, to convene the members thereof; and the said board shall thereupon examine and compare the said several assessment rolls, for the purpose of ascertaining, whether the valuations in one ward bear a just relation to the valuations in all the wards of the said city; and they may increase or diminish the aggregate valuations of real estates in any ward by adding or deducting such sum upon the hundred, as may, in their opinion, be necessary to produce a just relation between all the valuations of real estate in the said city; but they shall in no instance reduce the aggregate valuations of all the wards below the aggregate valuation thereof, as made by the assessors of the said wards respectively. *(a)*

§ 5. The said general board of assessors shall have power, by a vote of the majority of all the assessors, to alter or correct any such assessment roll, by increasing or diminishing the valuation of any property or any assessment therein contained. Alterations made by vote.

§ 6. After the said assessment rolls shall have been so examined and compared, or altered or corrected, the same shall be returned to the assessors of the several wards respectively, who shall cause fair copies thereof to be made out and left with one of their number, and shall proceed thereupon to give notice, according to law, of their having completed such assessments. Fair copies to be made.

§ 7. It shall be the duty of the secretary of the said general board of assessors, to deliver to the supervisors of the city of New York, at their first annual meeting, the Book of minutes.

(a) By sec. 17, laws of 1850, chap. 121, p. 191, as amended by sec. 1, chap. 319, laws of 1851, p. 611, the power given by this section is conferred on the tax commissioners. See post, p. 215.

book of minutes of the proceedings of the said board, and to attend before the said supervisors when required. *(a)*

Supervisors to examine rolls.

§ 8. The supervisors of the said city shall at their annual meetings examine the assessment rolls of the several wards, for the purpose of ascertaining whether the valuations in one ward bear a just relation to the valuations in all the wards of the said city; and they may increase or diminish the aggregate valuations of real estates in any ward by adding or deducting such sum upon the hundred as may in their opinion, be necessary to produce a just relation between all the valuations of real estates in the said city; but they shall in no instance reduce the aggregate valuations of all the wards below the aggregate valuation thereof as made by the assessors.

Pay of assessors and collectors.

§ 9. The compensation to be allowed to assessors and collectors of taxes in the city of New York, for their services, shall be determined by the supervisors of the said city, at such time or times as they may think proper. *(b)*

Tavern keepers, &c., to give names of boarders.

§ 10. All keepers of taverns, of boarding-houses, and other house-keepers, upon their being requested by any assessor of the ward in which such tavern, boarding-house, or other house may be situated, shall give such assessor a true account of all persons boarding or lodging or being tenants in such house, and their several names if known, to the end that any such person liable to taxation may be assessed according to law.

(a) Book of minutes to be delivered to tax commissioners, by sec. 12, chap. 121, laws of 1850, pp. 189, 190. And see sec. 7, laws of 1859, chap. 302, p. 680. See post, p. 229.

(b) Office of collector of taxes was abolished by chap. 230, laws of 1843, p. 314, sec. 1. The deputy tax commissioners to receive such compensation as may be determined by comptroller and board of commissioners, not to exceed $2,000 per annum. Laws of 1859, chap. 302, sec. 3, p. 679. See post, p. 228.

§ 11. If any person of whom such information is demanded, shall refuse to give the same, or shall willfully give erroneous account, such person shall forfeit and pay one hundred dollars to the collector of such ward, who may sue for and recover the same with costs in any court having cognizance thereof, and the sums so recovered shall be applied to make good any delinquency in the collectors of taxes in such ward. Penalty

---

CHAPTER CCCLXXXVII.

Laws of 1840, p. 336.

AN ACT *authorizing Mortgagees to redeem Real Estate sold for Taxes and Assessments, passed May* 14, 1840. *(a)*

The People of the State of New York, represented in Senate and Assembly, do enact as follows:

§ 1. No sale of real estate hereafter made for the non-payment of any tax or assessment shall destroy, or in any manner affect the lien of any mortgage thereon duly recorded or registered at the time of such sale, except as hereinafter provided. Mortgage not affected by sale of land for taxes, &c.

§ 2. It shall be the duty of the purchaser at such sale to give to the mortgagee a written notice of such sale, requir- Purchaser to give notice to mortgagee.

(a) By section 18 of article 3, of chap. 230, p. 326, of laws of 1843, it is provided that "this act shall not apply in cases in which the notice and affidavit therein provided for have been given and filed." And by section 19, of same chapter, that no person shall be entitled to the benefit of the 1st, 2d, and 6th sections of this act, unless the memorandum mentioned in the 12th and 13th sections of article 3 of same chapter shall have been filed, &c. See post, p. 202.

ing him to pay the amount of the purchase money, with the interest at the rate allowed by law thereon, within six months after the giving of such notice.

Effect of redemption by mortgagee.

§ 3. If such payment shall be made, the sale shall be of no further effect, and the mortgagee shall have a lien on the premises, for the amount paid, with the interest which may thereafter accrue thereon, at the rate of seven per cent. per annum, in like manner as if the same had been included in his mortgage.

Failure to redeem.

§ 4. In case the mortgagee shall fail to make such payment, within the time so limited, he shall not be entitled to the benefit of the first section of this act.

Construction of certain terms.

§ 5. The term "mortgagee," as used in this act, shall be construed to include assignees whose assignment shall be duly recorded, and personal representatives; and the term "purchaser" shall be construed to include assignees, and real or personal representatives, as the case may be.

Notice, how given.

§ 6. The notice required by this act may be given either personally, or in the manner required by law in respect to notices of non-acceptance or non-payment of notes or bills of exchange; and a notarial certificate thereof shall be presumptive evidence of the fact of such notice; such certificates may be recorded in the county in which the mortgage was recorded, in the same manner, and with same effect, as is by law prescribed in respect to deeds or other evidences of title of real estate. *(a)*

Evidence of notice.

(a) See Laws of 1859, p. 419.

COLLECTION OF TAXES.

[Laws of 1843, chap. 230, p. 314.]

AN ACT *for the Collection of Taxes in the City of New York.* Passed April 18, 1843, by a two-third vote.

The People of the State of New York, represented in Senate and Assembly, do enact as follows:

ARTICLE I.

Collectors of Taxes and of Arrears of Taxes abolished, and a Department created therefor.

§ 1. The office of collector of taxes, as created and established by the charter of the city of New York, and by the statutes of this State, and the office of collectors of arrears of taxes in the said city, as created and established by the Common Council of the said city, shall cease from and after the day when this act shall take effect; and all provisions by charter, statute, ordinance, resolution, or otherwise, creating such offices and imposing or defining the duties thereof, are hereby abrogated. The office of collector of taxes abolished.

§ 2. It shall be the duty of the common council of the said city, within twenty days after this act shall take effect, to establish an office for the collection of taxes in the city of New York, which shall be a branch of, and subordinate to, the department of finance of the said city, and which shall be conducted by a receiver of taxes, a deputy, and a suitable number of clerks, to be appointed as hereinafter directed, and whose duties are hereinafter prescribed. Office for the collection of taxes to be established.

Receiver of taxes to be appointed.

§ 3. It shall be the duty of the common council of New York, within twenty days after this act shall take effect, to appoint a suitable and discreet person, to be known as receiver of taxes in the city of New York, who shall hold his office during the pleasure of the Common Council, and until his successor shall be appointed, as hereinafter provided; and another person, to be known as deputy receiver of taxes in the city of New York, who shall hold his office for the like term, unless sooner in like manner removed. The said receiver of taxes shall receive an annual salary not exceeding the sum of two thousand dollars, and the said deputy receiver an annual salary not exceeding the sum of fifteen hundred dollars, to be paid to them respectively by the mayor, aldermen, and commonalty of the city of New York, on the usual quarterly days. (*a*)

He shall give bond with sureties.

§ 4. The said receiver of taxes shall, before entering upon the duties of his office, enter into a bond to the

(*a*) By laws of 1848, chap. 231, p. 329, the board of supervisors, within twenty days after act takes effect, were to appoint receiver and deputy receiver of taxes, for a term of four years from May 1, 1848, at the respective salaries of $2,000 and $1,500 per annum.

By the charter of 1849, laws of 1849, chap. 187, sec. 20, p. 283, receiver of taxes is to be nominated by the mayor, and confirmed by the board of aldermen.

By laws of 1851, chap. 148, p. 271, the deputy receiver of taxes is to be appointed in the same manner as the receiver of taxes.

By laws of 1851, chap. 543, p. 1002, the power of nominating the receiver of taxes to the board of aldermen is continued in the mayor.

By the amended charter of 1857, laws of 1857, chap. 446, vol. 1, p. 879, sec. 22, the receiver of taxes is continued at the head of a bureau in the finance department, and by sec. 21 the power of appointing chiefs of bureaux and their clerks is vested in the heads of the departments. The receiver, deputy receiver, and their clerks, are therefore at present appointed by the comptroller.

mayor, aldermen, and commonalty of the city of New York, with at least two sureties, to be approved by the chamberlain of the said city of New York, in the penal sum of twenty-five thousand dollars, conditioned for the faithful performance of the duties of his office as prescribed by this act; and every such bond shall be a lien on all the real estate held jointly and severally by the receiver or his sureties within the county, at the time of filing thereof, and shall continue to be such lien till the condition, together with all costs and charges which may accrue by the prosecution thereof, shall be fully satisfied; and the said deputy receiver shall also, in like manner, before entering upon the performance of the duties of his office, enter into a like bond with the like sureties, in the penal sum of ten thousand dollars, conditioned for the faithful performance of the duties of his office, as prescribed by this act; which said bonds, when so approved, shall be forthwith filed in the office of the comptroller of the said city.

First clerk to be appointed.

§ 5. The said receiver of taxes shall appoint a suitable person, to be known as first clerk in the office of the receiver of taxes, at a salary to be fixed and paid by the mayor, aldermen, and commonalty of the city of New York; and as many clerks, and at such rate of compensation, as the common council shall from time to time by ordinance designate. The said first clerk, before entering upon the duties of his office, shall enter into bonds in the like manner, and for the like amount, with the deputy receiver of taxes, conditioned for the faithful performance of the duties of his office. [*As amended by sec.* 2, *chap.* 238, *Laws of* 1844.]

Offices, where to be kept.

§ 6. The office of the said receiver of taxes shall be kept at such place in the said city, as shall be, from time to time, by ordinance of the said common council, assigned for that purpose; and shall be kept open on each day in the year (Sundays excepted), from the hour of eight in the forenoon till two in the afternoon.

Taxes paid at the office, how received.

§ 7. It shall be the duty of the said receiver of taxes, personally to receive all taxes which may be paid at the said office; and of the said deputy receiver, to retain the possession in the said office, and not elsewhere, of the warrants and assessment-rolls, which shall, from time to time, be delivered to the said receiver of taxes, by the supervisors or comptroller of the said city; and it shall be the duty of the said first clerk to keep all the books of accounts of the said office, and to assist the deputy receiver in the performance of all duties required of him by this act. [*As amended by section* 3, *chap.* 238, *Laws of* 1844.]

Suitable books to be procured.

§ 8. The said receiver of taxes shall enter into suitable books, to be kept by him for that purpose, the sums received by him for taxes, and at the expiration of the office hours for each day, and before three o'clock thereof, shall render a statement of the same to the chamberlain, and at the same time on each day pay over to the said chamberlain the amount received on such day; he shall also thereupon receive from the said chamberlain a voucher for the payment of such sums, which he shall forthwith on the same day exhibit to the comptroller of the said city. [*As amended by section* 4, *chap.* 238, *Laws of* 1844.]

Duty of deputy receiver.

§ 9. It shall be the duty of the said deputy receiver, from time to time, to enter in a column to be made for that purpose upon the assessment-rolls in his possession, opposite to the names of the persons mentioned therein, and who shall pay their tax as aforesaid to the said receiver of taxes, the fact of such payment, the amount thereof, and the day when paid, and to enter in suitable books to be kept by him for that purpose, on each day, such payments, with a statement of the ward for which the same were received; and the names of the parties respectively, on whose account the same were paid; and at the expiration of the office hours, and on the same day, shall furnish to the comptroller of the said city, a detailed statement of such sums, and of the ward for which received, and of the names of the parties respectively on whose account the same have been paid, which shall be filed by the said comptroller in his office. [*As amended by section* 5, *chap.* 238, *Laws of* 1844.]

§ 10. The said comptroller shall, on each day immediately after receiving from said deputy receiver the statement required by the last preceding section, compare the said statement with a voucher furnished to him by the receiver of taxes and the chamberlain, for the payment thereof to the chamberlain, and if the aggregate amounts thereof shall correspond, shall credit the said receiver of taxes, in his books, with such amount.

Credit to be given for payment.

§ 11. If the said receiver of taxes, or the said deputy receiver, shall on any day omit or neglect to furnish to the said chamberlain, or to the said comptroller respectively, the said statements and vouchers, or to make the daily payments hereinbefore prescribed, it shall be the duty of the said comptroller forthwith to suspend from office the party delinquent, and to report the same without delay to the mayor and to the president of each board of the common council of the said city, that the action of the said common council may be had thereon. In case of such suspension, the comptroller shall appoint a suitable person to perform the duties of the officer so suspended, who shall

Receiver and deputy to be suspended in case of omission or neglect.

continue to act as such officer, with all the powers conferred upon him by this act, until the party suspended shall be restored by the common council to his office, or another person shall have been appointed. On making such temporary appointment, the comptroller shall be required to take from the party so appointed a bond with two sufficient sureties, to be approved by the chamberlain, and filed with the said comptroller, in such penal sum as the said chamberlain may deem just, conditioned for the faithful performance of the duties of the office during the continuance of the person so appointed therein; and all the provisions of this act prescribing the duties of the said receiver of taxes, and the said deputy receiver, shall apply to the person or persons so appointed in their stead by the said comptroller.

Additional security may be required.

§ 12. If at any time during the continuance in office of the said receiver of taxes, or of the said deputy receiver, or of the said first clerk, the said common council shall deem the sureties of them or either of them insufficient, they may require the said receiver of taxes, or the said deputy receiver, or the said first clerk, to enter into a new bond with the like sureties, and to be approved in like manner as hereinbefore prescribed, within such time as they may direct, not being less than ten days after requiring such new bond to be given; and in case of the neglect or refusal of such officer to furnish such bond within the time so directed, the said common council may declare his office vacant. [*As amended by section* 6, *chap*. 238, *Laws of* 1844.]

Provision in case of their sickness or absence.

§ 13. In case of the inability of the said receiver, or of the said deputy receiver, to perform the duties of his office, by reason of sickness or absence from the city, the comptroller shall designate some suitable person to perform the duties of his office, during such inability, and shall, in his discretion, take from such person a bond, with sufficient sureties, in the manner prescribed in the eleventh section of this title.

ARTICLE II.

Of the Mode of the Collection of Taxes.

§ 1. The board of supervisors of the city and county of New York shall cause the corrected assessment roll of each ward of the said city, or a fair copy thereof, to be delivered to the receiver of taxes in the said city, on or before the 25th day of September, in each year. (*a*)

Assessment rolls to be delivered to receiver.

§ 2. To each assessment roll so delivered to the said receiver of taxes, a warrant under the hands and seals of the board of supervisors, or of any five or more of them, of whom the mayor and recorder shall always be one, shall be annexed, commanding such receiver to collect from the several persons named in the assessment roll the several sums mentioned in the last column of such roll, opposite to their respective names, and to pay the same from time to time, when so collected, to the chamberlain of the said city, according to the provisions of this act. (*b*)

With warrants annexed.

§ 3. The said receiver, upon receiving the said assessment rolls and warrants, shall proceed to collect and receive the said taxes from the several persons assessed in

Duty of receiver.

(*a*) The time for the delivery of the assessment roll to the receiver changed to on or before the first day of September, by laws of 1850, chap. 121, sec. 27, pp. 192, 193.

(*b*) By act of April 15, 1857, laws of 1857, vol. 2, p. 285, chap. 590, as amended by act of April 17, 1858, laws of 1858, chap. 321, p. 515, it is provided that the mayor and recorder shall cease to be members of the board of supervisors.

the said assessment rolls, in the manner hereinafter mentioned.

Persons paying tax previous to Nov. 1, entitled to reduction.

§ 4 If any person, who shall be assessed in any of the said assessment rolls, shall pay the amount of his taxes on or before the first day of November succeeding the delivery of the said assessment rolls and warrants to the said receiver, it shall be the duty of the said receiver to receive the same, and to deduct therefrom, at the rate of seven per cent. per annum, between the day of such payment and the first day of December then next succeeding. [*As amended by Laws of* 1850, *chap.* 121, *sec.* 29.]

Notice of taxes unpaid Nov 1.

§ 5. If any such taxes shall remain unpaid on the said first day of November, it shall be the duty of the said receiver of taxes to give public notice, by advertisement in six or more of the public newspapers printed in said city, that unless the same shall be paid to him at his office on or before the first day of December in such year, he will immediately after that day proceed to collect the same, as provided in the next section. [*As amended by Laws of* 1850, *chap.* 121, *sec.* 30.]

Percentage on unpaid taxes.

§ 6. If any such tax shall remain unpaid on the said first day of December, it shall be the duty of said receiver to receive and collect upon such tax so remaining unpaid on that day, in addition to the amount of such tax, one per cent. on the amount thereof, and to charge, receive, and collect, upon such tax so remaining unpaid on the fifteenth day of said month of December, one per cent. in addition on the amount thereof; and on the first day of January thereafter, a further addition or increase of one per cent. upon the amount of such tax; and such increase or percentage shall be paid over and accounted for, by such receiver, from time to time, as thereinbefore described, as a part of the tax collected by him. [*As amended by Laws of* 1850, *chap.* 121, *sec.* 31.]

§ 7. If any such tax shall remain unpaid on the first day of December, after the delivery of the assessment rolls and warrants to the said receiver, the said receiver shall immediately thereafter cause notice in writing to be given to the person from whom the same shall be due, specifying therein the amount of such tax, and the percentage which shall accrue thereon, and requiring such person to pay the same, to the said receiver, on or before the first day of January thereafter, at his office. [*As amended by Laws of* 1850, *chap.* 121, *sec.* 32.]

Personal notice of taxes unpaid December 1.

§ 8. Such notice shall be served upon such person, if he be a resident or engaged in the transaction of business within the said city, either personally, or by leaving the same at his residence or place of business, as the case may be, with some person of suitable age and discretion, at least eight days before the said first day of January. [*As amended by Laws of* 1850, *chap.* 121, *sec.* 33.]

Such notice how served.

§ 9. The said receiver shall, also, immediately after the said first day of December, give public notice in at least six of the public newspapers of the said city, to be published therein respectively at least ten days, notifying all persons who shall have omitted to pay their taxes to pay the same to him at his office, on or before the first day of January; and upon filing an affidavit of the service of the notice required by the sixth section of this act, as therein prescribed, in the office of the clerk of the city and county of New York, or that the person named therein could not, upon diligent search and inquiry, be found in the said city; and also upon filing an affidavit or affidavits of the publication of the notice required by the seventh section of this

Public notice of unpaid taxes December 1.

act, as therein prescribed, it shall be the duty of the said receiver to charge, collect, and receive, upon all taxes remaining unpaid on and after the said first day of January, an interest at the rate of twelve per cent. per annum, to be calculated from the day on which the said assessment rolls and warrants shall have been delivered to the said receiver. It shall also be lawful for the said receiver, if any such tax, with the interest thereon, as hereinbefore provided, shall remain unpaid on the *fifteenth day of the said month of January*, to issue his warrant under his hand and seal, directed to any constable or marshal of said city and county, commanding him to levy said tax, with interest thereon at the rate of twelve per cent. per annum, from the day of the delivering of the assessment rolls and warrants to the said receiver, to the time when the same shall be paid, by distress and sale of the goods and chattels of the person against whom the said warrants shall be issued, or of any goods and chattels in his possession, wheresoever the same shall be found within the said city, and to pay the same to the said receiver, and return such warrant within thirty days after the date thereof; and no claim of property to be made to such goods and chattels, so found in the possession of the said party, shall be available to prevent a sale. [*As amended by laws of* 1850, *chap.* 121, *sec.* 34.] (*a*)

Percentage, 12 per cent.

Warrant for taxes unpaid, January 1.

Duty of sheriff, constable, or marshal.

§ 10. The said sheriff, constable, or marshal shall give public notice of the time and place of sale, and of the property to be sold, at least six days previous to the sale, by advertisement to be posted up in at least three public places in the ward where such sale shall be made.

The sale shall be by public auction.

(*a*) The sections referred to in this section should be the seventh and ninth, instead of the sixth and seventh.

Property distrained to be sold.

§ 11. If the property distrained shall be sold for more than the amount of the tax, the surplus shall be returned to the person in whose possession such property was when the distress was made, if no claim be made to such surplus by any other person. If any other person shall claim such surplus, on the ground that the property sold belonged to him, and such claim be admitted by the person for whose tax the same was distrained, the surplus shall be paid to such owner; but if such claim be contested by the person for whose tax the property was distrained, the surplus moneys shall be retained by the said sheriff until the rights of the parties shall be determined by due course of law.

Provision in case of non-payment of tax for personal property.

§ 12. In case of the refusal or neglect of any person to pay any tax imposed on him for personal property, if there be no goods or chattels in his possession upon which the same may be levied by distress and sale according to law, and if the property assessed shall exceed the sum of one thousand dollars, the said receiver, if he has reason to believe that the person taxed has debts, credits, choses in action, or other personal property, not taxed elsewhere in this State, and upon which levy cannot be made according to law, may thereupon in his discretion, make application within one year to the court of common pleas of the county, or the Supreme Court, to enforce the payment of such tax.

Fine may be imposed equal to tax and costs.

§ 13. The court may impose a fine for the misconduct mentioned in the next preceding section, sufficient in amount for the payment of the tax assessed, and of the costs and expenses of the proceedings authorized by this act to enforce such payment, or to punish such misconduct; and the amount of such tax shall be paid out of such fine, to the said receiver, who shall pay the same in like manner as the tax was required to be paid; and costs and expenses of such proceedings shall be paid out of such fine to the said receiver who made the application to enforce the payment of the tax.

Order to prosecute to operate as an assignment of bond to receiver.

§ 14. Whenever any bond taken under the provisions of the last preceding section of this act, shall be ordered to be prosecuted, such order shall operate as an assignment of the bond to the said receiver, who shall be authorized to prosecute the same in any court of record, in his name as such receiver, as the assignee of the officer to whom the bond was given, in the same manner as in other actions on bonds with conditions to perform covenants other than for the payment of money; and the measure of damages in such action shall be the extent of such tax, and the costs and expenses of the proceedings to enforce the payment thereof, and shall be applied and paid in like manner as the fine mentioned in the next preceding section, as therein directed to be applied and paid; and in all such actions, if the plaintiff recovers, he shall recover all costs against the defendant.

Taxes on corporations, of whom demanded.

§ 15. The said receiver shall demand payment of all taxes assessed on incorporated companies in the said city, from the president or proper officer of such companies, and if not paid, shall proceed in the collection and payment thereof, in the same manner as in other cases, and his receipt shall be evidence of the payment of such tax.

To be paid out of company's fund.

§ 16. Such taxes shall be paid out of the funds of the company, and shall be ratably deducted from the dividends of those stockholders whose stock was taxed, or shall be charged upon such stock, if no dividends be afterwards declared.

In case of inability to collect taxes.

§ 17. If the said receiver shall not be able to collect any tax assessed upon an incorporated company, he shall return the same to the chamberlain, and at the same time make affidavit before him, or some other officer authorized to administer oaths, that he had demanded payment thereof from the president, or other proper officer of the company, and that such officer had refused to pay the same, or that he had not been able to make such demand, as the case may be; and that such company had no personal property from which he could levy such tax.

§ 18. The chamberlain shall thereupon certify such facts to the comptroller of this State, who shall pass to the credit of such chamberlain the amount of all taxes so returned and certified, as in the cases of taxes on the lands of non-residents.

The chamberlain to certify the same to State comptroller.

§ 19. The comptroller of the State shall furnish the attorney-general with the names of all companies refusing or neglecting to pay the taxes imposed on them, with the amount due from them respectively, and the attorney-general shall thereupon file a bill in the court of chancery against every such company, for the discovery and sequestration of its property.

The comptroller shall furnish names of companies to attorney general.

§ 20. The chancellor, on the filing of such bill, or on the coming in of the answer thereto, shall order such part of the property of such company to be sequestered as he shall deem necessary for the purpose of satisfying the taxes in arrear, with the costs of prosecution; and he may also, at his discretion, enjoin such company, and the officers thereof, from any further proceeding under their act of incorporation, and may order and direct such other proceedings as he shall deem necessary to compel the payment of such tax and costs.

Duty of chancellor on filing bill by attorney general.

§ 21. The attorney-general may also recover such tax,

Tax may be recovered in any court of record.

with costs, from such delinquent company, by action in any court of record in this State. (*a*)

ARTICLE III.

Sale of lands for Taxes.

Provision for the sale of lands for non-payment of taxes.

§ 1. Whenever any tax on lands or tenements in the said city shall remain unpaid on the fifteenth day of April in any year, and the affidavits prescribed by the ninth section of the second article of this title shall have been filed, it shall and may be lawful for the Comptroller of the city of New York, to take order for advertising the said lands and tenements, or any of them, for sale, and by such advertisements, the owner or owners of such lands and tenements respectively, shall be required to pay the amount of such tax so remaining unpaid, together with interest thereon, at the rate of 12 per cent. per annum to the time of payment, with the charges of such notice and advertisement to the receiver of taxes of the said city; and notice shall be given by such advertisements, that if default shall be made in such payment, such lands and tenements will be sold at public auction, at a day and place therein to be specified, for the lowest term of years at which any person or persons shall offer to take the same in consideration of advancing the said tax, and the interest thereon as aforesaid to the time of sale, and together with the charges of the above-mentioned notice and advertisement, and all other costs and charges accrued thereon. And if, notwithstanding such notice, the owner or owners shall refuse or neglect to pay

(*a*) See sections 16, 17, 18, 19, and 20, of title 4, of chap. 13, part 1, of Revised Statutes, 5th edition, as amended by laws of 1857, vol. 2, p. 2, chap. 456, ante pp. 155 and 156.

such tax, with interest as aforesaid, and the charges attending said notice and advertisement, then it shall and may be lawful to and for the said Comptroller to cause such lands and tenements to be sold at public auction for a term of years, for the purpose and in the manner expressed in the said advertisements; and such sales shall be made on the day for that purpose mentioned in the said advertisements, and shall be continued from day to day, if necessary, until all the lands and tenements so advertised shall be sold; and the mayor, aldermen, and commonalty of the city of New York shall give to the purchaser or purchasers of any such lands and tenements, a certificate, in writing, describing the lands and tenements so purchased, the term of years for which the same shall have been sold, the sum paid therefor, and the time when the purchaser will be entitled to a lease for the said lands and tenements. But no houses or lots, or improved or unimproved lands, in the city and county of New York, shall be hereafter sold or leased at public auction for the non-payment of any tax which may be due thereon, unless notice of such sale shall have been published once in each week for three months, in at least ten of the daily newspapers printed and published in the city of New York, one of which shall contain a particular and detailed statement of the property to be sold for taxes, and such as is now published by the street commissioner in one of the daily newspapers in the city of New York, or the said detailed statement or description shall be printed in a pamphlet, at the discretion of the said comptroller, in which case the pamphlets shall be deposited in his office and the office of the said receiver, and shall be delivered to any person applying therefor; and the notice provided for in this section to be given of the sale of houses and lots and improved and unimproved lands, shall also state that the detailed statement of the tax and ownership of the property assessed or taxed is published in one of the daily newspapers, naming the same, or in a pamphlet, as the case may be, and where the same will be deposited, to be delivered to any person applying for the same. *(a)*

Notice to be published, how lands may be redeemed.

§ 2. The said comptroller shall, at least six months before the expiration of two years after any such sale, cause an advertisement to be published, at least twice in each week for six weeks successively, in one of the daily public newspapers printed in the city of New York, in such form as he shall deem best calculated to give notice of such sale; and that unless the lands sold be redeemed by a certain day, they will be conveyed to the purchaser. And if the person claiming title to the said lands and tenements, or some other person, shall not within two years from the date of the above-mentioned certificate, pay to the said comptroller, for the use of the purchaser, his executors, administrators, or assigns, the sum mentioned in such certificate, together with the interest thereof, at the rate of 14 per cent. per annum, from the date of such certificate, the mayor, aldermen, and commonalty of the said city, shall, at the expiration of the said two years, execute to

(a) The portion of this section referring to the sale of houses and lots, and improved or unimproved lands, &c., and the proceedings thereon, is taken from sec. 9, of chap. 326, p. 272, of laws of 1840, which act, so far as it relates to the collection of taxes, is repealed by the general repealing clause in sec. 2, art. 4, of this act.

By the laws of 1853, chap. 579, sec. 3, p. 1065, it is provided that all duties heretofore required by law to be performed by the comptroller in relation to advertising, selling, and leasing for taxes, &c., and the redemption of property sold therefor, shall be performed by the clerk of arrears, under the direction of the comptroller. See post, p. 220.

the purchaser, his executors, administrators, or assigns, a lease under the common seal of the said city, of the lands and tenements so sold, for such term of years as the same shall have been sold: and such lease shall be conclusive evidence that the sale was regular, according to the provisions of this Act: and such purchaser or purchasers, his, her, or their executors, administrators, and assigns, shall by virtue thereof and of this Act, lawfully hold and enjoy the said lands and tenements in the said lease mentioned, for his, her, or their own proper use, against the owner or owners thereof, and all claiming under him, her, or them until such purchaser's term therein shall be fully complete and ended; and the said purchaser or purchasers, his, her, or their executors, administrators, or assigns, shall be at liberty to remove all the buildings or materials which he, she, or they shall erect or place thereon during the said term, within one month after the expiration of the said term, but leaving the lands and tenements, with the streets fronting the same, in the order required by the regulations of the common council. *(a) (b)*

Section 10, act of 1839, repealed.

§ 3. Section 10 of the act entitled "An Act to amend an Act entitled 'An Act to reduce the several laws relating particularly to the city of New York, into one act,'" passed April 20, 1839, so far as it relates to advertising and selling real estate, or other property, for non-payment of taxes, is hereby repealed. Nothing herein contained shall refer to assessments laid upon real estate or other property.

(a) Rate of interest on redemption changed to 12 per cent., by laws of 1853, chap. 579, sec. 15. See post, p. 225.

(b) The provision relative to the advertisement by the comptroller of the redemption notice, is substantially the same as sec. 10, chap. 326, laws of 1840, p. 274, amending sec. 2, of chap 115, laws of 1816, which said acts, as far as they relate to collection of taxes, are repealed by the general repealing clause in sec. 2, of art. 4, of this act.

Sales may be suspended by order of the Common Council.

§ 4. It shall be lawful for the mayor, aldermen, and commonalty of the city of New York, whenever they shall deem it expedient, by a resolution to be passed in common council, to suspend or postpone any sale or sales of lands and tenements, or any portion thereof, which shall have been advertised for sale in pursuance of the first section of this article, to any time not exceeding fifteen months from the day specified in any such advertisement. *(a)*

And may afterwards be made without further notice.

§ 5. All sales which shall be postponed or suspended by virtue of the last section, shall be made without further advertisement, other than a general notice of such postponement, to be published in two or more of the public newspapers in the city of New York, at least once a week, until the time of sale, and such sales, when made, shall be as valid and effectual as if the same had taken place at the time for that purpose first advertised.

Sales, how to be conducted.

§ 6. All sales of lands and tenements for taxes, under and by virtue of this act, may hereafter be conducted by the said comptroller or by his deputy, and it shall not be necessary to employ a public auctioneer for any such sales.

Lands may be sold, though warrant of distress may have been issued.

§ 7. The above-mentioned proceedings by advertisement and sale, may take place in any case of such unpaid tax, as is above mentioned, notwithstanding a warrant of distress may have been issued for the collection thereof, in the manner above mentioned, in case the whole or any part of such tax shall be uncollected thereupon. And nothing in

---

(a) Sections 4, 5, and 6, *supra*, are taken from sections 1, 2, and 3, of laws of 1830, chap. 2, p. 3, which act, so far as it relates to taxes, is repealed by the general repealing clause of sec. 2, art. 4, of this act. Sales are now to be conducted by clerk of arrears. Laws of 1853, chap. 579, sec. 3. See post, p. 220.

this act shall be construed to prevent the collection of any tax or taxes by distress and sale of the goods and chattels of the owner or owners, occupant or occupants, of any lands or tenements therein, or thereby assessed.

§ 8. In advertising houses and lots, improved or unimproved lands, to be sold for the non-payment of taxes, it shall be the duty of the said comptroller to advertise all the houses and lots, or other lands, lying contiguous to each other, and belonging to the same owners, in one parcel, unless otherwise requested by such owner. Lots, how to be advertised in parcels.

§ 9. Certificates of sale shall be made and delivered to the purchaser without charge, and no charge shall be made in the sale for the second advertisement and lease, but the former shall be paid by the owner at the time of redeeming, or by the purchaser when he shall receive a lease. The expense of drawing and executing a lease, shall be paid by the purchaser at the time of receiving the same, and not exceed fifty cents. Certificates of sale to be given without charge.

§ 10. The rate of interest allowed by law to the purchaser at the time of redemption on the amount of the purchase money, shall be reduced to 14 per cent. per annum; but no interest shall be calculated on a less portion of time than one quarter of a year; and in all cases where the property shall be redeemed during any fractional part of a year, the interest shall be calculated so as to include the quarter in which such redemption shall be made, the time to be computed from the day of sale. *(a)* Rate of interest to be allowed.

§ 11. In all cases where pieces or parcels of land shall have been sold for taxes, and any person shall claim to re- Parts of lots may be redeemed.

(a) Rate of interest on redemption changed to 12 per cent. by laws of 1853, chap. 579, sec. 15. See post, p. 225.

deem any portion of the same within the time limited for redemption, he shall be permitted to do so on paying the apportionment of the tax for which the property was sold, together with the interest on the same, and an equitable proportion of the expense; the apportionment to be made by the comptroller.

Notice to be given of redemption to mortgagees, &c.

§ 12. In cases of sales of real estate for the non-payment of taxes in the city of New York, it shall be the duty of the said comptroller, sixty days before the time limited by law for the redemption of any real estate from the effect of such sale, to cause notice to be given to all mortgagees of the real estate so sold, their assignees or personal representatives, and to all owners, lessees, or persons otherwise interested, who shall at any time, at least one month before the time for giving such notice, have filed in the office of the register of the city and county of New York, a memorandum of such mortgage, and of such real estate, containing a brief abstract designating the property, with the street numbers, if there be any, or such definite description or diagram as will enable the said comptroller to designate the said premises upon the city maps, and the name and residence of such mortgagee, assignee, or personal representative, and such owner, lessee, or person otherwise interested.

Notice, how to be sent to mortgagees.

§ 13. Such notice shall be given by putting into the post office in the city of New York, directed to such mortgagees, assignees, or personal representatives, at their places of residence, if known to the comptroller, and such owners, lessees, or persons otherwise interested, a printed list, describing all the property sold for taxes, and remaining unredeemed. Such description shall name the street or avenue on which the property may be situate, the side of the street or avenue, and between what streets or avenues, with the map or street numbers of the property, and in whose name assessed, together with the term of years and amount for which the same shall have been sold, and the day or days on which the time limited for the redemption of the property will expire, with a notice that unless the property shall be redeemed on or by such days, by the payment of the sums for which the same was sold, with all interest and expenses allowed by law, leases will be given to the purchasers, in accordance with the statute in such case made and provided.

§ 14. An affidavit of the service of such notice as is above required, before any officer authorized to take affidavits, to be read in a court of record, and filed in the office of the said register of deeds, or a certified copy thereof, under the signature of such register, shall be evidence of the fact of such notice.

Proof of service of notice.

§ 15. It shall be the duty of the said register of deeds to keep in his office a book, alphabetically arranged, for the registering of all such memorandums as aforesaid, which book shall be open to the inspection of any person desiring to examine the same, without charge.

Duty of register of deeds.

§ 16. The said register shall be entitled to receive twenty-five cents for performing the above services, and he shall make no other charge therefor, under any pretense whatever.

His fees.

§ 17. Such mortgagees, or their assignees, or personal representatives, shall be entitled to redeem the property sold, from the effect of such sale, at any time within two years from the date of such sale, and shall have a lien on the property for the amount paid, with the interest which may thereafter accrue thereon, at the rate of seven per

Mortgagees, &c., may redeem lands and have a lien for amount paid.

cent. per annum, in like manner as if the same had been included in such mortgage.

Act of 1840 not to apply to New York. § 18. The act entitled "An act authorizing mortgagees to redeem real estate sold for taxes and assessments," passed May 14, 1840, shall not apply to the city and county of New York, in any case in which the notice and affidavit herein provided for shall have been given and filed, as required by the tenth section of this article.

Persons entitled to the benefit of the act of 1840. § 19. No person shall be entitled to the benefit of the provisions of the first, second, and sixth sections of the act entitled, "An act authorizing mortgagees to redeem real estate sold for taxes and assessments," passed May 14, 1840, for any lands or tenements in the city of New York, sold for taxes, unless the memorandum mentioned in the twelfth and thirteenth sections of this article shall have been filed as therein provided; and in such case it shall only be necessary to give the notice in the manner therein designated. *(a)*

Notice to be served on occupants of lands sold by the grantee. § 20. Whenever any lands or tenements sold for taxes in the city of New York, and conveyed in the manner provided by law, shall, at the time of conveyance, be in the actual occupancy of any person, the grantee to whom the same shall have been conveyed, or the person claiming under him, shall serve a written notice on the person occupying such lands or tenements, and in all cases on the person last assessed as owner, whether the property be in occupancy or not, provided such person has a residence or actually resides in the city of New York, stating in substance the sale and conveyance, the person to whom made, and the amount of consideration money mentioned in the conveyance, with the addition of forty-two per cent. on such

(*a*) For this act, see ante, p. 179.

amount as the said lands or tenements were struck off for at the time of the sale, and the further addition of the sum paid for the lease and advertisements; and stating also that unless such consideration money, and the said forty-two per cent., together with the sum paid for the lease and advertisements, shall be paid to the said comptroller for the benefit of the grantee, within six months after service of such notice, the said conveyance would become absolute, and the occupant, and all others interested in the lands or tenements, be barred from all right and title thereto during the term of years for which such lands or tenements shall have been conveyed.

§ 21. Such notice shall be served personally, or by leaving the same at the dwelling-house of the occupant and person last assessed as owner, with any person of suitable age or discretion belonging to his family. Notice, how to be served.

§ 22. The occupant, or any other person, may at any time within the six months mentioned in such notice, redeem the said lands or tenements, in the same manner as now provided by law for the redemption of lands sold for taxes in the city of New York, by paying such purchase money, with the addition of forty-two per cent. thereon, and the amount that shall have been paid for the lease; and every such redemption shall be as effectual as if made before the conveyance of the lands or tenements sold. Land may be redeemed within the six months.

§ 23. In every such case of actual occupancy, the grantee or the person claiming under him, in order to complete his title to the land conveyed, shall file with the said comptroller the affidavit of some person residing in the city of New York, who shall be certified as credible by the officer before whom such affidavit shall be taken, that such notice as is above required, was duly served, specifying the mode of Affidavit to be filed with comptroller.

service; and a copy of such notice shall be attached thereto.

Conveyance, when to become absolute.

§ 24. If the said comptroller shall be satisfied by such affidavit that the notice has been duly served, and if the moneys required to be paid for the redemption of such land or tenements shall not have been paid as hereinbefore provided, he shall certify to the fact, and the conveyance shall thereupon become absolute; and the occupant and all others interested in the land or tenements shall be barred of all right and title thereto, during the term of years for which the same shall have been conveyed.

Construction of 22d section.

§ 25. The 22d section of this article shall be construed to authorize the computing of the forty-two per cent. named therein on the amount of sale and expenses authorized by law, and not to be in addition to, or upon the interest accruing after the sale. (*a*)

Divided or undivided parts of lots may be redeemed.

§ 26. If a sum of money in gross has been or shall be taxed upon any lands or premises in the city of New York, by virtue of any law of this State, any person or persons claiming any divided or undivided part thereof, may pay such part of the sum of money so assessed or taxed, and also of the interest and charges due or charged thereon, as the mayor, aldermen, and commonalty of the city of New York, in common council convened, may deem to be just and equitable; and the remainder of the sum of money so taxed, together with the interest and charges, shall be a lien on the residue of the land only, which may be sold in pursuance of the provisions of this article, to satisfy the

Taxes on remainder to be a lien thereon.

(*a*) Sections 12 to 25 inclusive, are taken from the acts of May 6, 1841, laws of 1841, chap. 170, p. 141, and May 25, 1841, laws of 1841, chap. 230, p. 210, which said acts, so far as they relate to the collection of taxes, are repealed by the general repealing clause of sec. 2, art. 4, of this act.

residue of such tax, interest, and charges, in the same manner which it could have been, provided the residue of said tax had been imposed upon the residue of said lands and tenements. *Provided always*, that nothing herein contained shall be so construed as to release the occupant of any such premises from his liability to pay the taxes upon the whole of the premises, which he is or shall be in the occupation of. (*a*) Proviso.

ARTICLE IV.

Repeal of other Provisions, and Time when this Act shall take effect.

§ 1. The provisions of chapter thirteen of the first part of the Revised Statutes regulating the collection of taxes, shall hereafter be inapplicable to the city and county of New York. Chap. 13 R. S., inapplicable to New York.

§ 2. All former laws, acts, and parts of acts, relating to the collection of taxes in the city of New York, or to the officers by whom the same shall be collected, and to the sale of property, real or personal, therefor, or to the redemption of real estate sold for taxes in the said city, and all other acts or parts of acts inconsistent herewith, are hereby repealed. Repeal.

§ 3. Neither of the two preceding sections shall in any manner be construed to affect any act done, or right accrued, or any proceeding, or any suit of prosecution for any offense, or for the recovery of any penalty, or forfeiture, commenced or pending under any of the provisions, acts, or parts of acts, thereby repealed, or declared inapplicable to the city and county of New York. Saving clause.

(*a*) Sec. 26 is substantially the same as sec. 1, chap. 149, of laws of 1821, which said act, so far as it relates to taxes, is repealed by the general repealing clause in sec. 2, of art. 4, of this act.

When to take effect. § 4. This act shall take effect immediately, except the provision to abolish the office of collector of taxes, which provision shall take effect on the first day of April, one thousand eight hundred and forty-four.

CHAPTER CCXXXV.

[Laws of 1843, p. 333.]

AN ACT *to authorize the Mayor, Aldermen, and Commonalty of the City of New York, to purchase lands for Taxes and Assessments in certain cases, and for other purposes.* Passed April 18, 1843, by a two-third vote.

The People of the State of New York, represented in Senate and Assembly, do enact as follows:

Lands may be bid in for city at sales for taxes or assessments. § 1. It shall be lawful for the comptroller of the city of New York, at any sale of lands for taxes in the said city, and for the street commissioner of the said city, at any sale of lands for assessments in the said city, held pursuant to law, to bid in, for the mayor, aldermen, and commonalty of the said city, every lot of land and premises by them put up, for which no person shall offer to bid; and certificates of such sale shall be made by the said comptroller and the street commissioner, in the several cases of such sale for taxes or assessments, which shall describe the lands purchased, and specify the term of years for which the same shall have been sold, and the time when the said mayor, aldermen, and commonalty will be entitled to a lease of such lands and premises. Such purchases shall be subject to the same right of redemption as purchases by individuals; and if the lands sold shall not be redeemed, or shall not have been assigned as hereinafter provided, the said comptroller in sales for taxes, and the said street commissioner in sales for assessments, shall execute a lease therefor, by virtue of the authority in them vested by this act, to the said mayor, aldermen, and commonalty, in the same form and with the same effect as in the cases of leases to individuals, as now authorized by law. (*a*)

Comptroller and Street Commissioner to bid in lands.

§ 2. It shall be the duty of the said comptroller, in all cases of purchases of land by the said mayor, aldermen, and commonalty, for taxes, and of the said street commissioner, in all cases of purchases of land by the said mayor, aldermen, and commonalty, for assessments, to assign any and all of such purchases to any person who shall, at any time within one year from the time when such purchases were made, offer to take the same, upon their paying to the said comptroller and street commissioner respectively, for the use of the said mayor, aldermen, and commonalty, the purchase money, with seven per cent. interest thereon.

Lands, how and on what terms redeemed.

§ 3. The persons receiving the assignments mentioned in the next preceding section, shall be entitled, upon the redemption of the property, to receive the amount paid by them to the said mayor, aldermen, and commonalty, with interest from the time of such payment, at the same rate and in the same manner as if they had purchased the property at a sale for taxes or assessments.

Time for redemption.

§ 4. In all cases of lands and premises purchased by the mayor, aldermen, and commonalty, for taxes or assessments, in which the same shall not have been assigned, as pro-

---

(*a*) By laws of 1853, chap. 579, sec. 3, p. 1065, the duties theretofore by law to be performed by the comptroller, in relation to advertising, selling, and leasing property, &c., for taxes, &c., are thereafter to be performed by clerk of arrears, under the direction of the comptroller. See post, p. 220.

vided in the second section of this act, any person may redeem the same previous to the time when the mayor, aldermen, and commonalty shall be entitled to a lease of such lands and premises, by paying, in the manner provided by law, for the use of the said mayor, aldermen, and commonalty, the purchase money, with seven per cent. interest thereon, together with any expense which shall have accrued since the sale.

Rights of mortgagees and lessees.

§ 5. In all cases where mortgagees of real estate sold for taxes and assessments in the city of New York, their personal representatives or owners, lessees, or persons otherwise interested in any lands or tenements so sold, shall file in the register's office of the said city, a memorandum of such mortgage or property, pursuant to the act entitled "An act in relation to the redemption of lands sold for taxes or assessments in the city of New York," passed May 6th, 1841, and of the act entitled "An act in addition to the acts respecting the collection of taxes and assessments in the city and county of New York," passed May 25th, 1841, the street commissioner shall cause the notice of such sale required by said acts to be given by such persons, by sending to them, in the manner therein provided, a printed list describing all the property sold for assessments or taxes, and remaining unredeemed. Such description shall name the street or avenue on which the property may be situated, the side of the street or avenue, and between what streets or avenues, with the map or street numbers of the property, and in whose name assessed, together with the term of years and amount for which the same shall have been sold, and the day or days on which the time limited for the redemption of the property will expire, with a notice that unless the property shall be redeemed on or by such days by the payment of the sums for which the same was sold, with all interest and expenses allowed by law, leases will be given to the purchasers, in accordance with the statute in such case made and provided; and it shall not be necessary for the street commissioner to give any other or further notice to the person aforesaid, than is herein contained. (*a*)

§ 6. The notice required to be given to the occupant of property sold for taxes and assessments in the city of New York, and the person last assessed as owner, by the grantees of such property, in accordance with the third and fourth sections of the last-mentioned act, shall be extended in all cases to the person last assessed as owner, whether the property be in occupancy or not; such person so to be notified shall be the person who shall have been last assessed as owner by the assessors of the ward in which the property shall be situate, at the time when such notice shall be actually given by such grantee; but such notice shall only apply to the persons assessed who have a residence or who actually reside in the city and county of New York.

Notice to occupant of property sold.

CORRECTION OF TAXES. (*b*)

CHAPTER CCL.

[Laws of 1844, pp. 383 and 384.]

* * * * * * *

§ 2. The board of supervisors in and for the city and

(*a*) The provisions of the acts referred to in section 5, *supra*, were incorporated into the act of April 18, 1843. See ante, pp. 199 and 203. Sections 12 to 25 inclusive, and the acts themselves, were repealed so far as they related to taxes, by sec. 2, of art. 4, of that act.

(*b*) Section 1 authorizes the supervisors to raise the annual tax.

14

Erroneous assessments to be corrected.

county of New York, may at any meeting of said board, at which the mayor or recorder shall be present, correct any erroneous assessment which may have been made by the assessors of either of the wards of the said city for the year eighteen hundred and forty-three, and may also correct any erroneous assessment which shall hereafter be made by any such assessors as aforesaid; provided application for such relief shall be made upon assessments in eighteen hundred and forty-three, within three months after the passage of this act, and in all other cases within the period of six months after the assessment rolls shall have been returned as required by law; and provided also proof is made to the satisfaction of such board of supervisors by the affidavit of the applicant or other legal evidence, that the said erroneous assessment did not result from any neglect on the part of the person or persons applying for relief. (*a*)

(*a*) By laws of 1859, chap. 302, sec. 10, p. 681, no reduction of assessments to be made by supervisors, unless it appear by oath or affirmation that the party aggrieved was unable to attend within the period prescribed for correction of taxes, by reason of sickness or absence from the city. By laws of 1850, chap. 121, sec. 28, p. 193, the remission to be made before collection of tax, and within six months from the time of delivery of books to receiver of taxes. See post, pp. 219 and 230.

CHAPTER CCCVIII.

[Laws of 1845, p. 329.]

AN ACT *to enable the Receiver of Taxes in the City of New York and the Comptroller of the said City to collect the Taxes remaining unpaid.* Passed May 14, 1845, by a two-third vote.

The People of the State of New York, represented in Senate and Assembly, do enact as follows:

Payments of taxes in arrears to be enforced.

§ 1. It shall be the duty of the receiver of taxes in the city of New York to collect all arrearages of taxes due and payable prior to the first day of October, one thousand eight hundred and forty-three, with interest thereon, and to enforce the payment thereof by distress and sale of the goods and chattels of the person against whom said tax has been assessed; and the provisions of the act entitled, "An Act for the collection of taxes in the city of New York," passed April 18, 1843, so far as the same relates to distress and sale of goods and chattels for the payment of taxes, shall be in full force, and applicable to the collection of such taxes under this section.

Costs to be collected in addition to tax.

§ 2. In all cases where the said receiver shall proceed by distress and sale of the goods and chattels of any person for the payment of any tax due and payable, as well before as after the said first day of October, one thousand eight hundred and forty-three, it shall be lawful for him to authorize and empower the officer making such distress and sale, to collect in addition to the tax and the interest thereon, the costs of such distress and sale.

Lands may be sold.

§ 3. It shall be lawful for the comptroller of the city of New York, to sell any lands or tenements in said city for the payment of any tax due thereon prior to the first day of October, one thousand eight hundred and forty-three; and all the provsions of article third of the said act entitled "An Act for the Collection of Taxes in the City of New York," passed April 18, 1843, shall be applicable to such sale, and the prior proceedings to effect the same.

Repeal. § 4. All acts and parts of acts inconsistent with the provisions of this act are hereby repealed.

§ 5. This act shall take effect immediately. (*a*)

CHAPTER CXXI.

[Laws of 1850, p. 188.]

AN ACT *in relation to the assessment and collection of taxes in the city of New York, and to amend the several acts in relation thereto.* Passed March 30, 1850—three-fifths being present.

The People of the State of New York, represented in Senate and Assembly, do enact as follows: (b)

* * * * * *

Assessment, when to be made. § 7. The assessors must, within ten days after the first day of January in each year, enter upon the performance of their duties, and must complete their assessments on or before the first day of April thereafter. (*c*) (*d*)

(*a*) By laws of 1853, chap. 579. sec. 3, p. 1065, the duties theretofore by law to be performed by the comptroller in relation to advertising, selling and leasing property, &c., for taxes, &c., are thereafter to be performed by clerk of arrears. See post, p. 220.

(*b*) Sections 1 to 6 of this act refer to the mode of election, classification, &c., of the assessors, and are therefore omitted.

(*c*) By laws of 1859, chap. 302, sec. 2, p. 679, see post, p. 227, the offices of ward assessors in the city of New York are abolished, and the powers and

§ 8. If an assessor neglect, or from any cause omit to perform his duties, the other assessor of the ward must perform such duties, and must certify to the tax commissioners hereinafter mentioned, with the assessment roll, the name of the delinquent assessor, stating therein the cause of his delinquency.

Duties of delinquent assessors, how performed.

§ 9. The assessors, before they assess the property in their respective wards, must meet together in the City Hall of the city of New York, at eleven o'clock in the forenoon, on the first Tuesday after been sworn into office, and appoint from among themselves a president and secretary and organize themselves into a board for the transaction business, to be called the board of assessors.

First meeting of assessors.

§ 10. The board of assessors may meet again at such time and place, and from time to time, as they may think fit; and the secretary thereof must keep a regular book of minutes of all the proceedings of the board.

Other meetings.

§ 11. The board of assessors, either at their first or any subsequent meeting, before the members thereof proceed to assess property in their respective wards, may adopt such rules or by-laws as may, in their opinion, be best calculated to produce equality and uniformity in the different valuations of property and assessments in the several wards, and to insure the assessment of all real and personal estate subject to taxation according to law.

Rules of assessment.

---

duties vested in and performed by those officers, are vested in and to be performed by the deputy tax commissioners created by that act, and the existing provisions of law in respect to the mode and manner of making assessments, so far as conformable to the supervision of the commissioners of taxes and assessments are made applicable to the deputy tax commissioners.

(*d*) By section 7, laws of 1859, chap. 302, p. 680-1, the deputy tax commissioners are to commence their assessments on the first Monday of September in each year. See post, pp. 227-230.

§ 12. The board of assessors can exercise no other powers than those conferred by law, and upon their final adjournment must cause their minutes to be filed with the tax commissioners.

Tax commissioners. § 13. The board of supervisors of the city and county of New York must, within twenty days after this ac takes effect, appoint three persons, to be known as tax commissioners of the city of New York. The persons so appointed must be classified by lot by the clerk of the board of supervisors, in the presence of the board, immediately after said appointments are made. The classes

Their term of office. must be numbered one, two, and three ; the commissioner of the first class shall hold his office until and including the thirty-first day of December, one thousand eight hundred and fifty-one ; the commissioner of the second class shall hold his office until, and including the thirty-first day of December, one thousand eight hundred and fifty-two ; and the commissioners of the third class shall hold his office until, and including the thirty-first day of December, one thousand eight hundred and fifty-three. The said board of supervisors must, also, in like manner, within thirty days before the expiration of the term of office of any tax commissioner, make a similar appointment for the next three years, and so on in like manner in every year thereafter.

Vacancies, how filled. If a vacancy occur in the office of either of the tax commissioners, it may be filled by a similar appointment, to continue in force until the expiration of the office of the person in respect to whom the vacancy occurred. (*a*)

Compensation. § 14. The said tax commissioners shall receive as a com-

(*a*) By sec. 1, chap. 302, laws of 1859, the mode of appointment of the commissioners of taxes and assessments is changed, and the compensation is made $3,500 per annum. See post, p. 227.

pensation for their services, a per diem allowance, to be fixed by the board of supervisors, for each day actually and necessarily employed in the discharge of their duties. The said board of supervisors must also assign them a suitable office in the City Hall, in the city of New York, to be known as the tax commissioners' office, which office shall be kept open the usual days and hours as the other city offices are by law required to be kept open for the transaction of business.

Their office

§ 15. The tax commissioners must keep in their office, in suitable books to be provided for that purpose by the supervisors, a record of all information which they may receive, or be able to obtain, in respect to the taxable property, or persons liable to taxation, in the city of New York, and of all changes in the divisions of real property in that city, of which they can obtain information; and must preserve all maps delivered to them for that purpose, and file all assessment-rolls furnished to them by the assessors. The books, records, maps, and papers, mentioned in this section, are public records, and must, at all reasonable times, be open to public inspection.

Books to be kept by commissioners.

§ 16. The tax commissioners must cause to be prepared and delivered, on or before the first day of January in each year, to the assessors of the several wards, the assessment-rolls for their wards respectively, with the printed blanks required by law.

Assessment rolls.

§ 17. On or before the first day of April in each year, after the assessment-rolls for the several wards have been completed by the assessors, according to law, they must be delivered to the tax commissioners, who must thereupon examine and compare them, for the purpose of ascertaining whether the valuations in one ward bear a just relation to

Equalization of rolls.

the valuations in all the wards of the city; and they may increase or diminish the aggregate valuations of real property in any ward, by adding or deducting such sum upon the hundred, as may, in their opinion, be necessary to produce a just relation between all the valuations of real property in the city; but they can in no instance reduce the aggregate valuations of all the wards below the aggregate valuation thereof, as made by the assessors of the wards respectively. [*As amended by sec.* 1, *chap.* 319, *Laws of* 1851, *p.* 611.] *(a)*

Notice of completion of rolls.

§ 18. Within ten days after the assessment-rolls are delivered to the tax commissioners, they must cause a notice to be published, which publication shall be continued for three weeks, and three times in each week, in such of the newspapers published in the city of New York as are, or may be employed by the corporation of said city, to the effect that the assessors have completed their assessment-rolls, and that the same are left with the tax commissioners, at their office in the City Hall, in the city of New York, where the same may be seen and examined by any person taxable in that city, during at least thirty days; and that the tax commissioners will meet at their office for a certain number of days, during the usual business hours thereof, to review the assessments, on the application of any person conceiving himself aggrieved.

Review and reduction of assessments.

§ 19. The tax commissioners must meet at the time and place specified in the notice; and on the application of any person conceiving himself aggrieved, must review the assessments; and when the person objecting has not previously been examined under oath, by any assessor or

---

(a) But see sections 7, 8, and 12, of laws of 1859, chap. 302. See post, pp. 229–231.

assessors, concerning his property, and made affidavit of the value thereof, according to law, must, after such examination shall have been had, and affidavit been made, reduce the assessment to the sum specified in the said affidavit. *(a)*

§ 20. The examination and affidavit mentioned in the last section, must be had and made before the tax commissioners, or one of them, either of whom is authorized to administer an oath for that purpose; and the tax commissioners shall reduce such examination to writing; and the same must thereon, together with the affidavit, be filed in their office. Affidavit, before whom made.

§ 21. The tax commissioners must thereupon correct the assessment-roll for each ward, and add thereto and assess according to law, any real or personal estate liable to taxation, which may not have been assessed by the said assessors, and when so corrected, must cause a fair copy thereof to be prepared, and must attach thereto and sign a certificate, in substantially the following form: "We certify that the preceding is a copy of the corrected assessment-roll of the ward." [*As amended by sec.* 2, *chap.* 319, *Laws of* 1851.] Corrected rolls.

§ 22. The rolls thus certified, must, on or before the first day of July in each year, be delivered by the tax commissioners to the comptroller of the city of New York, and be by him delivered to the supervisors, at a meeting to be held for that purpose, as provided in the next section. Rolls, when delivered to comptroller.

§ 23. The board of supervisors of the city and county of New York must meet at the city hall, in that city, Meeting of board of supervisors.

(a) But see section 10, laws of 1859, chap. 302. See post, p. 230.

on the second Wednesday of July in each year, at noon of that day. (*a*)

Descriptions of real property of non-residents to be examined.

§ 24. At such meeting, they must make such alterations in the description of real property belonging to non-residents, as may be necessary to render such descriptions conformable to the provisions of law; and if such alterations cannot be made, they must expunge the descriptions of such real property, and the assessments thereon, from the assessment rolls.

Assessment of tax.

§ 25. They must also estimate and set down in a fifth column, to be prepared for that purpose in the assessment-rolls, opposite to the several sums set down as the valuation of real and personal property, the respective sums, in dollars and cents, to be paid as a tax thereon, rejecting the fractions of a cent.

Statement of aggregate valuation to be sent to comptroller.

§ 26. They must also add up and set down the aggregate valuations of the real and personal property in the several wards, as corrected by them; and must trasmit to the comptroller of this State, by mail, a certificate of such aggregate valuations, showing separately the aggregate amount of the real and personal property in each ward, as corrected by the board.

Corrected roll to be delivered to receiver of taxes.

§ 27. They must also cause the assessment-roll of each ward, when corrected according to law, and finally completed, or a fair copy thereof, to be delivered to the receiver of taxes in and for said city, on or before the first day of September thereafter, with the proper warrant or warrants annexed, directing and requiring him to collect the several sums therein mentioned, according to law. The said

(*a*) Time changed to first Monday of July—laws of 1859, chap. 302, sec. 13—and rolls to be delivered by the commissioners to the supervisors. See post, p. 232.

receiver shall, immediately after he shall have received the said assessment-rolls, give public notice in six or more of the public newspapers printed in said city, that said assessment-rolls have been delivered to him, and that all taxes are then due and payable; and that in case of payment on or before the first day of November thereafter, the person so paying shall be entitled to the benefits mentioned in the 29th section of this act. Receiver to give notice.

§ 28. The board of supervisors may remit or reduce a tax imposed, as prescribed by law, for good cause shown by affidavit, taken before an officer authorized to administer oaths in the city of New York, and filed by them with the tax commissioners; and such reduction or remission must be made before the collection of the tax; but the application therefor must be made within six months from the delivery of the books to the receiver for the collection of such tax; and when, under the provisions of the existing law, any remissions of taxes shall be made by the common council of said city, the affidavit of the person applying shall be in like manner filed with the commissioners of taxes. [*As amended by sec.* 3, *chap.* 319, *Laws of* 1851. (a) Supervisors may remit tax.

* * * * * *

§ 35. If any officer or officers mentioned in this act, shall willfully refuse or neglect to perform any of the duties required of him by this act, he shall forfeit to the mayor, aldermen, and commonalty of the city of New York, the sum of one hundred dollars, to be recovered in a civil action; and shall also be punishable for a misdemeanor. Penalty.

§ 36. All acts and parts of acts inconsistent with the Repeal.

(a) Sections 29, 30, 31, 32, 33, and 34, amend sections 4, 5, 6, 7, 8, and 9, of article 2, chap. 230, of laws of 1843, and the amendments are incorporated into that act. See ante, pp. 188 and 189.

provisions of this act, be, and the same are hereby repealed.

§ 37. This act shall take effect immediately.

CHAPTER DLXXIX.

[Laws of 1853, p. 1065.] (*a*)

AN ACT *to simplify the manner of collecting arrears of taxes, assessments, and regular rents of Croton water, in the city and county of New York.* Passed July 20, 1853—three-fifths being present.

The People of the State of New York, represented in Senate and Assembly, do enact as follows:

Ward or block numbers.

§ 1. In all assessments for any improvements hereafter to be made, in addition to the known street numbers, if there be any, the same ward or block numbers shall be used to designate the lots, as are, or may be used to designate them in assessments for taxes, and no other numbers, except where no ward or block numbers exist.

Bureau of arrears.

§ 2. There shall be a bureau of arrears in the department of finance, at the head of which shall be a clerk of arrears.

(*a*) The act of 1852, chap. 282, qualifying the exemption from taxation of buildings for public worship and school-houses, &c.;

Also act of 1852, chap. 46, exempting the mint in the city of New York from taxation;

Also the act of 1853, chap. 406, exempting the assay office in the city of New York from taxation, are incorporated into chapter 13, title 1, part 1, of the Revised Statutes, and are therefore omitted in this part of the compilation.

See for these acts ante, pp. 118 and 119.

§ 3. All the duties heretofore required by law to be performed by the street commissioner and comptroller in relation to advertising, selling, and leasing for assessments, taxes, and regular rents of Croton water, and the redemption of property sold therefor, shall hereafter be performed by the clerk of arrears, under the direction of the comptroller. Duty of clerk of arrears.

§ 4. The street commissioner shall, without delay, furnish to the clerk of arrears an account of all property which has been sold for assessments, whereof the time for redemption shall not have expired. Duty of street commissioner.

§ 5. The comptroller shall, without delay, furnish the clerk of arrears with an account of all property which has been sold for taxes, or for regular rents of Croton water, whereof the time for redemption shall not have expired. Comptroller to furnish an account of property.

§ 6. No assessment for any improvement shall hereafter be deemed to be fully confirmed, so as to be due, and be a lien upon the property included in it, until the title thereof, with the date of confirmation, shall have been entered, with the date of such entry, in a record of the titles of assessments, to be kept in the street commissioner's office, and which may be used as an index to a record of assessments; and until the title of the said assessments shall have been also entered, with the date of confirmation and the date of such entry, in a record of the titles of assessments confirmed, to be kept in the office of the clerk of arrears. Confirming assessment.

§ 7. The street commissioner shall give to the clerk of arrears a separate return, with particulars of all arrears remaining unpaid on each and every assessment so entered, without delay, on the expiration of twelve months after Street commissioner to give a separate return.

the date of such entry thereof, as required in the preceding section, and of every assessment which was confirmed before the passage of this act, which has been due twelve months, or over; or as soon as they shall have been twelve months due; and he shall, at the same time, notify the comptroller of the aggregate amount of arrears of each assessment so returned, and balance, on his books, the accounts of arrears so returned, by charging the amount thereof to the bureau of arrears, and there shall thereafter be received no payments by him, or in his department, on account of arrears so returned, and he shall be entitled to draw on the comptroller for any amount, to the extent of the amount of arrears so returned, necessary to complete the payments due to the persons who were to be paid from the proceeds of said assessments, and also for the amount of compensation due thereon to the collectors, the amount or rate of which shall not be changed by the passage of this act.

§ 8. The clerk of arrears shall, without delay, make a requisition on the street commissioner for any returns required by section seven of this act, which may be omitted to be made.

President of Croton aqueduct board.

§ 9. The president of the Croton aqueduct board shall, annually, on the last day of the month of April, cause to be prepared, and transmitted to the clerk of arrears, a separate account for each ward, of all lots in which the said regular rents for that water year may remain unpaid, with the amount due on each lot, and shall include in such account which he shall first render after the passage of this act, whatever regular rents may remain unpaid of previous years, and shall, at the time, notify the comptroller of the aggregate amount of the regular rents so returned, and shall thereafter receive no payments on account of the same, but may, nevertheless, certify to the clerk of arrears, any over-charges which shall, upon such certificate, be remitted by the clerk of arrears, at any time before settlement. [*As amended by section* 1, *Laws of* 1854, *chap*. 335.]

§ 10. There shall be ruled in the yearly assessment rolls for taxes of each ward, a new column headed "regular rents," in which, immediately after the confirmation of such assessment rolls, the clerk of arrears shall cause to be entered, opposite to the ward numbers of the property on which the said arrears may be due, the amounts due for "regular rents," as transmitted to him, in accordance with the provisions of the preceding section, and the same shall be, and continue to be, with the charges thereon, until paid, a lien upon the property on which they may be due, and shall be collected at the same time, and in the same manner, with the taxes to which they shall be added.

Yearly assessment rolls.

"Regular rents."

§ 11. The receiver of taxes shall, on the first day of June in each year, make a return to the clerk of arrears, of all taxes on real estate, and of "regular rents" of Croton water, which have been added thereto, remaining unpaid, and shall notify the comptroller of the aggregate amount of arrears so returned, and balance on his books, the accounts of arrears, so returned, by charging the amount thereof to the bureau of arrears, and shall thereafter receive no payments on account of arrears so returned, but may, nevertheless, certify to the clerk of arrears any errors which shall, upon such certificate, be corrected by the clerk of arrears any time before settlement.

Receiver of taxes.

§ 12. There shall be ruled in the yearly assessment rolls of taxes in each ward, a new column, headed "arrears,"

Assessment rolls, "arrears."

in which the clerk of arrears shall, annually, before any taxes for the year are collected, cause to be entered the word "arrears," or "sold," according as the fact may be, opposite to the ward numbers on which any arrears of taxes, or of taxes with the regular rents of Croton water added, shall be due, or on which any assessment shall remain unpaid, which was due or confirmed thirteen months prior to the first of June, then last past, or which may have been sold for assessments, taxes, or regular rents of Croton water, and yet be redeemable.

Arrears.

§ 13. There shall be ruled a column headed "Arrears," in every bill rendered for taxes, for lots on which said arrears for assessments, taxes, or taxes with "regular rents" for Croton water added, may be due as aforesaid, or which may have been sold and be yet redeemable; in which shall be written opposite the entry of the ward number of said lots, "Arrears," or "Sold," according as the fact may be; and it is hereby delared to be the duty of the receiver of taxes to cause a record to be kept of the ward numbers of all lots so noted in said bill as in arrears or sold, when said bills are presented for settlement, and at the bottom of said bills shall be printed, "The column for arrears indicates lots sold for arrears, or to be sold therefor; arrears to be paid, and lots redeemed at the office of the clerk of arrears."

Record to be kept of lots in arrears, or sold.

When real estate may be sold.

§ 14. No real estate shall hereafter be sold for any arrears of taxes on real estate or assessments thereon, until after three years from the time when the same shall have become due; nor for any arrears of "regular rents" for Croton water, until four years from the time the same shall have become due. An omission of the entry of "Arrears," or "Sold," in any bill, as required in the preceding section, shall have no other effect than to postpone the time of sale of the property represented by the number opposite which the entry shall have been omitted, in cases of arrears for the further term of one year, and to extend the time for redemption two years in cases of property sold; but no bill shall be considered evidence of such omission unless paid and duly receipted.

§ 15. Interest shall hereafter be charged at the rate of twelve per cent. per annum, on all arrears of taxes and assessments returned to the clerk of arrears, from the time they become due until paid; and on the "regular rents" and charges for Croton water, from the time the taxes become due, to which they may be added, as required in section ten of this act, until paid.

Interest to be charged.

§ 16. The clerk of arrears, upon the requisition of any person, shall furnish a bill of all arrears of taxes, and of taxes with the "regular rents" of Croton water, added, on any lot or lots, due prior to the first of June, then last past, and of assessments which shall have been due twelve months or over, including the amount necessary to redeem it or them, if it or they have been sold for any arrears of assessments, taxes, or regular rents for Croton water, and be yet redeemable; and upon the payment of the said bill (which shall be called "a bill of arrears of assessments, taxes, and 'regular rents' for Croton water and for redemption"), his receipt thereon, which shall be conclusive evidence of such payment, countersigned by the comptroller, who shall cause to be kept a duplicate account of amounts so collected, or the certificate of the clerk of arrears, countersigned by the comptroller, that there are no such liens on said lot or lots, shall forever free the said lot or lots from all liens or taxes, or for taxes with the regular

Clerk to furnish bill of arrears of taxes when requested.

Lot to be free from lien for taxes on payment of bill.

rents for Croton water added, or for regular rents for Croton water added to the taxes, prior to the first of June, then last past; and for all assessments, due thirteen months or over, prior to the date of the said receipt or certificate, and from all liens in consequence of sales for assessments, taxes, or regular rents for Croton water, or for all of them, when the time allowed by law for redemption had not expired at the date or time of said payment or certificate.

Fees to be charged and paid into the city treasury.

§ 17. Fees for the searches, to be paid into the city treasury, shall be included in the bills mentioned in section seventeen of this act, and shall also be charged for certificates which shall be given by said clerk of arrears, respecting lots on which there may be no arrears, when searches are required; the said fees to be regulated by ordinance of the common council of the city of New York. (*a*)

Corporation to borrow to meet deficiencies.

§ 18. The corporation of the city of New York is hereby authorized to borrow, on the credit of the corporation, from time to time, such amounts as may be required to meet the deficiencies caused by delay in collecting arrears of assessments; the aggregate amount so borrowed not to exceed, at any time, the aggregate amount of said arrears then outstanding.

Repeal.

§ 19. All parts of acts, inconsistent with this act, are hereby repealed.

§ 20. This act shall take effect from the first January, eighteen hundred and fifty-four.

(*a*) The section referred to in this section must be 16 and not 17. See section 16.

CHAPTER CCCII.

[Laws of 1859, p. 678.]

AN ACT *in relation to taxes and assessments in the city of New York, and to amend the several acts in relation thereto.* Passed April 14th, 1859—three-fifths being present.

The People of the State of New York, represented in Senate and Assembly, do enact as follows:

Commissioners to be appointed.

SEC. 1. Immediately upon the passage of this act there shall be appointed by the comptroller of the city of New York three commissioners, who shall form a board and be designated commissioners of taxes and assessments for the city and county of New York, who shall hold their office for the term of five years, and until others are appointed in their places. Any vacancy in said board of commissioners, from death, or resignation, or otherwise, shall be filled by said comptroller, for the balance of the term for which such commissioners are appointed. The annual compensation for each commissioner shall be three thousand five hundred dollars, to be paid monthly by the comptroller out of the county treasury.

Ward Assessors abolished.

§ 2. The offices of ward assessors in the city of New York, and commissioners of taxes and assessments, as heretofore existing, are hereby abolished, and the powers and duties now or heretofore vested in and performed by the officers thereof, relative to the assessment of real and personal estate, shall hereafter be vested in and performed by the officers provided for by this act, and in the manner hereinafter provided; and the provisions now existing in respect to the mode and manner of making assessments in the city of New York, as far as the same are conformable to the supervision of the commissioners of taxes and assessments, are hereby made applicable to the officers provided for by this act.

Deputy Tax Commissioners. § 3. The board of commissioners of taxes and assessment shall appoint not to exceed twelve persons, to be known as deputy tax commissioners, who shall perform, under their direction and supervision, the duties heretofore performed by the assessors of the several wards of said city, or such other duties as they shall prescribe. They shall hold their office during the pleasure of the said commissioners, and shall receive such compensation as may be determined by the said comptroller and board of commissioners, not to exceed the sum of two thousand dollars per annum to each of said deputies, to be paid by the comptroller out of the county treasury.

Clerks. § 4. The said board of commissioners may appoint such number of regular and extra clerks as in their judgment may be necessary to perform such duties as may be prescribed by said commissioners, who shall hold their office during the pleasure of said commissioners, and shall receive for their services such compensation as may be fixed by the comptroller and the board of commissioners, not exceeding at the rate of twelve hundred dollars per annum for the time employed, to be paid by the comptroller out of the county treasury.

Surveyor. § 5. The said board of commissioners shall appoint a surveyor from one of the city surveyors, whose duty it shall be to make the necessary surveys and corrections of the ward maps, and also all new maps which may be required for the more accurate assessment of real estate. He shall hold his office at the pleasure of the commissioners, and shall receive for his services three thousand dollars per annum.

§ 6. The board of supervisors of the city and county of New York shall provide for and assign to the commissioners and their deputies, a suitable and convenient office or offices in any of the public buildings in the city of New York, or elsewhere in the city of New York, together with the requisite and necessary books, stationery, lights, and fuel, and which said office or offices shall be kept open during the usual days and hours, as the other offices are by law required to be kept open, for the transaction of business. The books, maps, assessment rolls, and other papers now pertaining to the office of commissioner of taxes and assessments, shall be transferred to the custody and control of the commissioners of taxes and assessments appointed under this act, and shall continue to be public records, and at all reasonable times shall be open to public inspection. Offices to be assigned.

§ 7. It shall be the duty of the deputy tax commissioners, under the direction of the commissioners of taxes and assessments, to assess all the taxable property in the several districts that may be assigned to them for that purpose by said commissioners, and shall furnish to them, under oath, a detailed statement of all such property, that said deputies have personally examined each and every house, building, lot, pier, or other assessable property, giving the street and ward map number of such real estate embraced within said districts, together with the name of the owner or occupant, if known; also, in their judgment, the sum for which such property, under ordinary circumstances, would sell, with such other information, in detail, relative to personal property, or otherwise, as the said commissioners may from time to time require. Such deputies shall commence to assess real and personal estate on the first Monday of September, in each and every year. Duty of deputy tax commissioners.

Annual record to be kept.

§ 8. The said commissioners shall keep in their office books, to be provided for that purpose by the comptroller, to be called "the annual record of the assessed valuation of real and personal estate," in which shall be entered, in detail, the assessed valuations of such property within the city and county of New York, and which said books shall be open for examination and correction from the second Monday of January until the first day of May in each and every year; but on the said last-mentioned day, the same shall be closed, to enable the commissioners to prepare assessment rolls of the several wards, for delivery to the supervisors, as hereinafter provided.

Advertising by commissioners.

§ 9. The said commissioners, previous to and during the time the said books are open for inspection, shall advertise the fact in the several newspapers, or in such manner as they may deem most advisable; and the charges therefor, certified by the commissioners, shall be audited and allowed by the supervisors as a county charge.

Books to be kept open, &c.

§ 10. During the time the books shall be open to public inspection, as hereinbefore provided, application may be made by any person considering himself aggrieved by the assessed valuation of his real or personal estate, to have the same corrected. If such application be made in relation to the assessed valuation of real estate, it must be made in writing, stating the ground of objection thereto; and thereupon the commissioners shall examine into the complaint; and if, in their judgment, the assessment is erroneous, they shall cause the same to be corrected. If such application be made in relation to the assessed valuation of personal estate, the applicant shall be examined, under oath, by the said commissioners, who shall be authorized to administer such oath or any of them; and if, in his or their judgment, the assessment is erroneous, they shall cause the same to be corrected, and fix the amount of such assessment as they may believe to be just, and declare their decision thereon, within thirty days after such application shall have been made to them. No reduction shall be made by the board of supervisors, of any assessment on real or personal estate, imposed under this act, unless it shall appear, under oath or affirmation, that the party aggrieved was unable to attend within the period prescribed for the correction of taxes, by reason of sickness or absence from the city.

Intention of act.

§ 11. It being the intention of this act to provide for the better equalization of the taxation in the city and county of New York, the commissioners may at any time before the second day of April in each year, increase or diminish at any time before the closing of the books of annual record on the first day of May in each year, the assessed valuation of any real or personal estate in said city, as in their judgment may be necessary for such equalization; but they shall not increase such valuations after said books are open for correction and review, except upon notice being given to the party affected by such increase, twenty days before the closing of said books.

Valuations.

Assessment rolls to be made.

§ 12. On the first day of May in each year, the commissioners shall cause to be prepared from the books of annual record of assessed valuations of real and personal estate in the city of New York, assessment rolls for each of the several wards of said city, in the same form as the same are now by law directed to be prepared, and shall annex to each of said rolls their certificate, that the same is correct, in accordance with the entries in said books of record.

Rolls to be delivered to the supervisors.

§ 13. The rolls thus certified must, on the first Monday of July in each year, be delivered by the said commissioners, to the supervisors of the city and county of New York, who shall meet at noon on that day, at the city hall, in said city, for the purpose of receiving the same, and for the purpose of performing such other duties in relation thereto as are prescribed by law.

Erection of buildings,&c.

§ 14. Whenever any permit shall be granted by the proper officer of the city government, for the erection of any building, pier, or bulkhead within said city, a copy of such permit shall be furnished by the said officer to the commissioners of taxes and assessments.

Assessors.

§ 15. The said commissioners of taxes and assessments shall appoint three skillful and competent disinterested persons, citizens of the United States, and residents of the city of New York, who shall constitute a board, to be known as the board of assessors, and who shall be charged with the duty of making the estimates and assessments required by law for building wells, erecting pumps, pitching, paving, regulating, and repairing streets, constructing sewers, fencing vacant lots and public slips, and all other improvements directed by corporation ordinance, for which an assessment may be made.

Board of assessors.

§ 16. The said board of assessors, or a majority thereof, shall make all estimates and assessments, give all notices, receive and pass upon all objections, and certify to the common council, in accordance with the existing laws relative to all such matters. The said assessors shall each receive an annual compensation of two thousand dollars, to be paid by the comptroller of the city of New York, from the city treasury, and which shall be in lieu of all other compensation. The said assessors shall hold their office during the pleasure of the appointing power, and no longer. The common council of the city of New York shall provide for, and assign to said assessors, a suitable and convenient room or rooms for the transaction of their business, and shall provide the said assessors with the requisite and necessary stationery, lights, and fuel. It shall be lawful for the said commissioners of taxes and assessments to appoint a clerk to assist said assessors in the performance of their duties, and who shall receive an annual compensation, to be fixed by said commissioners, not exceeding the sum of twelve hundred dollars, to be paid by the comptroller out of the city treasury.

Assessment list and duty of common council.

§ 17. Whenever any assessment list shall be certified by the assessors to the common council of the city of New York, for confirmation, as provided by law, it shall be the duty of the common council to proceed forthwith to confirm such assessment, or refer the same back to the said board of assessors, if necessary, for revisal and correction; and all such matters shall have precedence to all other matters before the common council, or in either board thereof.

Record.

§ 18. The said board of assessors shall cause to be entered in books to be provided for that purpose by the common council, a full and complete record in detail, of all assessments confirmed by the Supreme Court, or by the common council, which shall, at all convenient times, be open to public inspection.

Duties of assessors.

§ 19. All the powers and duties now possessed by the street commissioner in the city of New York, or by his department, in regard to making and perfecting assessments, shall devolve upon the assessors appointed under the provisions of this act.

§ 20. A certiorari to review and correct on the merits, any decision or action of the said commissioners, under section ten or eleven of this act, shall be allowed by the supreme court, or any judge thereof, directed to the said commissioners, on the petition of the party aggrieved, and shall, with the return, be heard and decided forthwith by said court, in preference to all other matters, actions, or proceedings.

§ 21. The act entitled "An act in relation to assessments in the city of New York, and to amend the several acts in relation thereto," passed April sixteenth, eighteen hundred and fifty-seven, is hereby repealed; and also all laws and acts, and parts of acts, so far as the same are inconsistent with this act, are hereby repealed; provided, however, that nothing contained in this act shall be so construed as to repeal any act or law now exempting real or personal estate from taxation.

§ 22. This act shall take effect immediately.

MISCELLANEOUS PROVISIONS.

CHAPTER LXXXVI.

AN ACT *to reduce several laws relating particularly to the city of New York into one act.* Passed April 9, 1813. 2 Revised Laws, 1813, p. 342–399.

COLLECTION OF TAXES. (*a*) (*b*)

§ 150. *And be it further enacted*, that the mayor, recorder, and aldermen of the city of New York, shall be the supervisors of the said city, and as such shall annually on the second Tuesday of July, meet together at the city hall of the said city, and at such other times and places as they shall find necessary, and examine and ascertain what sums of money are by law imposed on the said city, in that year, for the maintenance of the poor, for defraying the contingent charges of said city, and for other purposes, and shall cause the same to be raised, levied, and collected in the said city, in the same manner as the contingent charges of the several counties of this State are directed to be levied and collected by the act entitled "An act for defraying the public and necessary charges in the respective counties of this State," and the same shall in like manner be paid to

Mayor, recorder, and aldermen to be supervisors for city of New York.

Their duty as to taxes

(*a*) By act of 1857, chap. 590, as amended by laws of 1858, chap. 321, it is provided that the mayor and recorder shall cease to be supervisors of the county of New York. See post, p. 237.

(*b*) By laws of 1850, chap. 121, the time of the meeting of the supervisors to impose tax was changed to the second Wednesday of July in each year. See section 23. And by chap. 302, sec. 13, laws of 1859, the time was again changed to the first Monday of July. Ante, pp. 217 and 232.

the chamberlain of the said city, and the said mayor, aldermen, and commonalty, and chamberlain, shall respectively proceed relative thereto in like manner and subject to the like restrictions and regulations as the supervisors and treasurers of the other counties of this State, are by the said act respectively required to do in relation to the contingent charges of the said counties. *(a)*

* * * * *

Penalty on supervisors for neglect of duty.

§ 154. *And be it further enacted*, That if any mayor, recorder, or alderman of the said city and county of New York, shall willfully neglect or refuse to perform any of the duties required of him by the four last preceding sections of this act, he shall for every such offense incur the like forfeiture, as in the case of such refusal or neglect, by any supervisor in the other counties of this State, by virtue of the said act, and to be recovered and applied in like manner.

(a) Sections 151 and 152 of this act refer to the duties of the chamberlain and are to be found at p. 241.

Section 153 defines the number of supervisors necessary to constitute a quorum, and is virtually repealed by section 2, of laws of 1857, chap. 590, as amended by laws of 1858, chap. 321. Post, pp. 238 and 239.

CHAPTER DXC.

[Laws of 1857, vol. 2, p. 285.]

AN ACT *relating to the board of supervisors of the county of New York.* Passed April 15, 1857. (*a*)

The People of the State of New York, represented in Senate and Assembly, do enact as follows:

§ 1. The mayor and recorder of the city of New York shall cease to be members of the board of supervisors of the county of New York; the members now composing the said board of supervisors shall continue to be members thereof, as hereinafter mentioned; on or before the first Monday of May, eighteen hundred and fifty-eight, the present members of said board shall meet at their usual place of meeting in said county, and the six members thereof, elected by the votes of the electors, shall then and there, in the presence of the mayor of said city, classify themselves respectively, by lot, into six classes, and the six members of said board, appointed in December, eighteen hundred and fifty-seven, by the mayor of said city, shall also classify themselves respectively, at the same time and place, and in the same presence and manner, into six classes; the terms of office of the two members of the first class shall expire on the thirty-first day of December, eighteen hundred and fifty-eight; the term of office of the two members of the second class shall expire on the thirty-first day of December, eighteen hundred and fifty-nine; the term of office of the two members of the third class shall expire on the thirty-first day of December, eighteeen hun-

Mayor and Recorder to cease to be members of board of supervisors.

Classes.

Expiration of term of office.

(*a*) The amendments to this act, by laws of 1858, chap. 321, are incorporated herein.

dred and sixty; the term of office of the two members of the fourth class shall expire on the thirty-first day of December, eighteen hundred and sixty-one; the term of office of the two members of the fifth class shall expire on the thirty-first day of December, eighteen hundred and sixty-two; and the term of office of the two members of the sixth class shall expire on the thirty-first day of December, eighteen hundred and sixty-three. At the general election to be held in the city of New York in this year, and at every succeeding general election, two supervisors shall be voted for upon a separate general ticket, but only one name for supervisor shall be on any one ticket, and any ticket having thereon more than one name for supervisor, shall not be counted. The person having the highest number of votes, shall be declared elected by the board of county canvassers, who shall canvass the votes, and all the provisions of law relating to the election of county officers in said county, are hereby applied to the election of supervisors. On or before the fourth Wednesday of December, in each and every year, the mayor of said city shall appoint, as supervisor, the person who received the highest number of votes for supervisor, next to the votes received by the supervisor having the return of the board of county canvassers, as having been elected at the election last held. [*As amended by Laws of* 1858, *chap.* 321.]

Supervisors, how elected.

§ 2. The vote of seven of the members of the said board of supervisors in the affirmative, or in favor thereof, shall be necessary to pass any ordinance or resolution appropriating money, or to fill any vacancy in said board, or to do any act or thing, except to adjourn from day to day, and every act, ordinance, or resolution, which shall have passed the said board of supervisors, except such as levy any special tax or taxes, or fill a vacancy in said board, before it

Vote of seven members, &c.

shall take effect, shall be presented, duly certified, to the mayor of the city of New York, for his approval; if he approve, he shall sign it; if not, he shall return it, with his objections, to the board, within ten days thereafter, or if said board be not in session, at its next meeting after that period; the board shall enter the objections at large on their journal, and cause the same to be published in one or more of the daily papers of the city of New York. [*As amended by Laws of* 1858, *chap.* 321.]

§ 3. The board shall, after the expiration of not less than ten days thereafter, proceed to reconsider the same; and such act, resolution, or ordinance, if approved by a majority of all the members elected to the board, shall thereupon take effect. In all such cases the votes of the board shall be determined by ayes and noes, and the names of the persons voting for and against its passage, shall be entered on the journal of the board.

§ 4. If the mayor shall not return any act, resolution, or ordinance so presented to him, within the time above limited for that purpose, it shall take effect in the same manner as if he had signed it.

*§ 3. In case of any vacancy in said board, by death, resignation, or otherwise, the same shall be supplied by the remaining members thereof, and the person thus appointed shall hold his office as a member of said board for the unexpired term of the member thereof in whose place he shall have been appointed. [*Laws of* 1858, *chap.* 321.]

Expenses, &c.

§ 5. No money shall be drawn from the treasury, except the same shall have been previously appropriated to the purpose for which it is drawn; and no expense shall be incurred, whether it shall have been ordered by the board or not, unless an appropriation of moneys then in the treasury, sufficient to cover such expense, shall have been previously made.

Finance department.

§ 6. The finance department of the mayor, aldermen, and commonalty of the city of New York, and its officers, shall have the like powers, and perform the like duties in regard to the fiscal concerns of said board, as they possess in regard to the local concerns of the said mayor, aldermen, and commonalty. All moneys drawn from the treasury, by authority of the board of supervisors, shall be upon vouchers for the expenditure thereof, examined and allowed by the auditor, and approved by the comptroller and no such moneys shall be drawn therefrom, except on the warrant drawn by the comptroller, and countersigned by the mayor and clerk of the board, and no other warrant shall be necessary for such purpose.

§ 7. No allowance or payment, beyond legal claims, shall ever be allowed by the board.

§ 8. The members of the board of supervisors, whenever attending as members of the board of county canvassers, shall not receive compensation for a greater period than ten days, for canvassing the votes at any election; nor shall any person receive any compensation for services as a supervisor for the said county of New York.

Legal adviser.

§ 9. The counsel to the corporation of the city of New shall be the legal adviser of the said board of supervisors, and shall receive such compensation for his services as shall be fixed by said board, not exceeding the sum of two thousand dollars per annum.

§ 10. This act shall take effect immediately. (*a*)

THE CHAMBERLAIN AND HIS DUTIES. (*b*)

CHAPTER LXXXVI.

AN ACT *to reduce several laws relating to the city of New York into one act.* Passed April 9, 1813.

§ 151. *And be it further enacted*, That the chamberlain of the said city, shall in respect to all moneys so to be levied and collected, and also in respect to all moneys to be levied and collected in the said city, for the use of this State, perform the like duties as the treasurers of the several counties of this State are by the said act required to do and perform, and be accountable in like manner to the said mayor, recorder, and aldermen, as the supervisors of the said city, and once in every year, between the third Tuesday of November and the first Tuesday of December, and at such other times and at such places as the said mayor, recorder, and aldermen shall direct, exhibit to them his books and accounts, and all vouchers relating to the same, to be examined and audited; and shall also, before entering upon the execution of his office, give the like security by

Chamberlain to be treasurer of city, and subject to like regulations as other county treasurers.

(*a*) For the general duties and powers of the boards of supervisors in the several counties of this State, see chap. 12, part 1, title 2, art. 1, of the Revised Statutes (1 R. S.), page 847, 5th edition.

(*b*) For duties of chamberlain, relative to taxes, &c., under Revised Statutes, see ante, pp. 137-139.

16

bond, to the mayor, aldermen, and commonalty of the said city, and the obligors in such bond, their heirs, executors, or administrators, shall jointly and severally be liable to be prosecuted on such bond, and such chamberlain shall also be liable to such other actions, and in the like cases, as the said treasurers of the other counties of this State, and their sureties are respectively liable to by the said act, and the moneys recovered in any such action shall be paid and applied in the like manner; and in case of the death, resignation, or removal from office of such chamberlain, all the books and papers belonging to his office, shall be delivered to his successor in office, upon oath, in like manner as in the case of death, resignation, or removal from office of the treasurer of any other county, and upon refusal or neglect so to do, when lawfully demanded, every person so refusing or neglecting, shall forfeit the like penalties to the mayor, aldermen, and commonalty of the said city, to be recovered and applied in like manner as in the case of such refusal or neglect, on the death, resignation, or removal from office of the treasurer of any other county.

How moneys received by him shall be paid.

§ 152. *And be it further enacted*, That all moneys which shall come to the hands of the chamberlain of the said city, for the maintenance of the poor, and for defraying the other contingent expenses of the said city, or for any other purpose in the said city, and for any penalties or forfeitures incurred by virtue of this act, and appropriated hereby to the use of the said city, shall be paid by him to such persons, and in such manner, as the mayor, aldermen, and commonalty of the said city, in common council convened, by warrant under the hand of the mayor or recorder of the said city, presiding in such common council, shall from time to time direct; and the said chamberlain shall be entitled

His salary.

to retain for his services the sum of five hundred dollars

per annum; and he shall annually, on the first Monday of December, publish in one or more of the public newspapers in the said city, a statement of all moneys received by him for the use of the said city, and the purposes to which the same have been applied, as mentioned in such warrants. (*a*)

Annually to publish an account of receipts and expenditures.

(*a*) By sec. 22, of chap. 446, laws of 1857, vol. 1, pp. 879, 880, the chamberlain is made the head of a bureau in the finance department. And by sec. 21, of same act, he is to be appointed by the mayor, with the consent of the board of aldermen, and may be removed in same manner as heads of departments.

By the act aforesaid, warrants on the chamberlain are to be drawn by the comptroller, and countersigned by the mayor and aldermen of the common council.

By 1 R. S., p. 863, 5th edition, every county treasurer, before he enters upon the duties of his office, is to give a bond to the supervisors, with two or more sufficient sureties, to be approved of by the board of supervisors, and in such sum as they shall direct, conditioned that such person shall faithfully execute the duties of his office, and shall pay according to law all moneys which shall come to his hands as treasurer, and render a just and true account thereof to the board of supervisors, or to the comptroller of this State, when thereunto required. Such bond, with the approbation of the said board of supervisors, indorsed thereon by their clerk, shall be filed in the office of the county clerk.

By 1 R. S., p. 865, chap. 12, part 1, title 2, sec. 101 (sec. 29), the chamberlain of the city and county of New York is made the county treasurer thereof.

That chapter, article 2, prescribes the general duties of county treasurers. See 1 R. S., pages 863 to 865, 5th edition.

Laws of 1859, p. 411, the chamberlain is required to give a bond to the board of supervisors, with three sureties, in such sum as directed by the supervisors, &c.

PART III.

NOTES OF CASES RELATING TO THE SUBJECT OF TAXATION.

WHAT IS A TAX?

1. The word "taxes" means a contribution in *money*, not labor or personal service.

Overseers of Amenia, vs. Overseers of Stanford, 6 Johns. R. p. 92.

2. Taxes are burthens, charges, or impositions, set on persons or property, for public uses.

Matter of the Mayor, &c., of New York, 11 Johns. R. p. 77.

3. The distinction between a *tax* properly so called and an assessment, is stated and considered per Bronson J. in

Sharp vs. Speir, 4 Hill, page 76; and see matter of Mayor, &c., of New York, 11 Johns. R. p. 77.

4. Taxation exacts money from individuals as their share of a public burthen, and the tax-payer receives, or is supposed to receive, just compensation in the benefits conferred by government and in the proper application of the tax.

Taxation operates upon a community, or upon a class of

persons in a community, and according to some rule of apportionment.

The People, &c., vs. the Mayor, &c., of Brooklyn, 4 Comstock, p. 419, overruling the People, &c., vs. the Mayor, &c., of Brooklyn, 6 Barbour, p. 209; also reversing People vs. the Mayor of Brooklyn, 9 Barbour, p. 535.

NATURE AND EXTENT OF THE POWER OF TAXATION.

1. The taxing power of a State is one of its attributes of sovereignty—

And where there has been no compact with the Federal Government, or cession of jurisdiction for the purposes specified in the Constitution, this power reaches all the property and business within the State, which are not properly denominated the means of the general government.

Nathan vs. Louisiana, 8 Howard, U. S. R. p. 82, per McLean, J.

And see Providence Bank vs. Billings, 4 Peters R., p. 514.

McCullough vs. Maryland, 4 Wheaton, p. 429.

Mager vs. Grima, 8 Howard U. S. R., p. 493.

Dobbins vs. Commissioners of Erie Co., 16 Peters R., p. 435.

Catlin vs. Hull, 21 Vermont, p. 152.

See also, Thomas vs. Leland, 24 Wendell R., p. 69, remarks of Cowen, J.

2. The power to tax implies the power to *apportion*

the tax as the legislature shall see fit, and the power of apportionment has no limit where there is no constitutional restraint.

There is nothing in the constitution of this State which requires that taxation shall be general, so as to embrace all taxable persons within the State, or within any district or territorial division of the State, or that it shall be equal, as in the case of a capitation tax, or that it shall be in proportion to the value of the property of the persons taxed, or that it shall not be apportioned according to the benefit which each tax-payer is supposed to receive from the object on which the tax is expended.

The People, &c., vs. The Mayor, &c., of Brooklyn, 4 Comstock, p. 419 and 420.

3. A statute giving a municipal corporation the power to assess the owners and occupants of lands benefited by an improvement in proportion to the amount of such benefit, declared to be constitutional, and a proper exercise of the power of taxation vested in the State government.

Ib. overruling
The People, &c., vs. The Mayor, &c., of Brooklyn, 6 Barbour, p. 209. (*a*)

4. The legislature of this State has power to levy a tax upon the taxable property of a town, and appropriate the same to the payment of a claim made by an individual against the town.

The Town of Guilford vs. Supervisors of Chenango Co., 3 Kernan, p. 143.
Affirming same case, 18 Barbour, p. 615.

(*a*) In this case all the cases relative to assessments for local improvements are reviewed, and the distinction between the power of taxation and eminent domain, discussed and pointed out per Ruggles, J.

Neither is the statute imposing the tax void, although the claim had been rejected by the voters of the town when submitted to them at town meeting, under an act of the legislature, authorizing such submission, and declaring that their decision should be final and conclusive.

Ib.

5. A tax upon a particular business may be levied for the benefit of a public charity, and may be made payable directly to the persons having charge thereof—accordingly held,

The act of the legislature of the State of New York, passed February 21st, 1837, requiring the agent in the city of New York of any individual or association, not incorporated by the laws of this State, although incorporated by any other State or country, to pay an annual tax into the State treasury, as a condition to the right of effecting insurances against losses by fire, and the act subsequently passed, requiring, under a penalty, such payment to be made to the treasurer of the fire department, for the use and benefit thereof, were constitutional.

See Session Laws of 1837, chap. 30, p. 21.
The Fire Department vs. Noble, 3 E. D. Smith R., p. 440.
And see The Fire Department vs. Wright, 3 E. D. Smith R., p. 453.
The latter case affirmed in Court of Appeals, not reported. (*a*)

(*a*) The act of February 21, 1837, and the provisions of the Revised Statutes, sections 3, 4, 5, 6, 7, title 21, chap. 20, part 1, so far as they relate to fire insurance companies, were repealed by Laws of 1849, chap. 178, p. 239. The act of 1849, sections 1, 2, 3, and 4, so far as applicable 1 R. S., p. 714.

6. The power of the State to tax all property within its limits, whether real or personal, is unquestionable.

Wilson vs. The Mayor, &c., of New York, 4 E. D. Smith R., p. 675.

In the State of New York the constitution recognizes the existence of the power, but leaves to the legislature to determine upon what descriptions of persons and property, and in what ratio, the imposition shall be made.

Ib.

It would be competent for the legislature to tax the personal property owned within this State by non-residents.

Ib. (*a*)

7. A power to tax real and personal estate, according to law, authorizes the taxation of a species of property liable to taxation at the time of the assessment, although not taxable under the law when the power was granted.

Ontario Bank *vs.* Bunnell, 10 Wend., p. 186.

ACTION.

1. Where a collector of taxes voluntarily and without the request of defendant pays his tax, he cannot afterwards maintain an action against him for money so paid.

Overseers of Wallkill vs. Overseers of Mamakating, 14 Johns. R., p. 87.

And see Beach vs. Vandenbergh, 10 Johns. R. p. 361.

---

to New York, was repealed by Laws of 1857, chap. 548, vol. 2, p. 171, and the provisions of that act substituted for said sections. The act of 1857 was amended by Laws of 1858, chap. 255, p. 405.

See note to taxation on incorporated companies, ante, p. 156.

(*a*) This decision was rendered in July, 1854. In 1855 the Legislature passed an act taxing non-residents doing business in this State upon all sums of money invested in said business. Laws of 1855, chap. 37, p. 44.

See ante, p. 116, and Constitutional Law, post, p. 272.

2. A county treasurer refusing to pay money without cause, is liable to an action. County treasurer.

Boice vs. Russell, 2 Cowen, p. 444.

3. Where the illegality of an assessment and taxation of property appears upon the face of the warrant for the collection of a tax, trespass will lie against the collector who levies upon the property for the payment of such tax.

Bank of Utica vs. City of Utica, 4 Paige R., p. 399.

4. See Supervisors of Albany vs. Durant, 9 Paige R., p. 182.

AFFIDAVIT.

1. The applicant for a reduction of the assessed valuation of his personal estate, must make affidavit that the value of the personal estate owned by him, after deducting his just debts, &c., does not exceed a certain specified sum. The statute does not sanction a statement upon *belief.*

An affidavit presented by a *trustee* for the purpose of procuring a reduction of the assessment upon property held by him in trust, which merely states the value of each of the estates specified in the schedule annexed to such affidavit, and alleges that the statements are just and true, according to the best of the deponent's knowledge and belief, is defective. Trustee.

Such affidavit should specify the value of the property possessed by the applicant, or under his control by virtue of the trust, after deducting the just debts due from him, and the stock held by him in incorporated companies liable to taxation in that capacity.

People, &c., vs. Supervisors of Westchester, 15 Barbour, S. C. R., p. 608. (*a*)

AGENT.

Agent.

1. Where one is the agent of another for the sale of real estate in his vicinity, and for making contracts for sales, and for receiving the consideration agreed to be paid by the purchasers, and as such agent he has in his possession contracts for the lands, executed by his principal, who resides in another place, and by the several purchasers of the land, the amount owing by the purchasers upon such contracts, is not subject to taxation against the agent, as personal estate in his possession or under his control as such agent.

Lord vs. Arnold, 18 Barb., p. 104.

ASSESSMENTS.

1. The tax law prescribing that every person shall be assessed in the town or ward where he resides for all personal estate owned by him, including all personal estate in his possession as executor, &c., such last estate to be carried out separately, and assessed to the person in his representative character; and having provided for the correction of any errors that might occur, if a party neglects to avail himself of the mode of correction given by the act, he is concluded from questioning the assessment in any other manner.

(*a*) The section of the Revised Statutes referred to in this case relative to affidavits (15 and 16, 1 R. S., p. 392, 1st edition), are repealed by Laws of 1851, chap. 176, sec. 3, p. 333.

The regularity of the assessment cannot be impeached, in an action against the collector for a neglect of duty, by a plea that there were other executors who acted jointly with the person upon whom the tax was imposed.

Williams vs. Holden, 4 Wendell R., p. 223–4.

2. Where a person occupies one entire farm, and a division line between two adjoining towns passes through the same, such farm can be assessed for taxes only in the town where the owner or occupant resides, although the farm comprises portions of distinct lots, and such lots lie in different towns. The words *farm* and *lot*, as used in the act of 1823, in this particular are synonymous. Farm or lot

Saunders and others vs. Springsteen, 4 Wendell R. p. 429. (*a*)

3. A banking corporation, located in a village authorized by law to raise money by tax for certain purposes, is liable to pay its proportion of the village taxes, and its real and personal estate is accordingly subject to taxation. Banks.

Where such village taxes are directed to be assessed upon the freeholders and inhabitants of the village, according to law, a moneyed or stock corporation having its banking house or office for the transaction of business within the bounds of such village, is an inhabitant within the meaning of the act; and a conformity in the assessment to the general law on the subject of the assessment and collection of taxes, as it exists at the time of the assessment, is a compliance with the direction that it be made according to law; although the general law as it exists at Inhabitant.

(*a*) The provision of the act of 1823, is the same as 1 R. S., p. 908, sec. 4, 5th edition.

the time of the assessment, declares property subject to taxation, which according to universal usage was not deemed subject to tax under the general law as it existed at the time when the act was passed authorizing the assessment.

Assessment. Where a party justifies the taking of property to satisfy a village tax imposed upon a bank, it is no objection to the defense that the personal property of the bank was assessed at double its value; the remedy of the bank was to have applied to the assessors for a reduction of the assessment.

The Ontario Bank vs. Bunnell and others, 10 Wendell R., p. 186.

Accumulations. 4. In ascertaining the sum to be inserted in the assessment roll, no regard should be had either to accumulations or losses of capital in the course of the business of the company, but only to the amount of capital stock paid in and secured to be paid, after deducting expenditures for real estate, and such of the stock as the statute exempts from taxation. *(a)*

To entitle a corporation to have its name stricken from the assessment roll, pursuant to 1 R. S., chap. 416, sec. 9, the affidavit presented to the board of supervisors must show that the company is not in the receipt of *any* profits

---

(a) By Laws of 1851, chap. 456, sec. 3, vol. 2, p. 2, the surplus profits or reserved funds of every incorporated company exceeding ten per cent. of its capital, after deducting the assessed value of its real estate, and shares of stock in other corporations owned by such company which are taxable upon their capital stock, are to be assessed and taxed, &c.

These provisions are incorporated into the last edition of the Revised Statutes. See ante, p. 153.

or income; an affidavit showing that it is not in the receipt of any *net* profits or income is insufficient. *(a)*

The People vs. the Supervisors of Niagara, 4 Hill R., p. 20.

5. The fifth subdivision of section 12, of 1 R. S., p. 391, does not dispense, where the land to be assessed is a full lot, with the particularity required by the previous parts of the section in the designation of the lands of non-residents; it relates simply to the description of the quantity of land assessed, providing that if such quantity be a full lot, the designation of the lot is sufficient; otherwise, the quantity must be designated by boundaries, or in some other way, by which it may be known.

Sec. 12, 1 R. S., p. 910, 5th ed. See ante, p. 127.

The same as to the second subdivision of that section.

Hubbell vs. Weldon and Weldon, Lalor's sup. to Hill and Denio, p. 139.

Unoccupied land.

6. In order to take a person's unoccupied land from him, for the non-payment of a tax, the law requires that if the township, patent, or tract of which it is a part, has been subdivided into lots, such land shall be assessed by the *number* of the lot, if that can be ascertained.

Dike and others vs. Lewis, 2 Barbour, p. 344.

Lot assessed by wrong number

If assessors assess a lot belonging to a non-resident, by a *wrong number*, and it is advertised and sold by such wrong number, the rights of the owner will not be defeated by the sale; nor will any title pass to the purchaser by the comptroller's deed.

Ib.

(a) The provisions of the Revised Statutes above referred to were amended by Laws of 1853, chap. 654, p. 1240, and as thus amended were repealed by Laws of 1857, chap. 456, vol. 2, p. 1, sec. 1.

Lot No. of. assessment roll, correction of by supervisors.

7. After an assessment roll has been delivered to the board of supervisors, at their annual meeting, and been finally acted upon by them, and a warrant has been issued to the collector of the town, with a copy of the assessment roll annexed, commanding him to collect the taxes apportioned according to such roll, the roll has passed from the jurisdiction of the supervisors, and they have not the power to correct it.

The People vs. Supervisors of Westchester, 15 Barbour, p. 608.

Non-resident lands.

8. An assessment for taxes of non-resident lands, is fatally defective, if it contain such a falsity in the description of the parcel assessed, as might probably mislead the owner, and prevent him from ascertaining, by the published notices, that his land was to be sold or redeemed.

Description.

Tallman vs. White, 2 Comst., p. 66, per Ruggles, J.

Ib.

Where a lot of land, intended to be assessed, is part of a tract which has a known name, and the assessment describes the lot as situated in a different tract, a comptroller's deed, given upon a sale for non-payment of the tax, is void; although there be other matter of description which, if the name of the tract were rejected, would sufficiently identify the lot.

Ib.

ASSESSORS—Liabilities of.

1. The duty of assessors in determining the value of taxable property (where such value is not sworn to as authorized by law), is in its nature judicial.

Weaver vs. Devendorf, 3 Denio R., p. 117.

A public officer is not responsible in a civil suit for a judicial determination in a matter over which he had jurisdiction, however erroneous it may be, or however malicious the motive which produced it. Public officer.

Accordingly held,

That an action could not be maintained against the assessor of a town for refusing to give the plaintiff, who was a taxable inhabitant, the benefit of the exemption allowed by law, on account of his being a minister of the Gospel, or for assessing his property at a higher rate than that at which they assessed the property of other inhabitants, though the conduct of the defendant was alleged to be willful and corrupt. Minister.

Ib.

2. As to liability of assessors for penalty imposed by statute, see

Spafford vs. Hood, 6 Cowen, p. 478.

3. In order to enable a minister of the Gospel to maintain an action against assessors, for assessing his property and thereby subjecting him to the payment of taxes, he must show affirmatively—1. That he is a minister of the Gospel, or priest of some denomination; and, 2. That the value of both his real and personal property does not exceed $1,500. Minister or priest.

Assessors have no authority to enter upon the assessment roll the name of any person whose property is by law exempt from taxation, nor to impose an assessment thereon. They have no jurisdiction whatever over such persons, or their property. Nor can they acquire any, by any act or decision of their own.

Accordingly *held*,

Minister or priest. That assessors have no jurisdiction over the person or the property of a minister of the Gospel not having real and personal estate exceeding the value of $1,500; which will authorize them to impose an assessment upon his property.

Assessment. The assessment of property is a judicial act, upon which a certiorari will lie. But, to make an assessment legal, the Certiorari. assessors must have jurisdiction of the particular case. If they transcend the limits of their authority, and undertake to assess property exempt by statute, they cease to be judges, and are responsible for all the consequences.

In determining whether they have jurisdiction or not, in a given case, assessors do not act judicially.

Jurisdiction. No officer can acquire jurisdiction by deciding that he has it. In all such cases, every officer, whether judicial or ministerial, decides at his peril.

Per Johnson, P. J. Prosser vs. Secor, 5 Barbour, pp. 607–8.

And see 19 Barbour, p. 22.
24 Barbour, p. 419.
15 N. Y. Reports, 1 Smith, p. 316.

Real estate. 4. The only facts necessary to the jurisdiction of assessors are, in reference to real estate, that it be situate in the Personal estate. town or ward, and in reference to personal property, that the owner be an inhabitant of the town or ward.

Jurisdiction. If lands assessed are situated within the town in which the assessors reside, the assessors have jurisdiction of the subject matter. And in making an assessment upon such lands, they perform a judicial act, in a matter within the limit of their authority.

However much assessors may have erred in the performance of their duty, yet having jurisdiction of the subject matter, their error may be corrected, in a court of review, but will not render their proceedings void.

Occupied lands, which are owned by persons who are not residents of the town or ward where they are situated, are liable to taxation. And the legislature having omitted to prescribe the manner in which the assessment of such lands shall be made, it is proper for the assessors to specify who is the occupant, as well as the name of the owner. Occupied lands owned by non-residents. How assessed.

Either would be a sufficient compliance with the law. They may regard the occupant as owner, and assess the lands as owned by a resident of the town; or they may, without noticing the occupant, assess them as the lands of a non-resident owner.

Van Rensselaer vs. Cottrell, 7 Barbour, p. 127. Affirmed by Court of Appeals, Dec. 1852. Not reported.

5. Assessors are not liable, in a civil action, for assessing property which is by law exempt from taxation.

For all the purposes of the assessment, assessors have *jurisdiction* over all the inhabitants of their town. The inquiry which they are required by the statute to make, preparatory to their assessment, is a *judicial act;* and no action can be maintained against them for any error which they may commit in the performance of their duty. Jurisdiction. Action.

Vail vs. Owen, 19 Barbour, p. 22.
And see Prosser vs. Secor, 5 Barbour, p. 608.

6. In determining the question as to the residence of a person owning real estate subject to taxation, assessors act Assessors.

judicially; and when acting judicially, within the scope of their authority, they are not liable to an action, although they err.

Accordingly, where the plaintiff's farm lay partly in the county of Otsego, and partly in the county of Herkimer, his residence being in the latter county, and the defendants, assessors of a town in Otsego county, assessed the whole of the farm to him in that county, and upon a warrant issued for the collection of a tax, the plaintiff's property was taken and sold; it *was held*, that no action would lie against the defendants for such erroneous assessment.

Action.

Brown vs. Smith, 24 Barbour, pp. 419–20.
And see Prosser vs. Secor, 5 Barbour, p. 608.

Jurisdiction. Non-resident.

7. Assessors have not jurisdiction to assess a person for his personal estate, where he is not a resident of their town at the time when the assessment is made.

One assessor cannot make the assessment; it must be made by all the assessors, or by a majority of them, upon a meeting of all.

And where one of the assessors, while engaged in ascertaining the names of the taxable inhabitants, and the taxable property, called in May upon a person then a resident of the town, and made an entry of his name and the value of his taxable personal estate at $10,000, and so informed him, and such person soon thereafter removed to another county; and afterwards, and in July, the assessors prepared and completed the assessment roll, in which he was assessed for personal property to the value of $10,000; *held*, that the assessment was not made till July, and that the assessors had no jurisdiction to make it.

Where, on such an assessment, the board of supervisors of the county impose a tax upon the party, which is collected by a seizure and sale of his property upon their warrant issued to the collector, the assessors are liable to him in an action for the amount of the tax and expenses of collection. Action.

But in such a case the supervisors cannot be compelled by writ of mandamus to audit and allow to the person, thus wrongfully assessed, the amount of the tax collected from him, and direct it to be levied upon the town or county. Supervisors. Mandamus.

People, &c., ex rel. Mygatt vs. Supervisors of Chenango County, 1 Kernan R., p. 563.

Assessors who enter upon their assessment roll as liable to be taxed for personal property, the name of a person not a resident of their town or ward at the time the assessment is made, act without jurisdiction, and are liable for the damages resulting from the collection of a tax founded on such entry. Jurisdiction.

The words of the statute, "the time the assessment is made," relate to the binding and conclusive act of the board of assessors, which designates the tax-payers and the amount of taxable property. Assessment, when complete.

It seems, that this time is the first day of July, the assessors being required to complete their preparatory inquiries in the months of May and June. Per Denio, Chief J.

Mygatt vs. Washburn, 15 N. Y. Reports, 1 Smith, p. 316.

See Wilson vs. Mayor, &c., of N. Y., 4 E. D. Smith C. P. R., p. 675.

Prosser vs. Secor, 5 Barbour, pp. 607–8.

Weaver vs. Devendorf, 3 Denio, p. 117.

Vail vs. Owen, 19 Barbour, p. 22.

Brown vs. Smith, 24 Barbour, p. 419.

ASSESSORS—Duty of.

Affidavit to reduce assessment.

1. When an affidavit is presented to the assessors by the owner of rents subjected to taxation, for the purpose of reducing the amount of the tax, it is their duty to correct the assessment, in accordance with such affidavit. They should pursue strictly the directions contained in the 15th section of the article of the Revised Statutes.

The assessors have no discretion to reject such an affidavit, when tendered by the person assessed. They are bound to receive it, and to strike out the assessment accordingly.

If assessors, in estimating the value of annual wheat rents, commit an error to the prejudice of the owner by estimating wheat at a greater sum per bushel than it is worth, the supreme court has no jurisdiction to review it. The assessors act judicially, and if their judgment be honestly exercised, it is conclusive upon all interested, except so far as the affidavit of the owner of the rents may serve to correct it. (*a*)

Livingston vs. Hollenbeck, 4 Barbour, pp. 9 and 10.

Correction of assessment roll.

2. Assessors have the power to correct an assessment (except to increase an estimate of property, after the roll has been deposited with one of their number for inspection) at any time before their roll is delivered to the supervisor.

Affidavit, how sworn to.

An affidavit presented to assessors, for the purpose of procuring a reduction of an assessment, can only be sworn to before the assessors, or one of them.

(*a*) See note *a*, next page.

A justice of the peace has no authority to administer an oath in such a case.

When assessors have deposited a copy of the assessment roll with one of their number, and given public notice that they have done so, and that they will meet at a specified time and place to review their assessments, and a person complaining of the assessment in respect to his property, fails to produce at that time his affidavit or other proof, showing that his property has been over-estimated, but subsequently, and before the assessors have delivered the assessment rolls to the supervisor, such person produces to the assessors affidavits which are not in conformity with the statute, it is not compulsory upon the assessors to reduce the assessment. When to be produced to assessors.

They have at least a discretion on the subject, and with the exercise and result of that discretion, the supreme court will not interfere. *(a)*

The People &c., vs. Supervisors of Westchester, 15 Barbour, p. 608.

3. It is the duty of assessors to estimate and assess that section of a railroad which lies within their town, at its full and true value. In ascertaining this value, the superstructure and fixtures, and every thing annexed to the land, is to be taken into the account. But whether the stock of the Railroads how assessed.

(*a*) By laws of 1851, chap. 176, the 15th section of title 2, of part 1, of chap. 13, of the Revised Statutes, which rendered it compulsory upon the assessors to reduce an assessment upon an affidavit presented by the party assessed, at any time before the completion of their assessment, showing that the assessment was greater than the actual value of his real estate, &c., was repealed. For the mode and manner of applying to the assessors to reduce an assessment, and for the duty of the assessors upon such application, see *§ 21, 1 R. S., 912, 5th ed. Ante, pp. 130–132.

This case arose before the amendment of 1851.

company is above or below par, or whether the business of the road is productive or unproductive, are questions with which the assessors have nothing to do.

So long as the assessors confine themselves within the above rule, however grossly they may err in their estimate, their valuation is conclusive. Like the verdict of a jury, the amount is not to be questioned.

The tax based upon the assessment is like a judicial sentence, and can only be attacked for fraud or an excess of jurisdiction.

Railroads how assessed. But when assessors, after estimating and assessing that part of a railroad lying within their town, with the superstructure and erections thereon, at its full and true value, proceed to add any thing to the valuation, by reason of the increased cost of the road, or on account of its income or productiveness, so far as they transcend their authority, their act is void.

Where the property assessed is a railroad, the omission of the assessors to state the number of acres of land assessed to the company in their town, is not such a defect in their proceedings as to deprive them of jurisdiction.

In such a case, *it seems* the requirement of the statute will be complied with, by stating the number of miles of road, without adding the *quantity* of land.

Albany and West Stockbridge R. R. Co. vs. Town of Canaan, 16 Barbour, p. 244.

Certificate. 4. Where a statute prescribes the form of a certificate to be signed by the assessors, and attached to their assessment roll, a substantial compliance with its terms is Jurisdiction. necessary to give jurisdiction to the board of supervisors to impose a tax and issue their warrant to the collector thereon.

The warrant to the collector consisting in part of the assessment roll, of which the proper certificate is a necessary element, the want of the latter is a defect apparent upon its face, and renders the process no protection to the officer. Warrant. Officer.

Van Rensselaer vs. Witbeck and Sharp, 3 Selden R., p. 517.

5. The assessors and collector are not in any legal sense the agents of the town, in its corporate capacity, in the assessment and collection of taxes, and the town is not responsible for any mistake or misfeasance by them in the performance of their duties. Agent.

Accordingly, where land not situate within the town, but in an adjoining county, was erroneously assessed by the assessors, and payment of the tax by the owner enforced by the collector of the town; *held*, that the town was not liable in an action by the owner to recover the amount of the tax. Town.

Lorillard vs. The Town of Monroe, 1 Kernan R., p. 392.

Affirming the same case, 12 Barbour, p. 161.

ASSOCIATIONS.

1. Associations formed under the *general banking law* of this State are *corporations*, and as such liable like other moneyed institutions to be taxed on all lands and personal estate owned by them. Corporations.

Exparte, The Bank of Watertown vs. The Assessors of the Village of Watertown, 25 Wendell R., p. 686.

Corporations. 2. Associations formed under the general banking law are *corporations*, and as such liable to taxation on their capital.

The People, &c., vs. Watertown, 1 Hill, p. 616.

Ib. 3. The constitution of this State, § 1, art. 8, declares that *corporations* may be formed under general laws, and by section 3, it is declared that the term "corporations," as used in this article, shall be construed to include all *associations* or *joint stock companies* having *any* of the *powers* or *privileges not possessed by individuals or partnerships*. The legislature, in 1849 and 1854, passed laws authorizing generally the formation of associations or joint stock companies under this provision of the constitution. [Laws of 1849, p. 390. Laws of 1854, p. 558.] These acts conferred on the associations thus formed many powers and privileges not possessed by individuals or partnerships. But the act of 1854 declares that that act should not be construed to give such association any rights and privileges as corporations. *Held*, that these joint stock associations were, nevertheless, corporations within the meaning of the constitution, and as such liable to taxation on their capital.

Edward S. Sandford, Prest. Am. and European Joint Stock Express Co. vs. The Board of Supervisors of N. Y., 15 How. P. R., p. 172.

And see the People vs. Suprs. of Niagara, 4 Hill, p. 20.

Same case affirmed, 7 Hill, p. 504.

BANKS AND BANKERS.

Individual banker, how assessed. 1. An individual banker, doing business under the general banking law of this State, who assumes a special name by which his business as banker is characterized and known, may be assessed by that name, and the warrant for the collection of the tax, issued against such name, may be levied upon the money or property used in the business of such banker.

Officer

Process.

The question whether such banker was taxable in the town or ward in which the assessment was made, cannot be raised to affect the validity of process regular on its face, against the officer executing it; nor—where the process is against an individual bank, by the name in which it does business, which name is apparently that of a corporation, and such bank has a place of business within the jurisdiction of the assessors, and of the officer executing the process—can its owner be permitted, as against the officer levying on the money or property of the bank, to claim that it is not a lawful corporation, and not taxable by its apparently corporate name.

Patchin vs. Ritter, 27 Barb., p. 34.

2. A *bank* located in a village, may be assessed for a *village tax* voted previous to the bank going into operation, if, before the *assessment* be made, the bank is deriving an income from its capital stock.

Oswego Bank vs. Oswego Village, 12 Wendell R., p. 544.

BOARDING-SCHOOLS.

1 R. S., 906, 5th ed., § 5 and *§ 6. Ante, p. 118.

1. A building erected for the use of and occupied as a private boarding-school, is not exempt from taxation by the statute [1 R. S., 388, § 4] exempting every school-house and every building erected for the use of a college, incorporated academy, or other seminary of learning.

The school-houses referred to in this statute, are those used for the public common schools.

Buildings erected and used for private unincorporated seminaries of learning, are not exempt from taxation.

The dictum of Ruggles, J., in Chegaray vs. Jenkins [1 Seld., 376], overruled.

Chegaray vs. The Mayor, &c., of New York, 3 Kernan, p. 220.
Reversing, 2 Duer, p. 521.

2. The act of April 6, 1825, respecting the collection of taxes in the city of New York, which declared or limited the meaning of the act for the assessment and collection of taxes, passed on the 23d of April, 1823, by providing that "the exemption from taxation of any building for public worship, or any school, under and by virtue of the third section of the act of 23d of April, 1823, shall not extend or apply to any such building or premises in the said city, unless the same shall be exclusively used for such purposes, and exclusively the property of a religious society, or the New York free school society," is still in force, and was not affected by the general repealing act. [3 R. S., 165, sec. 398, 1st ed.]

Premises in the city of New York, occupied by the lessee as a boarding and day-school for young ladies, are liable to taxation, and are not exempted therefrom by the provisions of the Revised Statutes. [1 R. S., 387, sec. 4.] (*a*)

Chegaray vs. Jenkins, 3 Sandford S. C. R., p. 409.

(*a*) This case was affirmed in the Court of Appeals on the ground that the defendant, being a constable, was protected by the warrant issued by the receiver of taxes in levying upon the goods and chattels of the plaintiff. There

CAPITAL.

1. A moneyed corporation liable to taxation on its capital, is to be assessed upon the whole *nominal amount* paid in and secured to be paid, after deducting expenditures for real estate, and such of the stock as the statute exempts. Assessment of capital of moneyed corporations.

No deduction is to be made for losses of capital sustained by the corporation, nor for debts due from it.

Nor can a deduction be made for such part of its capital as is invested in the stock of other corporations liable to taxation. Semble. (*a*)

Farmers' Loan and Trust Co. vs. Mayor, &c., of New York, 7 Hill R., p. 261.

2. Mutual insurance companies are liable to taxation on their capital, the same as other moneyed corporations. Mutual insurance companies.

Such capital consists, in the first instance, of such amount of premiums as, by their act of incorporation, they are required to have subscribed before commencing business, and afterwards, of such sums as they may accumulate from premiums earned, and other sources of profits, and which are used by them as capital in the business of insurance. (*b*) Capital of.

Sun Mutual Ins. Co. vs. The Mayor, &c., of New York, 8 Barb., p. 450.

---

was a dictum of Ruggles, C. J., that the exemption in the Revised Statutes applied to all school-houses, whether used for public or private schools. This dictum was overruled in Chegaray vs. The Mayor, &c., of New York, 3 Kernan, p. 220, and the decision in the Supreme Court approved. Ante, pp. 117 and 174, 175, 265.

(*a*) By Laws of 1857, vol. 2, chap. 456, sec. 3, shares of stock of companies which are taxable under the laws of this State on their capital stock, owned by another company, are to be deducted from the assessment on the surplus profits, &c., of the company owning such stock. Ante, p. 153.

(*b*) By Laws of 1857, chap. 456, vol. 2, p. 2, sec. 4, the accumulation on life insurance companies, so far as the said accumulations are held for the exclusive benefit of the assured, are exempt from taxation. Ante, p. 153.

Mutual insurance companies. Premium notes.

3. The deposit or premium notes of a mutual insurance company constitute its capital stock; and if the company becomes insolvent, and a receiver is appointed, it is his duty to proceed and collect the amounts due upon such notes, as capital stock, unless he is excused from so doing, by an order of the Court.

Van Buren, Att'y Gen'l, vs. Chenango Mut. Ins. Co., 12 Barb., p. 671.

Mutual life insurance companies.

4. Mutual life insurance companies, incorporated previous to the year 1849, are liable to taxation upon their accumulations, as capital.

Tax commissioners.

And where a company of that description, having a fund, employed in its business, amounting to nearly three millions of dollars, was taxed by the assessors upon only $100,000 of personal property, it *was held* that the tax commissioners, on reviewing the assessment roll, had the power to add $900,000 thereto, making the amount of personal property belonging to the company, liable to taxation, one million of dollars, and that the board of supervisors was right in refusing to restore the original assessment, and in confirming the judgment of the commissioners.

Mandamus.

A judgment, entered at a special term, denying an application for a *mandamus*, to compel the board of supervisors to restore or reduce the assessment to the sum of $100,000, and to apportion or fix the tax upon that amount, instead of one million of dollars, and to correct the tax accordingly, was therefore affirmed. (a)

People, &c., ex rel. Mut. Life Ins. Co. of N. Y. vs.

(a) But see Laws of 1857, vol. 2, p. 2, chap. 456, sec. 3. Ante, p. 153.

Bd. of Suprs. of the City and County of N. Y., 20 Barb., p. 81.

Affirmed, 16 N. Y. Reports (2 Smith), p. 424. See post, p. 271.

5. The Buffalo Mutual Insurance Company, a corporation, possessed a fund of $100,000, arising from premiums earned upon fire and marine policies of insurance, which was invested pursuant to an authority contained in the charter, in bonds, mortgages, and stocks, so as to yield an income to be divided among the members; but the company had no other capital or effects. This fund could not, according to the charter, be withdrawn and divided among the members. *Held*, that the corporation was liable to taxation on account of such fund as capital.

Such a corporation is a "moneyed or stock corporation, Capital.
deriving an income or profit from its capital, or otherwise," within the meaning of the statute concerning the assessment of taxes on incorporated companies.

Money paid in as premiums to an insurance company, Ib.
not liable to be withdrawn and divided, but forming the basis of its business operations, is capital, and as such is liable to taxation.

But surplus earnings or profits, over and above the amount retained as permanent capital, *it seems*, are not liable to be taxed. (a)

Mut. Ins. Co. of Buffalo vs. Suprs. of Erie Co., 4 Comstock R., p. 442.

(a) By Laws of 1857, vol. 2, p. 2, ch. 456, sec. 3, surplus profits and reserved funds of incorporated companies exceeding ten per cent. of their capital, after deducting the value of their real estate, &c., are subject to taxation. Ante, p. 153.

Accumulations

6. Where a mutual insurance company is authorized to accumulate from its profits a fund to continue liable for its losses during the term of its existence, and to issue certificates to its members setting forth their interest therein, the accumulation becomes capital, and the certificates do not represent a debt, but the interest of the members in the capital. *(a)*

Such a company is liable to taxation upon the capital so accumulated.

Sun Mut. Ins. Co. vs. Mayor, &c. of N. Y., 4 Selden R., p. 241.

Mutual life insurance companies.

7. A mutual life insurance company was authorized by its charter to accumulate, from premiums received and from the profits of their investment, a fund to continue liable for its losses during the term of its existence. The representatives of each person insured are entitled to receive from such fund the amount for which his life was originally insured, and a proportionate share of all the profits of the company accumulated during the duration of the policy. *Held*, that the accumulation of premiums and profits made by the company, is capital, within the provisions of the Revised Statutes [1 R. S., p. 414, sec. 1], for taxing corporations.

Accumulations.

1 R. S., 5th ed., p. 944

The act of June 29, 1853 (ch. 469), providing that such company should be subject to taxation in the same manner as if incorporated under the general law for the incorporation of insurance companies, with a capital of $100,000, brought it into the category of ordinary moneyed corporations, subject to any changes in the general law relating to taxation, and consequently liable to be assessed, under the

---

(a) But see Laws of 1857, vol. 2, p. 2, ch. 456, sec. 3. Ante, p. 153.

act of July 21, 1853 (ch. 654), for the amount of all surplus profits or reserved funds exceeding ten per cent. of its capital, in addition to its capital, as fixed at $100,000.

The act of March 24, 1855 (chap. 83), declaring it to have been the intention and the true construction of the act of June 29, 1853 (chap. 469), that the life insurance companies therein mentioned should be subject to taxation in the sum of $100,000, "and no more," introduces a new rule for the taxation of such companies after the passage of the declaratory act, but is ineffectual in regard to the interpretation of the prior acts in controversies pending the courts. The legislature has no judicial authority, and cannot control the courts in respect to the construction of statutes in cases arising before the declaratory statute. Construction of statute.

People, &c., ex rel. Mut. Life Ins. Co. of New York vs. Suprs. of New York.
16 New York Reports (2 Smith), pp. 424–5.
See ante, p. 149.

CONSTITUTIONAL LAW.

1. An act of the legislature imposing a tax upon a *local* district of the State, in reference to a public improvement, such as a canal, is *valid* and *constitutional*, notwithstanding that previous to the passage of such act, a number of individuals of such district had entered into a *bond* to the State, by which they bound themselves to pay the whole expense of the improvement.

Thomas vs. Leland, 24 Wendell R., p. 65.

2. The act of the legislature "to equalize taxation," passed May 13, 1846, is not unconstitutional.

Livingston vs. Hollenbeck, 4 Barb., p. 10.
Le Couteulx vs. Suprs. of Erie Co., 7 Barb., p. 249.
Approved in Le Couteulx vs. City of Buffalo, 1 Smith, 15 New York R., p. 451.

Act to apportion taxes, &c.

3. The act (chap. 327 of 1855) "to provide for the due apportionment of taxes and assessments, and for the sale of real and personal estate to pay the same," is constitutional; and a sale under it, by the judgment of the supreme court, in an action to which all persons having vested estates at law or in equity are made parties, or are proceeded against, by the publication of notice, as unknown owners, cuts off estates contingent or vested, including the possible interests which might, under contingent limitations, vest in persons not yet in being, as well as vested estates, and transfers to the purchaser a fee simple absolute.

Jackson vs. Babcock, 16 New York Reports (2 Smith), p. 246.

See ante, pp. 165-6.

Constitutional law.

Non-residents.

4. The act of 1855 (chap. 37, p. 44, Laws 1855), providing that non-residents "doing business in this State as merchants, bankers, or otherwise," &c., shall be assessed and taxed on all sums invested in their business, the same as if they were residents of the State, is not repugnant to any of the provisions of the Constitution of the United States.

Injunction.

An injunction to restrain the receiver of taxes of the city and county of New York from collecting the taxes imposed upon the capital invested by the plaintiff in the firm of James G. King & Sons, bankers, in the city of New

York, the plaintiff being a resident of the State of New Jersey, was therefore denied.

Denning Duer vs. Wilson Small, Receiver of Taxes. United States Circuit Court, Feb. 1859. Per Ingersoll, J.

17 Howard P. R., p. 201.

5. The act of April 12, 1855, imposing a State tax of a mill and a quarter on each dollar of the valuation of real and personal property, taxable in this State [Laws of 1855, p. 611], was valid and constitutional.

The direction in that act, that the money raised shall "be paid into the treasury of the State, to the credit of the *general fund*," is a sufficient statement of the *object to which the tax is to be applied*, within art. 6, sec. 13, of the constitution.

People, &c., ex rel. Burrows, Compt., vs. Supervisors of Orange Co., 27 Barbour, p. 575.

CORPORATION.

1. A corporation is liable to be rated and taxed as a person or inhabitant within the meaning of the statute. Person or inhabitant.

People vs. The Utica Insurance Co., 15 Johnson, 382.

And see State of Indiana vs. Woram, 6 Hill, p. 33, per Bronson, J.

2. Moneyed or stock corporations, deriving an income or profit from their capital, *are liable to taxation*, although

the *income* be not equal to the *expenditures* of such companies for the twelve months preceding the taxation.

The People, ex rel. The Commercial Insurance Co. of the city of New York vs. The Supervisors of the city and county of New York, 18 Wendell, p. 605.

Affidavit. 3. To entitle a corporation to have its name stricken from the assessment roll, pursuant to 1 R. S., 416, sec. 9, the affidavit presented to the board of supervisors must show that the company is not in the receipt of *any* profits or income; an affidavit showing that it is not in the receipt of any *net* profits or income is insufficient. Semble. (a)

The Supervisors of Niagara vs. The People, 7 Hill, p. 504.

Railroads. 4. Railroad companies are not taxed upon their *capital*, but upon the valuation of their *real estate* in the several towns through which the road passes; and, *semble*, they are liable to be so taxed, though not in the receipt of any profits or income. Per Bronson, J.

The People vs. The Board of Supervisors of Niagara, 4 Hill, 20.

See 4 Paige, 384, post, p. 275.

Ib. 5. The real estate of a railroad company liable to taxation, must be assessed in each town at the actual value merely, of that part thereof which lies within the said town, detached from the remainder of the road, and without reference to the income or profitableness of the road.

(a) Sec. 9, above referred to, was amended by laws of 1853, chap. 654, p. 1240; and, as amended, was repealed by laws of 1857, chap. 456, vol. 2, p. 1, sec. 1.

Such property is to be appraised in the same manner as the adjacent lands belonging to individuals.

The Albany and Schenectady R. R. Co. vs. Osborn and others, 12 Barbour, 223.

6. A railroad corporation is not liable to taxation upon its capital, as personal estate, for that part thereof which is vested in the lands over which the road runs, and in the railways and other fixtures connected therewith; but that part of the corporate property is to be taxed in the several towns and wards in which the same is situated, as real estate, and at its actual value, at the time of the assessment thereof. Railroads.

The capital stock of a railroad corporation which is not invested in its railways or other real estate, is to be taxed as personal property, in the town or ward where the principal office or place for transacting the financial concerns of the company is situate.

Injunction.

Where the president of a railroad corporation furnished the statement, required by the statute, to be delivered to the assessors of the town in which the corporation was liable to be taxed upon its capital, but by a mistake as to the law, omitted to deduct as a part of the real estate of the corporation, that portion of its capital which was invested in the railways and other fixtures, and the corporation was assessed and taxed in that town, in conformity with such statement, the court of chancery refused to restrain the collection of the tax.

The Mohawk and Hudson R. R. Co. vs. Clute and others, 4 Paige, 384–5.

7. A corporation which is liable to taxation upon its capital, cannot be taxed for its surplus profits remaining Surplus profits.

on hand and undivided. It can only be taxed for so much of its capital stock paid in, or secured, as will remain after deducting therefrom the actual cost of the real estate of the company. (*a*)

The Bank of Utica vs. The City of Utica, 4 Paige, 399.

8. The estate of a corporation which is taxable as personal property, is only that portion of its capital which is not invested in real estate. But the capital of a corporation embraces the whole of its stock paid in, or secured to be paid, whether it is invested in real or personal property.

The principle of the Revised Statutes in regard to the taxation of corporations is, to tax the real estate of each corporation, except as to canal, turnpike, and bridge companies, at its *actual* value, for the benefit of the inhabitants of the town and county where it is situated, in the same manner as the property of individuals is taxed; and to tax the residue of its capital, after deducting the *cost* of its real estate, as personal property, for the benefit of the inhabitants of the town and county where the financial concerns of the corporation are carried on. (*b*)

The Utica Cotton Manufacturing Co. vs. the Supervisors of Oneida Co., 1 Barbour, Ch. R., 432.

Foreign life and health insurance companies.

9. By section 15 of the act entitled "An act to provide for the incorporation of life and health insurance compa-

(*a*) But see laws of 1857, vol. 2, p. 2, chap. 456, sec. 3. Ante, p. 153.

(*b*) Sections 7, 11, 12, and 13, of 1 R. S., p. 417, 1st ed., referring to the exemption of turnpike, bridge, &c., companies, were repealed by laws of 1853, chap. 654, p. 1240.

The residue of this case refers to the manner of making application under the 9th section of the 4th article of chap. 13, part 1, of the Revised Statutes; that section was repealed by laws of 1857, vol. 2, p. 1, and that part of the case is therefore omitted.

nies, and in relation to the agencies of such companies," passed June 24, 1853, laws of 1853, chap. 463, it is provided, that any company organized under the laws of any foreign government is authorized to do business within this State, upon depositing with the comptroller of this State, for the benefit of the policy holders of such company, citizens or residents of the United States, securities to the amount of one hundred thousand dollars, of the kind required by section 6 of that act, for similar companies of this State, and upon appointing an attorney in this State representing the company, upon whom all legal process can be served.

By laws of 1855, chap. 37, it is provided, that "*all persons* and associations doing business in the State of New York, *as merchants, bankers, or otherwise, either as principals or partners, whether special or otherwise, and not residents of this State, shall be assessed and taxed on all sums invested in any manner in said business, the same as if they were residents of this State;* and said taxes shall be collected from the property of the firms, persons, or associations, to which they severally belong." See ante, p. 116.

Persons.

Non-residents.

Associations.

Two foreign life insurance companies complied with the provisions of the act of 1853, and deposited with the comptroller of the State, each the sum of $100,000 in the securities required by the act, and each established an agency for the transaction of business in the city of New York.

Of the sum deposited by one of the companies, $50,000 was invested in stocks of the United States.

Corporations.

The commissioners of taxes and assessments assessed each of the companies for the year 1858, in the sum of $100,000, as liable to taxation, on that amount of personal property.

Upon a certiorari obtained under the 24th section of the act of April 16, 1857, laws of 1857, chap. 677, to review such assessment,

Capital. *Held*, That the $100,000 thus deposited with the comptroller, was capital within the meaning of the Revised Statutes, in reference to taxation on corporations.

1 R. S., p. 944, 5th ed Ante, p. 149.

Act of 1855 construed. That the language of the act of 1855, in reference to the taxation of non-residents doing business in this State, was sufficiently comprehensive to embrace corporations, and that the $100,000 in stock deposited with the comptrollor, was invested in the business of the companies in this State.

U. S. stock not taxable. That the $50,000 in United States stocks was not, however, liable to taxation.

The assessment of the tax commissioners on that sum, was therefore reversed, and as to the residue, affirmed.

[The case of the People vs. Utica Insurance Co., 15 Johns. p. 258. Affirmed.]

General term, December 31, 1858, Davies, P. J., Clerke and Mullen, JJ.

The People ex rel. The International Insurance Co. vs. Commissioners of Taxes.

The People ex. rel. British Commercial Life Insurance Co. vs. the same.

17 Howard P. R., p. 206.

Laws of 1849, p. 441, chap. 308. Mutual insurance companies. 10. The premium notes required by the fifth section of the act of April 10, 1849, "to provide for the incorporation of insurance companies," to be received by mutual marine and fire insurance companies, in the county of

New York or Kings, before commencing business, although not payable until within twelve months from the date thereof, are the main capital of such companies under such act, and the cash capital which may be raised under the 21st section of said act, is additional capital merely.

Premium notes. Capital. Corporation.

Such companies are, therefore, liable to assessment and taxation upon such premium notes as capital, under the provisions of the Revised Statutes.

N. Y. City Insurance Co. vs. Mayor, &c., of N. Y., June, 1854, per Hoffman, J. Not reported. (*a*)

COUNTY TREASURER.

1. Interest runs on arrears of taxes owing by a county to a State, to be calculated after thirty days from the time when the account current is made up and rendered by the Comptroller, pursuant to the statute. [Sess. 38, chap. 29, sec. 4.]

Interest.

The People vs. County of New York, 5 Cowen, p. 331. (*b*)

2. A county treasurer is chargeable with interest on all sums in his hands, which he omits to account for at the annual meeting of the supervisors of his county.

(*a*) This case was affirmed both by the general term of the Superior Court and by the Court of Appeals, but no opinion was written in either court, that I have been able to discover.

(*b*) 1 R. S., vol. 1, p. 926, 5th edition. Comptroller is to state accounts to several county treasurers on the 1st of May of every year, and whenever any part of a State tax shall appear to be unpaid by any county treasurer, the comptroller shall transmit by mail to such county treasurer a copy of his account, requiring him to pay the balance within thirty days.

This section does not apply to New York.

See 1 R. S., p. 939, sec. 127, 5th edition.

Commissions. A county treasurer is not entitled to *commissions* on moneys *not* received by him, as on *collectors' fees* retained by the collectors, *bad taxes*, and taxes levied on *non-residents'* lands returned to the comptroller's office.

Supervisors of Chenango vs. Birdsall, 4 Wendell R. p. 453. (*a*)

DISTRESS.

1. A town collector may seize, not only the goods and chattels of the person taxed, but any goods and chattels in his possession.

Sheldon vs. Van Buskirk, 2 Comstock, p. 473. (*b*)

DOMICILE.

Residence. 1. The terms "domicile" and "residence" are not synonymous.

A person can have but one domicile, but he may have two places of residence which he occupies in succession.

The act of the 25th March, 1850, relative to the assessment of taxes, contemplates and provides for such cases. [Laws of 1850, p. 142.] Ante, p. 123.

Held, that under the provisions of that act, the plaintiff, by his own showing, was properly taxed as a resident of the city of New York, and was therefore not entitled to an injunction to restrain the collection of the tax, which had there been imposed upon him.

Bartlett vs. the Mayor, &c., of N. Y., 5 Sandford, S. C. R., p. 44.

(*a*) See 1 R. S., p. 864, sec. 92, 5th edition.

(*b*) The statute passed upon in the above case is similar to section 9, of article 2, Laws of 1843, chap. 230, as amended by Laws of 1850, sec. 34, chap. 121. See ante, p. 189.

EXECUTOR.

1. The *individual* property of an *executor*, administrator, or trustee, may be taken for a *tax* imposed upon him in his *representative character*, when no property of the testator, intestate, or *cestui que trust*, can be found.

Williams, Supervisor of Batavia, vs. Holden, 4 Wendell, p. 223.

EXEMPTIONS.

1. An assessment for a supposed benefit, is not a tax or talliage within the meaning of the act of April 8, 1801, 2 R. L. 15, sec. 28. And the lands of churches, benefited by an improvement in opening and enlarging streets, are liable to be assessed for such improvement. Church lands. Assessment on.

Matter of Mayor, &c., of N. Y., 11 Johns R., p. 77.

2. Prosser vs. Secor. See assessors, ante, pp. 255--6. Minister of the Gospel.

3. Chegaray vs. Jenkins, 3 Sandford S. C. R., p. 409. 1 Selden R., p. 376. Boarding schools.

Chegaray vs. Mayor, &c., of N. Y., 3 Kernan R., p. 220.

4. *Lots* "appropriated, set apart, and devoted as a situation for a building for public worship to be erected thereon," and lots "appropriated to the uses and purposes of a *cemetery* or *keeper's house*, and *chapel* erected for religious services at interments," are not exempt from *taxation* under the statute in relation to the assessment and collection of taxes. [R. S., p. 388, 1st ed.] Church lands.

Because, the statute declares that every building for "*public worship*, and the several lots whereon such build-

are situated, shall be exempt from taxation." Now, "vacant lots" is not a building for public worship, however appropriately dedicated to be used for the erection of such a building; neither is a "chapel," erected for religious services at interments in a cemetery, a place of "public worship," in the sense contemplated by the statute, and of course the lots appurtenant to the chapel, as well as the chapel itself and the keeper's house, are subject to taxation.

Action. Assessment. Where taxes have been *assessed without objection or appeal*, although subsequently paid under protest, they cannot be recovered back.

The Rector, &c., of Trinity Church vs. Mayor, &c., of N. Y., 10 Howard P. R., p. 138.

U. S. stock not taxable. 5. United States stock is not liable to taxation, whether held by incorporated companies or individuals.

1 Kent's Com., 9th edition, p. 474.

Weston vs. City of Charleston, 2 Peters U. S. R., p. 449.

The People, ex rel. the British Commercial Life Insurance Co., vs. Tax Commissioners.
Supreme Court, General Term.
17 Howard, P. R., p. 206.

INCOME.

Profits 1. The word *income* means that which is received from any business or investment of capital, without reference to outgoing expenditures. Otherwise, as to the term *profits*, which generally means the gain made upon any business or investment, when both receipts and payments are taken into account.

People vs. Supervisors of Niagara, 4 Hill, p. 20, per Bronson, J.

INTEREST.

Interest upon tax warrants issued under the act to equalize taxation cannot be collected.

Where a judgment creditor, whose execution was junior to some of the tax warrants in the sheriff's hands, and older than others—held, that on a sale of defendant's property, under the tax warrants, the judgment creditor not desiring to advertise under his execution, all the tax warrants in the sheriff's hands, must first be paid out of the proceeds of the sale, and next the execution of the judgment creditor. Tax warrants.

Ellice vs. Van Rensselaer, 6 Howard P. R., p. 116.

INCORPOREAL HEREDITAMENTS.

1. Incorporeal heraditaments are not subject to taxation by the provisions of the Revised Statutes concerning the assessment and collection of taxes. Property not subject to taxation

They are not *land, real estate, or real property*, nor are they *chattels*, or *personal property*, as defined in the tax law.

Accordingly held, that where a municipal corporation having the right to land on the shore and under the water of a river or harbor, granted the land under water, from high-water mark, to A in fee, reserving so much of the soil under water as was required for a street, which was to become the exterior line of the filling up of such land, and the same, as well as the wharves built out therefrom, were to be public streets and wharves, and which grant contained a covenant of the corporation, that A and his heirs, &c., fulfilling their covenants, might have and enjoy the wharfage and all the advantages of the wharves to be Land, real estate, real property. Wharfage. Wharves.

erected, such grant conveys conditionally in respect of the wharf or bulkhead made by the street an interest, which is real property, and it is not to be considered as a mere covenant.

Such an interest is an incorporeal hereditament.

Boreel vs. the Mayor, &c., of N. Y., 2 Sandford, S. C. R., p. 552.

LEVY FOR TAXES.

Tenant in common.

1. The interest of a tenant in common in personal property can be levied upon under a warrant for the collection of taxes.

Dinehart vs. Wilson, 15 Barb. R., p. 595.

2. Property taken to satisfy a tax cannot be replevied.

People, &c., vs. Albany Common Pleas, 7 Wendell, p. 485.

Code, sec. 207, subdiv. 4.

Warrant.

3. A collector of taxes under a warrant to collect taxes against the lands of non-residents, cannot levy upon any personal property of non-residents, inasmuch as his warrant only authorizes him, "in case any person named *in the assessment roll* shall refuse or neglect to pay the tax, to levy the same by distress and sale of the goods and chattels of such person." The warrant does not authorize the seizure and sale of property of persons not named, or whose name it is apparent from the face of the paper, the assessors had no right to set down.

In such a case, the want of a requisite power to seize and sell the personal property of the person assessed, appears upon the face of the instrument to which the warrant refers, as explanatory of the directions which it contains.

The New York and Harlem R. R. Co. vs. Lyon, 16 Barbour, p. 651. (*a*)

MONEYS IN COURT.

1. The register, assistant register, and clerks of the court of chancery, are not liable to be assessed as trustees, for the funds and securities belonging to suitors, in that court standing, in the names of such officers. Neither can the court be assessed and taxed, as the trustee of such funds or securities. Trustee.

Where moneys are deposited in court, or securities taken for the same in the names of any of the officers of the court, in their official characters, the owners of such funds or securities are liable to be assessed and taxed therefor, at the places of their residence, as a part of their personal estate. Moneys, how taxed.

In the matter of Kellinger, Collector, &c., 9 Paige R., p. 62.

NON-RESIDENTS.

1. Assessors are not authorized by the statute, to insert in the assessment rolls the names of non-resident owners of real estate. In the case of a non-resident, the *land* is to be assessed, without naming the owner. Lands of.

Consequently, no person is charged with, nor rendered

(*a*) See as to warrant issued to constables in New York, and the directions therein contained, Laws of 1843, chap. 230, art. 2, sec. 9, as amended by sec. 34, Laws of 1850, chap. 121. Ante, p. 189.

liable to pay, the taxes imposed upon the lands of non-residents.

New York and Harlem R. R. Co. vs. Lyon, 16 Barbour R., p. 651.

OFFICER.

Warrant. 1. A warrant in due form issued to a constable, by the receiver of taxes in the city of New York, directing the collection of a tax, protects the officer executing it, whether the tax was lawfully assessed or not.

Chegaray vs. Jenkins, 1 Selden, p. 376.
And see Alexander vs. Hoyt, 7 Wendell, p. 89.
Van Rensselaer vs. Cottrell, 7 Barbour R., p. 127.
Sheldon vs. Van Buskirk, 2 Comstock R., p. 473.
And see N. Y. and Harlem R. R. Co. vs. Lyon, 16 Barbour, p. 651.
Wheeler vs. Anthony, 10 Wendell, p. 346.
Thomas vs. Clapp, 20 Barbour, p. 165.
Abbott vs. Yost, 2 Denio R., p. 86.

RENTS.

Affidavit. 1. A person entitled to receive rents subjected to taxation by the act to equalize taxation, passed May 13, 1846, has a right to avail himself of his own affidavit, as to the value of his property, under the provisions of the Revised Statutes, for the purpose of correcting an assessment upon such rents.

The act of 1846 merely adds a new subject for taxation, which is left to be governed by the general law regulating the assessment and collection of taxes, in every respect;

except those in which a different mode is prescribed by statute.

The general law is unrepealed, and that law and the act of 1846 must be construed together; and full effect is to be given to both.

Affidavit. Either of the affidavits required by the 15th section of the article of the Revised Statutes, relative to the assessment and collection of taxes, would be sufficient to correct an error in the valuation of rents. But the legislature having, by the act of 1846, declared such property personal estate, they have, by so doing, directed which affidavit is to be adopted. (*a*)

Lease. Rents reserved in a lease for a term exceeding twenty-one years, continue to be taxable till the expiration of the term. And the fact that at the time of the assessment, such leases have but a few years more to run, will not exempt the rents from taxation.

Landlord. Nor can the landlord avail himself of an agreement between him and his tenant, that a new lease shall be executed for the unexpired term.

Livingston vs. Hollenbeck, 4 Barbour, pp. 9 and 10.

Lease. 2. A lease for a term of thirty years, executed before the passage of the act of May 13, 1846, took effect, is within the provisions of the act, and the rents therein reserved are liable to taxation, although at the passage of the act the lease had less than twenty-one years to run.

Le Couteulx vs. Suprs. of Erie Co., 7 Barb., p. 249.
See also as to taxation on rents, Van Rensselaer vs. Denniston, 8 Barb., p. 23.

(*a*) Section 15 of the article of the R. S. referred to in this case, was repealed by Laws of 1851, chap. 176, sec. 3.

Rents. 3. The statute (ch. 327, Laws of 1846) making rents reserved by certain leases, taxable as personal estate, makes no discrimination between agricultural or city lands, nor in the taxation of city rents thus reserved, is any made between taxes for county and State, and those for city purposes.

Term. Such rents are taxable, although less than twenty-one years of the original term remains unexpired at the time of the assessment.

City of Buffalo vs. Le Couteulx, 15 N. Y. Reports (1 Smith), p. 451.

The cases of

Livingston vs. Hollenbeck, 4 Barb., p. 9.
And Le Couteulx vs. Suprs. of Erie Co., 7 Ib., 249.
Approved, per Comstock, J.

RAILROADS.

Assessors. Railroad corporations. The classified list of real estate of railroad corporations, specifying various particulars, required by statute, to be delivered to town assessors of the towns in which the real estate lies, on or before the first day of May in each year, must be regarded by the assessors as *prima facie* evidence of value, if delivered to them any time after the first day of May, before the completion of their roll, according to law, in like manner as if it had been delivered before the first day of May.

If not delivered until after the completion of the roll, according to law, the assessors are not bound to allow it any effect.

Assessment roll. The roll is complete when the assessors are prepared to make a fair copy for public inspection, and give notice of their meeting for a review of their assessments.(a)

The People, &c., vs. Ross et al., 15 How. P. R., 63.

REAL ESTATE.

1. Where the charter of a village authorized the trustees to raise money by tax, to be assessed on the estates, real and personal, within the corporation, and collected from the several owners thereof, to pay the contingent and other expenses of the corporation, and the trustees imposed and assessed taxes against the defendant on certain premises, of which the corporation had given a lease to another for 990 years, for $400 in hand paid, and for the annual rent of three pepper corns if demanded, of which premises the defendant was in possession, having acquired the interest of the lease therein: *Held*, that the premises were rightfully taxed to the defendant, as real estate, of which he was the owner. Assessment.

Trustees of the Village of Elmira vs. Dunn, 22 Barbour, p. 402.

REMEDIES

AGAINST ILLEGAL ASSESSMENT AND TAX.

1. A certiorari will not lie to a ministerial officer [*e. g.*, a collector of taxes], for the purpose of examining Certiorari.

(a) This case arose under Laws of 1857, chap. 536, vol. 2, p. 122. That chapter, so far as it required special notice to be given in case an assessment roll includes property belonging to a railroad corporation, was repealed by chap. 110, Laws of 1858, p. 209.

his right to proceed upon process under which he is acting.

People vs. Supervisors of Queens Co., 1 Hill, p. 195. Explaining, People vs. Works, 7 Wendell, p. 486.

Certiorari. 2. A certiorari will not be allowed, where another direct remedy, by appeal, is given.

Matter, Mount Morris Square, 2 Hill, p. 14.

Injunction. 3. A court of equity has no power to restrain by injunction the collection of taxes irregularly or erroneously assessed.

Livingston vs. Hollenbeck, 4 Barbour, p. 10.
Van Rensselaer vs. Kidd, 4 Barbour, p. 17.
Chemical Bank vs. Mayor, &c., 1 Abbott, p. 79.
New York Life Insurance Company vs. Supervisors of New York, 4 Duer, p. 192.
Wilson vs. the Mayor, &c., of New York, 4 E. D. Smith, p. 675.

[Where all the cases on the subject are cited.]

Action. 4. A person can recover from a county money collected from him for a tax illegally levied, and caused to be collected by the board of supervisors, and paid to the county treasurer, as money had and received by the county to his use.

Per Allen, J. Hill vs. Supervisors of Livingston County, 2 Kernan, p. 52.

Ib. 5. An action may be maintained against the assessors by a party illegally assessed and taxed.

Mygatt vs. Washburn, 1 Smith N. Y. R., p. 316.
Wilson vs. the Mayor, &c., of New York, 4 E. D. Smith, p. 675.
Prosser vs. Secor, 5 Barbour, pp. 607–8.

6. A mandamus may in some instances be granted. Mandamus.

Adriance vs. the Mayor, &c., of New York, 12 How. P. R., p. 224.

Bank of Utica vs. City of Utica, 4 Paige, p. 399.

Wilson vs. the Mayor, &c., of New York, 4 E. D. Smith, p. 675.

7. The process first issued and levied upon personal property, and the sale under such process, conveys to the purchaser the title to the property, to the same extent as the sheriff or officer could have given title, *on the day he made the levy;* that is, the sale by the officer relates back to the date of the levy, and conveys all the title to the property which the officer obtained the day the levy was made. Levy by sheriff. Levy.

And such sale cuts off all *lien for taxes* upon the property, where the levy for the taxes was made subsequent to the levy by the officer on the execution upon which the property was sold. Lien of taxes cut off by prior levy of sheriff under judgment.

In the city and county of New York the warrant to the receiver of taxes to collect the tax, does not authorize him to make a levy. The statute prescribes the mode of making such distress, by issuing a warrant to an officer, &c.; and until such warrant is delivered to the officer and levied, there can be no lien for such tax on personal property of the party assessed. Warrant to receiver of taxes.

A purchaser of personal property, on a sale under an execution, may have an injunction, *pendente lite*, to restrain the taking of such property for taxes claimed to be a lien thereon. Injunction.

Fuller vs. Allen, 16 Howard P. R., p. 247.

8. A party assessed for the same personal property in Interpleader.

two different counties—held, that a bill of interpleader against the two collectors is proper.

Thomson vs. Ebbets and others, 1 Hopkins, C. R., p. 272.

Certiorari. 9. A certiorari will not lie to remove and correct the proceedings of a board of supervisors in assessing town and county taxes.

People vs. Supervisors of Queens Co., 1 Hill, p. 196.
People vs. Works, 7 Wendell, p. 486.

Prohibition. 10. A writ of prohibition does not lie to a ministerial officer (*ex gratia*, a collector of taxes), to stay the execution of process in his hands.

Ib.

Ib. 11. A writ of prohibition will be granted to prevent the collection of a tax illegally imposed at a town meeting.

People vs. Works, 7 Wendell, p. 486.

Certiorari. 12. A writ of certiorari may in some cases be granted to review an assessment for taxes.

Wilson vs. the Mayor, &c., of New York, 4 E. D. Smith, p. 675.

[All the cases as to remedies against illegal assessments and taxes are cited in the opinion of Judge Woodruff in this case.] (*a*)

(*a*) By section 20, Laws of 1859, chap. 302, it is provided that a certiorari to review or correct on the merits, any decision of the commissioners of taxes, relative to the assessment of property for taxation, may be allowed by the supreme court or any judge thereof, on the petition of the party aggrieved, &c. Ante, p. 234.

RESIDENCE.

1. The plaintiff, in the year 1850, and for several years before, resided in a hired house in the city of New York, during the winter and spring, and at his country-seat in the town of Flushing, Queens county, during the summer and autumn. In the winter of 1850, he was assessed in New York for a tax on his personal estate, and in the summer was assessed for a similar tax in Flushing, which he paid. He resisted the payment of the tax in New York, and filed his complaint to restrain its collection.

Held, that whether the domicile of the plaintiff was or was not at Flushing, he was a resident of New York, and liable to be taxed as such when the tax for the city was assessed. Domicile.

Douglass vs. The Mayor, &c., of New York, 2 Duer, p. 110.

2. An individual having "his principal place of business" in the city of New York, and with his family residing in Newburgh, in which latter place he is taxed for his *personal property*, is not entitled to an *injunction* to restrain the collection of such tax, whatever the law may be, applicable to the proper assessment of such tax, where he does not show that he is taxed in both places for the same property, nor that there is any injustice in the matter. Residence. Injunction

Skeel vs. Thompson, 9 Howard P. R., p. 478.

SALES.

1. To divest the owner of lands by a sale for taxes, every preliminary step must be shown to be in conformity with the statute. It is a naked power, not coupled with

an interest, and every pre-requisite to the exercise of that power must precede it.

Leggett vs. Rogers, 9 Barbour, p. 411.
Williams vs. Peyton's Lessee, 4 Wheat. p. 77.
Stead's Ex. vs. Course, 4 Cranch, p. 403.
Rollendorf vs. Taylor, 4 Peters, p. 349.
Gaines vs. Stiles, 14 Peters, p. 322.
Bloom vs. Burdick, 1 Hill, p. 130.
Jackson vs. Shepard, 7 Cowen, p. 88.
Sharp vs. Speir, 4 Hill, p. 76.
Sharp vs. Johnson, 4 Hill, p. 92.
Doughty vs. Hope, 3 Denio, p. 594; same case, 1 Comst., p. 89.
Striker vs. Kelly, 2 Denio, p. 323.
Varick vs. Tallman, 2 Barbour, p. 113.
Tallman vs. White, 2 Comst., p. 66.
Bush vs. Davison, 16 Wendell, p. 550.
Jackson vs. Esty, 7 Wendell, p. 148.
Hubbell vs. Weldon, Lalor's Sup. to Hill and Denio, p. 139.

Publication of redemption notice.

2. The publication of the redemption notice required by statute of 1816, p. 114, sec. 2, *as amended by statute* of 1840, p. 274, sec. 10, after a sale for a tax or assessment, must be fully completed before the commencement of the last six months of the two years succeeding the sale, and an omission in this respect will invalidate the purchaser's title.

Redemption notice.

Where the redemption notice is not published according to law, a regular notice served after the execution of the lease given upon the sale, pursuant to statute of 1841, p. 211, sec. 3, and the certificate by the street commissioner, required by section 7 of the same act, do not confirm the title.

The statute, which declares that the lease given upon a sale for taxes or assessments in the city of New York, "shall be conclusive evidence that the sale was regular," &c. (statute of 1816, p. 115, sec. 2), refers only to the *notice of sale* and the proceedings *at the auction.*

Doughty vs. Hope, 1 Comst., p. 79, affirming same case, 3 Denio, p. 594.

See also Striker vs. Kelly, 7 Hill, p. 9, as to lease. (*a*)

3. Same point as to the publication of redemption notice, was decided by the Superior Court in Bennett vs. City of New York, 1 Sand., S. C. R., p. 485. Description of land.

4. The description of land sold for non-payment of taxes should be, substantially at least, as full and definite in the notice of sale, as the description required to be given in the assessment roll. Ib.

Hubbell vs. Weldon, Lalor's Sup. to Hill and Denio, p. 140.

5. Where lands are sold under a tax sale, the owner or occupant is to be regarded after that, as holding in subordination to the title of the purchaser—as quasi tenant to him, like a defendant in possession after sale of his real estate on judgment and execution. Owner after sale.

Hubbell vs. Weldon, Lalor's Sup. to Hill and Denio, p. 139.

(*a*) The acts of 1816 and 1841, above referred to, as far as they relate to taxes, are repealed by sec. 2, of art. 4, chap. 230, Laws of 1843. See ante, p. 205. But the provisions of those acts were incorporated into article 3 of that act, and the above cases are therefore in point, as construing the provisions of the act of 1843.

SALES

UNDER ORDER OF COURT TO PAY TAXES AND ASSESSMENTS.

Object of the act.

1. The object of the act of May, 1841 (*a*), to authorize the sale of real estate, in certain cases, to pay assessments and for other purposes, was not to throw upon the court of chancery the burthen of deciding all questions as to the validity of assessments and sales of property in cities and villages, where the property assessed is held by several persons as tenants in common, or by persons having different estates or interests therein; but to enable a person, who is not the absolute owner, in fee, of the whole premises assessed, to compel other persons, having estates or interests therein to contribute their rateable proportions of the assessments which have been legally and properly made upon the premises. And to entitle a complainant to file a bill for contribution, under that act, he must show that a valid assessment has been made upon the premises, upon which the defendants are interested with him; and that under such assessment the premises have been sold, or are liable to be sold.

For this act see 3 R. S., p. 264, 5th ed. Ante, pp. 161-163.

What must be shown to obtain order of court.

Where the premises have been sold for the non-payment of an assessment, the complainant, to entitle himself to an order of the court, extending the time for redemption, must not only show that a valid assessment has been made, and that the premises have been properly sold, but he must also verify his bill by oath; his bill, also, must contain a distinct offer, that in case he discontinues the suit, or his bill is dismissed, he will redeem the premises and pay the interest upon the redemption money from the expiration of the original period of redemption; or if the premises are

(*a*) See ante, pp. 161-163.

not redeemed, that he will pay the interest on the redemption money, for the term of such extension.

Security.

And where the complainant who applies for an extension of the time for redemption is irresponsible, the court ought not to grant an order of extension, without requiring security from him, that he will comply with the terms of the offer contained in his bill.

Where lands have been sold for taxes or assessments, during the existence of a law which entitled the purchaser to an absolute deed, or to a lease for a limited term, in case the premises were not redeemed within a specified time, it is not competent for the legislature to extend the time for the redemption, and thus to deprive the purchaser of the right to the possession and enjoyment of the premises, without providing an adequate compensation to the purchaser, for his loss of the use of the premises during the time of such extension.

Act, how far unconstitutional.

The provisions of the act of the 26th of May, 1841, authorizing an extension of the time for the redemption of certain lands, in cities and villages, which have been sold for taxes or assessments, are unconstitutional and void, so far as they relate to sales which had been made previous to the passage of that act.

Dikeman vs. Dikeman, 11 Paige R., pp. 484–6.

Sales under order of court to pay assessments and taxes.

Real estate must have been sold, or be thereafter sold, or liable to be sold, to authorize order of court.

2. Under the statute of 1855 (Sess. Laws of 1855, ch. 327), in which authority is given to the court to order a sale of real estate, or a portion thereof, in order to pay off the assessments and taxes imposed thereon, the only cases in which the court can order such sale, is, where the real estate or any part of it, has been sold, or where it shall thereafter be sold, or where it is or shall become liable, in case of default, to be sold to satisfy a tax or assessment.

Where taxes paid, statute does not apply. The statute does not apply to cases where the taxes and assessments have been *paid* and the land discharged therefrom, and it is sought by an application to the court for a sale to *reimburse* the parties who have made such payments.

Constitutionality of act. The *constitutionality* of this act cannot be questioned successfully; besides, the Court of Appeals have settled that question, by an express adjudication, in the case of Jackson vs. Calder (MS. opinion, 1857), per Johnson J.

Power to authorize sale is confined to real estate in city and village. And the sale which the court is authorized to order, is confined to the real estate within the *city* or *village* where the real estate is, which is assessed, either in whole or in part, and no authority is given to sell any property out of the city or village which is not assessed. (*a*)

Norsworthy vs. Bergh, 16 How. P. R., p. 315.

What may be sold. 3. Where land situated within the bounds of any city or village, in which several persons are interested, is ordered by the Supreme Court to be sold, under and in pursuance of the act of May 26, 1841, "to authorize the sale of real estate, in certain cases, to pay assessments," &c.; or under the act of April 12, 1855, "to provide for the due apportionment of taxes and assessments, and for the sale of real estate to pay the same;" one parcel taxed or assessed may be sold by the referee, to satisfy a tax or assessment on a different parcel.

Nature of power of sale. The power of sale conferred by the statute, in such cases, is for a special and limited purpose, that of either paying the taxes, before a sale for taxes takes place, or of redeeming from such a sale, after it has been made, or both. When these purposes have been subserved, when

(*a*) For this act, see 3 R. S., p. 267, 3d ed. Ante, pp. 165-168.

the taxes and assessments have been paid and satisfied—the power of sale is gone. The remaining land, therefore, cannot be sold, though it may be deemed by the referee, or by all the parties, to be more advantageous to convert the land into money than to retain the same unsold.

Powers et al. vs. Barr et al., 24 Barb., p. 142.

SUPERVISORS.

1. It is the duty of the board of supervisors, at their annual meeting, to examine the several assessment rolls returned to them, and to compare them with each other, and thus to ascertain what relation they bear to each other. Having done this, they are authorized to add to, or deduct from, the aggregate valuation of the real estate in any town or ward, such amount as in their opinion, will be necessary, in order to produce a just relation between all the towns and wards. Duty to examine and compare assessment rolls.

If they determine it to be necessary to add to the aggregate valuation of the real estate in a particular town, the letter of the law requires them, instead of adding a gross sum to the aggregate valuation, to add to the assessed valuation a specified sum upon each one hundred dollars. Valuations.

Thus, where a board of supervisors, deeming it necessary to add $300,000 to the aggregate valuation of the real estate of a particular town, resolved to add that sum in gross to the assessed valuation of the town—*it was held*, that the board should have voted to add $19.54 to every hundred dollars, amounting in the aggregate to $300,000, instead of voting to add $300,000, amounting to $19.54 upon every hundred dollars of the assessors' valuation; but Ib.

that this was not a material departure from the requirement of the statute.

May appoint committee to annex warrants to rolls.

It seems, that it is competent for a board of supervisors, after having determined all the questions within their jurisdiction, relating to the assessment rolls and collectors' warrants, to appoint a committee with power to annex the warrants to the rolls, when the clerical operation of extending the taxes shall be completed, and to deliver them to the collectors.

Tallmadge vs. Supervisors of Rensselaer county, 21 Barbour, R., p. 611–12.(a)

Affidavit of receipt of no profits, &c.

2. The statute having provided, that if the president or other proper officer of a corporation named in an assessment roll, shall show to the satisfaction of the board of supervisors, at their annual meeting, by affidavit, that such corporation is not in the receipt of any profits or income, the name of such corporation shall be stricken out of the assessment roll, and no tax shall be imposed upon it; and that the assessment of any corporation from which no such affidavit shall be received, shall be *conclusive evidence* that such corporation was liable to taxation, and was duly assessed; if the officers of a corporation whose property has been assessed, neglect to furnish the affidavit mentioned in the statute, at the proper time, a *mandamus* will not be issued, directing the supervisors to erase the name of the corporation from the assessment roll.

After taxes have been assessed and warrants issued and delivered to the collectors, the supervisors have no further control over the assessment roll, their power

---

(a) By Laws of 1843, chap. 230, art. 2, sec. 2, the warrant to be delivered to the receiver of taxes, is to be under the hands and seals of the board of supervisors, or of any five of them, &c. Ante, p. 187.

being spent; consequently, a mandamus, directing them to strike any particular name from the roll, would be nugatory. *(a)* Mandamus.

Colonial Life Assurance Society vs. the Supervisors of New York, 24 Barbour R., p. 166.

3. The board of supervisors of a county may file a bill in equity, in the nature of a creditor's bill, to collect a tax, legally assessed against the defendant, out of his equitable interests and choses in action, upon the return of the collector, that the defendant has no visible property out of which the tax can be levied. Tax may be collected out of equitable interests, &c.

Supervisors of Albany County vs. Durant, 9 Paige R., p. 182.

4. In the city of New York the board of supervisors in some respects has greater powers than those in the country. Supervisors of New York.

The power of correcting an erroneous assessment, or of remitting or reducing a tax imposed by law, it is well known, is exercised by the *new board*, after the term of the officers composing the board which imposed the tax has expired. This power, too, is given by law to the board of supervisors, as a *quasi* corporation, as a body known to the law as always in existence, however the members of it may change. Although the assessment rolls may have passed out of the hands of the supervisors of the city and county of New York, they have the power, on a proper application, to correct them, whether the supervisors in other counties have that power or not. Remission or reduction of tax. Quasi corporation. Supervisors have power to correct rolls, although they have passed out of their hands.

(*a*) The sections of the Revised Statutes referred to in this case—sections 9 and 10, of title 4, chap. 13—were repealed by Laws of 1857, vol. 2, p. 1.

Tax commissioners have no power to increase assessors' valuation.

The tax commissioners of the city and county of New York have no power to *increase* the assessors' *valuation* of property; their power under the act of 1851, authorizes them to add and assess, according to law, any real or personal estate liable to taxation, which may have been *omitted by the assessors*, or (in the language of the act) "*which may not have been assessed*" by the assessors. It was not intended that this should be an appellate power to *increase* the assessors' valuation; it is limited by its terms to cases in which the estate has not been assessed by the assessors, or in which, by accident or otherwise, they have not exercised their judgment. Therefore, *Held*, that where the tax commissioners *increased* the assessed valuation of the estate, as made by the assessors, the board of supervisors could be compelled, by mandamus, to correct the assessment by conforming it to the original assessment, as made by the assessors.

Power limited to property not assessed by the assessors.

Mandamus.

Affidavit of owner.

The *affidavit* alone of the owner to reduce the valuation of his property below that imposed by the assessors, without the *examination, or without the examination being reduced to writing*, either before the assessors or before the tax com missioners, as required by law, is of no avail as evidence to reduce the tax.

Matter of Isaac Adriance vs. Supervisors of New York, 12 Howard P. R., p. 224. (*a*)

(*a*) But by sec. 11, of chap. 302, Laws of 1859, p. 682, it is provided that the commissioners of taxes and assessments may at any time before the second day of April in each year, increase or diminish, at any time before closing books of annual record on first day of May in each year, the assessed valuation of any real or personal estate in said city, as in their judgment may be necessary for such equalization; but they shall not increase such valuations after books are open for correction and review, except upon notice to party affected by increase, twenty days before closing of books. Ante, p. 231.

TAXES—WHEN DUE.

1. In the city of New York, taxes are *due* and *payable* on the 15th of January in each year, at which time a warrant for the collection of those remaining unpaid is issued and placed in the hands of the collector.

Manice vs. Miller, 26 Barbour, p. 41.

See act of 1843, chap. 230, ante, p. 189.

WARRANT.

Supervisors.

1. A warrant issued by the supervisors of a county for the collection of taxes, is valid, although the persons signing it are not described therein as supervisors, and although their names are signed to it without any official designation.

Sheldon vs. Van Buskirk, 2 Comst., p. 473.

ANNUAL TAX BILLS

FOR THE

CITY AND COUNTY OF NEW YORK,

SINCE 1813.

1813, Laws of 1813, page 61.
1814, Laws of 1814, page 188.
1815, Laws of 1815, page 164.
1816, Laws of 1816, page 75.
1817, Laws of 1817, page 179.
1818, Laws of 1818, page 190.
1819, Laws of 1819, page 119.
1820, Laws of 1820, page 69.
1821, Laws of 1821, page 61.
1822, Laws of 1822, page 88.
1823, Laws of 1823, page 167.
1824, Laws of 1824, page 79.
1825, Laws of 1825, page 295.
1826, Laws of 1826, page 75.
1827, Laws of 1827, page 230.
1828, Laws of 1828, page 370.
1829, Laws of 1829, page 255.
1830, Laws of 1830, page 162.
1831, Laws of 1831, page 167.
1832, Laws of 1832, page 75.
1833, Laws of 1833, page 348.

1834, Laws of 1834, page 77.
1835, Laws of 1835, page 40.
1836, Laws of 1836, page 277.
1837, Laws of 1837, page 59.
1838, Laws of 1838, page 73.
1839, Laws of 1839, page 58.
1840, Laws of 1840, page 8.
1841, Laws of 1841, page 265.
1842, Laws of 1842, page 55.
1843, Laws of 1843, page 170.
1844, Laws of 1844, page 383.
1845, Laws of 1845, page 16.
1846, Laws of 1846, page 99.
1847, Laws of 1847, page 282, vol 1.
1848, Laws of 1848, page 429.
1849, Laws of 1849, page 402.
1850, Laws of 1850, page 123.
1851, Laws of 1851, page 482.
1852, Laws of 1852, page 72.
1853, Laws of 1853, page 520 and 1132.
1854, Laws of 1854, page 580.
1855, Laws of 1855, page 221.
1856, Laws of 1856, page 271.
1857, Laws of 1857, page 157, vol. 1.
1858, Laws of 1858, page 487.
1859, Laws of 1859, page 1123.

INDEX TO ASSESSMENT LAWS.

INDEX TO PART I. OF TAX LAWS.

COMPTROLLER OF THE STATE OF NEW YORK:

INDEX TO PART II. OF TAX LAWS.

* The office of Marshal was abolished by Laws of 1846, chapter 302.

Receiver of taxes in the city of New York:

Sale of lands for non-payment of taxes :

SUPERVISORS OF THE COUNTY OF NEW YORK:

* The act of March 30, 1850, prescribing and defining the duties of assessors, and the tax commissioners of the city of New York, has been inserted in this compilation, because the act of 1859, Laws of 1859, chapter 302, provides that the existing provisions of law in relation to the mode and manner of making assessments, &c., so far as conformable to the supervision of the commissioners of taxes and assessments, shall be applicable to the officers provided for by that act. See ante, p. 212, et seq., and 227.

INDEX TO PART III. OF TAX LAWS.

(a) The Act of 1859, chap. 302, sec. 20, provides that a certiorari shall he allowed by the Supreme Court, or any judge thereof, on the petition of the party aggrieved, to review and correct, on the merits, any decision, &c., of the commissioners of taxes and assessments in making or reviewing assessments. [Ante, p. 234.]

www.ingramcontent.com/pod-product-compliance
Lightning Source LLC
LaVergne TN
LVHW011149110826
845150LV00006B/1195

* 9 7 8 1 4 2 5 5 4 6 7 3 1 *